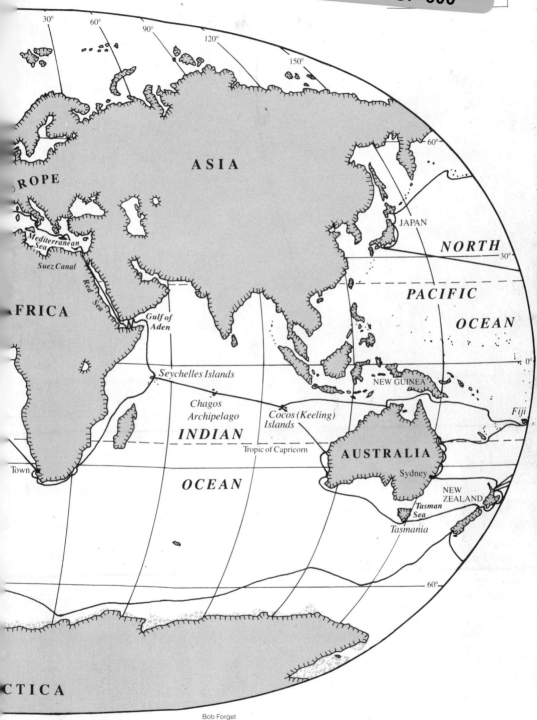

30°   60°   90°   120°   150°

ASIA

EUROPE

Mediterranean
Sea

Suez Canal

Red Sea

AFRICA

Gulf of
Aden

JAPAN

60°

NORTH

30°

PACIFIC

OCEAN

0°

Seychelles Islands

NEW GUINEA

Fiji

Chagos
Archipelago

Cocos (Keeling)
Islands

INDIAN

Tropic of Capricorn

AUSTRALIA

Sydney

OCEAN

Town

NEW
ZEALAND

Tasman
Sea

Tasmania

60°

CTICA

Bob Forget

BLUE
WATER

BLUE WATER

A guide to self-reliant sailboat cruising

by Bob Griffith
with Nancy Griffith

Sail Books, Inc.

BOSTON

Distributed to bookstores by W. W. Norton and Company, Inc.

Library of Congress Cataloging in Publication Data:

Griffith, Bob.
  Blue water.

  Includes index.
  1. Sailing. I. Griffith, Nancy, joint author.
II. Title.
GV811.G73   797.1'24   79–10264
ISBN 0–914814–19–2

For our son Reid Kenneth Higgins Griffith, brave and loyal shipmate for most of his 21 years, who was killed on November 17, 1975, in a climbing accident at Bay Marquesienne, Nuku Hiva, in the Marquesas Islands. He knew the challenge of the horizon, the press of the wind, the bite of the spray, and the power of a sailing vessel. We shall miss him for the rest of our lives.

Contents

FOREWORD. The sailing life   9

PART I. THE SEAWORTHY YACHT   13

  1. Hull design   21
  2. Deck structures   28
  3. Standing rigging   37
  4. Running rigging   47
  5. Sails   57
  6. Engines and electricity   67
  7. Equipment and gear   74
  8. Accommodations and stowage   85

PART II. VOYAGING   91

  9. Planning a voyage   104
  10. Preparing to navigate   120
  11. Provisions   127
  12. Lines and knots   141
  13. Sailhandling   147
  14. Life at sea   163
  15. Health   179
  16. Vermin   189
  17. Fishing and skin diving   193
  18. Emergencies   200
  19. Anchoring   222
  20. Arriving   253
  21. The rewards of cruising   258

  About the authors   261
  List of voyages   263
  Index   265

The sailing life

Damned if I know why I went sailing with you," a former crew member recently wrote, "but it was the best and biggest event in my life. The past 10 years—or has it been 12?—have been colored by those months sailing the Pacific, making landings, meeting real people, exploring, swimming, cooking, and everything both good and bad that went into making the trip what it was. I may not have been your best crew, but I remembered most of what you taught and I learned how to adjust to the conditions and like them (well, maybe accept them)."

A person who cruises the ocean in a small boat is never quite the same again. Captain or crew, he has faced personal responsibility and made decisions that matter. And he has used and been abused by two of the most powerful forces we know on this planet. They interact to form his world: the strong wind and the mighty sea.

I have always wanted to write a sailing book. Now after 20 continuous years of voyaging in two cutters and a ketch, the first and hundredth landfalls have been made, many things have been learned, and some forgotten. The sea still calls and the horizon still intrigues. Personal experience, study, and thought have formed the judgments that make up this book. I hope that many sailors will benefit from my opinions; they are not absolutes, but they are from my heart, and they work for me. Each day at sea differs from the one before. I'm still learning about sailing and I never expect to know it all. Every landfall is still a promise and a danger.

I wouldn't have it any other way. In fact, for me, there is no other way. I am a veterinarian by profession (not your lap dog type, but a large-animal doctor). The growth of my Northern California practice brought with it an increase in blood pressure, which would have completed its fatal work except for the sea. For some folks, a night off the south coast of Tierra del Fuego would cause blood pressure to soar, but for others the pressures of business life are worse. I am the latter type; the direct and tangible dangers of wind and sea, rock and shoal do not raise mine. I have chosen the real and lasting satisfaction of a free and self-determined life, augmented by an acceptance of total personal responsibility. With this choice my health has returned.

This is not unusual. I know dozens of men and women who have mentally detoxified and physically reconditioned themselves on small boats. They have found a sense of well-being they had never felt before. Slocum said he felt ten years younger after his epic solo circumnavigation in 1898, and at 54 years he was no spring chicken. Physical strength and agility are not absolute requisites for the determined sailor. Howard Blackburn twice sailed the Atlantic single-handed after losing all the fingers of both hands, all his toes, and half a foot to frostbite on the Grand Banks. Chichester found impaired health and age surmountable barriers in a circumnavigation that might well have stopped a more physically fit man.

If you take up a sailing life, you will have to give up many things, including some dearly held values. You will give up some comfort and conveniences. Few boats provide the insulation from the elements that you find at hearth and home. You will give up privacy. On a small boat you share continually with others; sailing is a twenty-four-hour-a-day joint effort with your shipmates. You may even give up your income. Most of us cannot cruise extensively and maintain a regular income.

Cruising the world's seas has in some ways made me more wealthy and satisfied than any amount of "success" could have. Taking action to pursue my own goals has given me more than can be held in the hand or stored in a warehouse. How have I done it? The answer is absurdly simple. All it takes is the doing.

I have tried to adopt the attitude that I don't need money. That attitude, of course, is a necessary illusion. But I find that I am able to avoid a surprising number of both small and large expenses by the time-honored devices of holding fast, making do, and thinking of another way. My "junk collection" of parts and pieces is often wondered at by the unknowing. It is admired by blue-water sailors.

My crew and I do virtually all the work on *Awahnee*. We do the bottom at low tide while on a grid, or next to a dolphin or pier. I step my own mast, make and tune my own rigging, and repair my sails insofar as possible. I invest in supplies and equipment in large quantities at favorable prices wherever practical all over the world.

But there always comes a day, and sometimes more than one, when plain hard cash is all that can save your boat, your trip, your freedom from the rat race. On a voyage I always try to keep $1,000 in small bills in reserve. With it I can get 50 men into the water, or on a heavy line, to save the boat. Cash will work in places where a credit card, a traveler's check, or a personal check mean nothing at all.

When should you go cruising? When young and single, without the responsibilities of a family? It seems ideal. But if you contemplate sailing alone, my advice is: don't. A single-handed voyage is often lonely and joyless; you will be without any reserve of ability, strength, or watchfulness. A single-hander must be ready to die, scared or not, each time he lays down his head to sleep. Self-steering rigs keep no lookout.

Should a couple wait until their children are out of school? Definitely not, in my opinion. Infants thrive on sailing. Children have everything to gain and practically nothing to lose by going cruising with their family. My son Reid sailed three times around the world between the ages of five and sixteen. He graduated in three years from public high school in the United States as a National Honor Student and then attended the University of California.

In our society, young children are often deprived of their ability to contribute to the welfare of the family. Nonetheless, a child recognizes the difference between being entertained and supplying valuable help in the day's work. He will be proud to accept real responsibility. On a boat, the very young can fetch and carry, even steer a little. By the age of seven or eight a girl or boy is a capable hand; at ten or eleven years he is responsible: he knows the wind, the weather, the boat.

But what about school? Some families let their children skip a year or so if they are going to be away for a limited amount of time. It is not always easy to sit a child down to a correspondence lesson the morning after you arrive at a fascinating new port. When we're sailing fast and spending relatively little time in port, we make every sailing day a school day and every port day a free day.

Correspondence school, faithfully taught, will combine with travel and experience to give an excellent education to any child at the elementary school level, as long as he keeps up with his age group. I do believe, however, that a student should attend a proper school for at least half his high school years. There is no shipboard equivalent of laboratory sciences, movies and demonstrations, a library, sports, or music. Nor does correspondence school compensate for qualified teachers in the higher levels, especially in subjects like language, the physical sciences, and math.

Now I have two little children, Tenoi'i and Fiona, who have about 15,000 miles of cruising north and south of the equator in their wake. My wife recently ordered correspondence kindergarten for them.

But children are by no means the only ones who learn at sea. Everyone who casts off on a voyage will learn lessons from the sea: what it's like to be free, how to be self-reliant, the value of competence. It may cost a lot, but no price can be put on the satisfaction of a successfully completed voyage.

Sailing the ocean . . . that, my friends, is living.

PART ONE

The Seaworthy Yacht

It is not within the scope of this book to review all aspects of the design, construction, and rigging of offshore yachts, but simply to set forth what in my experience has most contributed to satisfactory cruising. A boat that casts off to cross an ocean will sail far beyond the horizon and the scope of predictable conditions. The ability to sail under adverse conditions is the most necessary quality of an ocean-cruising yacht, for ability is safety. The only real criterion is performance: an ocean-cruising yacht must be able to claw off a lee shore when embayed in 50 knots of wind. This is a simple statement, but it carries a lot of meaning. The world's best crew cannot keep a boat off the rocks if she won't sail.

For instance, after two and a half circumnavigations, Harry Pidgeon wrecked his *Islander* in the New Hebrides Islands when he lost his shelter at anchor in the rising, shifting winds of an approaching hurricane. Natives vividly described to me several years ago how the onshore drive of the wind and sea forced him to try to sail out. He got underway and sailed across the bay, but *Islander* was not able to come about in that strength of wind. There was no room to jibe. She drove ashore just short of clearing the entrance at Hog Harbor on Espiritu Santo Island. I later found the keel; I carry a piece of it aboard my boat to remind me that there, but for the grace of a boat that can sail, might lie *Awahnee*.

A cruising boat that may be years on a voyage should have little in the way of nonessential or exotic equipment. I prefer our 53-foot conservatively rigged cutter because it is the largest boat I would care to sail single-handed. Yet at the same time she has room enough to carry a complement of six, seven, or more in comfort. The 542-square-foot mainsail can be worked by one man, as can the jibs. Even in difficult conditions we are able to sail with the helmsman alone in the cockpit. The main and staysail are self-tending; the jibsheet is the only line that must be handled in tacking. The main can carry three reefs, and the storm main, carried on a separate track on the mast, can be set conveniently in still heavier winds.

Awahnee is no showpiece of nautical pulchritude. She is a working boat, sea kindly and able. She has no fancy gear, but everything she does have works. We can maintain and repair her ourselves. We sail *Awahnee* with oiled woodwork, a hand-operated bilge pump, and no refrigeration, while others sit in port varnishing and looking up repairmen.

I have owned two 53-foot cutters named *Awahnee*. In the original we twice averaged more than 200 miles per day for five consecutive days. The first was a run of 1,040 miles from the Seychelles Islands to Cape Guardafui on the horn of Africa in five days flat, an average of 8.66 knots. The second was during her 1963 transatlantic passage from the Cape Verde Islands to Antigua in 11 days 22 hours, a record yacht passage. In 1960 with only three aboard she sailed from the Marquesas Islands to Hawaii in 11 days 20 hours, also an unequalled record. And I will never forget the exhilarating day and a half after departing the Cocos-Keeling Islands on my first circumnavigation. In that 36 hours she sailed 359 miles to a four-star fix, an average of ten knots flat over the bottom.

Strangely enough, this fine boat was known in San Francisco Bay as the boat that couldn't sail and the boat with the dirty sails (they were flax). She had been home-built there by a man grown too old to embark on a new voyage. Double-ended, she was rather deep and narrow in comparison to the beamy shoal-draft, transom-sterned designs of the day. Armed only with a reading knowledge of offshore design, I recognized that *Awahnee* was what I was looking for in a boat. She was simple, able, and sea kindly—a vessel capable of sailing practically anywhere the sea is deeper than her draft.

The second *Awahnee,* designed with slightly more beam and length, and less draft, has performed a little less well, possibly because she's met fewer favorable conditions. However, she sailed a passage of 7,500 miles from the South Orkney Islands in the far south Atlantic Ocean to New Zealand in 58 days, which included 20 days spent wholly or partially lying to drogues because of storms or iceberg danger. Incidentally, this passage was the last leg of an all-time record for sailing vessels, including clipper ships: 111 days around the world. *Awahnee* sailed from Bluff, New Zealand,

and back between December 23, 1970, and April 11, 1971. Twenty-three days were spent partially or wholly in port. Eighty-eight were full sailing days.

Many people today do not appreciate the wonderful hull designs of the small ocean-going boats of the 1920's and 30's, when the designer's only concern was that the boat perform well in wind and wave. In spite of the softenings and infirmities of age, every so often a boat from that era shows her mettle. *Niña* won the Transatlantic Race and the Fastnet in 1928, then came back in 1962 to win the Bermuda Race. Other performances of boats designed in that time are still outstanding: *Dorade* made a windward Atlantic passage of 22 days 15 hours from the Scilly Islands to Pollock Rip in 1933; *Pursuit,* built in 1930, sailed the Transpacific Race of 1969 from San Pedro, California, to Honolulu in 10 days 14 hours at an average of 221 miles per day for the passage (but ran fourth behind *Blackfin, Windward Passage,* and *Mir,* despite breaking her boom, both spinnaker poles, her rudder, and her emergency rudder); and the first *Awahnee* made remarkable Atlantic, Pacific, and Indian Ocean passages.

Many people dream of cruising but only a few actually commit themselves to voyaging on the briny deep. Everyone who has spent time around a yacht harbor knows of long-planned voyages that never passed beyond the planning stage, building projects that lasted beyond a man's vigor and sense of adventure or his wife's courage, and cruises that went awry soon after casting off. This creates a dilemma for naval architects: the problem of designing and building seagoing vessels for clients who in many if not most cases will never take them out of soundings. To increase comfort and convenience for weekends and vacations aboard, concessions are often made that compromise a boat's suitability for long-term cruising.

There are the boats with everything inside, shaped more like footballs than sea-going vessels, with high cambered decks to give extra headroom in shoal-draft hulls that contain the accommodations of a mini-condominium—difficult to push to windward, difficult to anchor, and an electrician's nightmare. And there are the boats with almost nothing inside which have large sailplans mounted on hulls as small as possible, hulls that taper in from the deck in all directions. Such boats are too tender to sail safely through a squall, too light to carry through well in a seaway, and wet and bouncy down below.

The public's idea of a good cruising boat is often influenced by successful offshore racing boats, but these too are often unsuitable for extended cruising. With few exceptions, offshore races are all downwind. Racing boats are built to a measurement rule that can make unseaworthy characteristics advantageous: transoms instead of faired sterns, split rigs on boats small enough for any man to handle sails on a single mast, construction so light that structural failures can occur in normal weather.

The strong, quiet, and slow-moving boat is frequently favored for serious cruising. More often than not, the hull is a heavy, fat tub that needs a gale to move it out of its own way. Designers and owners of these boats swear they can go anywhere—that is, anywhere a broad reach or run will take them. Tahiti ketches and their variations are the most outstanding example of this type of boat. Aside from the wonderful name, the popularity of these boats came from the fact that in the 1930's they could be built in a backyard for less than $1,000. Many Tahiti ketches have gone downwind around the world, but that is more a testament to the determination of their owners than to their boats' ability. There are three choices when you find yourself a few thousand miles downwind in a boat that won't make to windward: sell it, ship it home on a freighter, or sail it the rest of the way around. I have seen all three happen. I think every designer of a cruising boat should himself make good 500 miles to windward in his brain child before presenting it as a "go-anywhere" boat.

It was the same with *Spray*. Her charm for Joshua Slocum, that grand old man, was largely that the hull was free for the taking. That he rebuilt her and sailed the boat on the first single-handed circumnavigation shows what a fine seaman he was, but this is scant incentive for today's sailor. *Spray* was a horrible design. Because Slocum used a broken alarm clock for a chronometer is hardly reason for anyone else to. Slocum spun a good yarn, and he saw no reason to volunteer that navigating by the outdated method of lunar distances required no timepiece at all.

Another type of vessel variously praised and maligned for cruising purposes is the multihull, especially the trimaran. Their speed, spaciousness, reputed low cost, ease of construction, shallow draft, and light weight make them a favorite of neophyte sailors. Actually, few trimarans have performed as well as ordinary monohulls; there is a great deal of wetted hull surface, which, combined with extreme beam, makes them difficult to maneuver, expensive to maintain, and slow in light air. The extreme light loading required for even moderate-to-fair wind performances means imprudently short supplies of food, water, general stores, spares, fuel, and ground tackle. They are notoriously lacking in windward ability, and they have to be babied through beam seas. One fellow sailed with us more than 2,000 miles to windward from Samoa to Hawaii to buy some chain, an anchor, and some bottom paint rather than attempt the passage in his trimaran. He flew back.

Trimarans are good fun in mild conditions, but they are not suited for ocean passages, where they may be unable to avoid heavy seas and very strong winds. The support of the water, upon which all multihulls depend for stability, can be lost under extreme conditions. If a big swell falls away under a trimaran, her stability becomes close to zero until her hulls are back in the water. If a heavy sea strikes on only one hull, the forces generated can be very destructive. Trimarans cannot heel to a hard gust of wind, spilling pressure from their sails. In extreme conditions the wind may catch the underside of the wing area and flip a trimaran over. In January 1969, the 60-foot trimaran *Wakatoru* was found floating upside down in the Tasman Sea, dismasted but without any hull damage, her nine-man crew unaccounted for. I know of trimarans that flipped over at their moorings in South Africa and in New Zealand.

Cats are a different breed. The catamaran is inherently a far healthier hull configuration than a trimaran because her two hulls bear similar loads and are located at the ends of the connecting beams. Often there is less decked-over area forward and aft on cats than on tris. However, they have the same stability problems, and their accommodations below deck, except in quite large boats, tend to be cramped.

So if you are looking for a cruising boat, don't always go for the popular design. A capable cruising boat may seem odd, different, or old-fashioned. She will be designed to move, not to sit still. Her element is the sea and the wind, and they are the same now as they always have been.

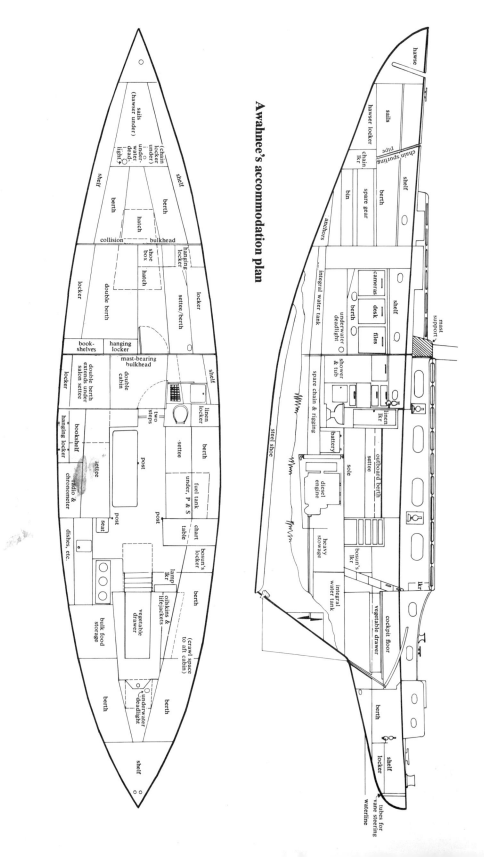

A wahnee's accommodation plan

Deck plan labels (top):

sails (hawser under)

(chain locker under)

i-o- under- water dead-light

shelf

shelf

berth

berth

hatch

collision — bulkhead

shoe box

hanging locker

hatch

locker

settee/berth

double berth

locker

book-shelves

hanging locker

mast-bearing bulkhead

shelf

double cabin

double berth extends under salon settee

linen locker

locker

two steps

berth

settee

bookshelf

hanging locker

settee

post

radio & chronometer

post

seat

post

dishes, etc.

fuel tank under, P & S

chart table

bosun's locker

lamp lkr

oilskins & lifejackets

berth

vegetable drawer

bulk food storage

(crawl space to aft cabin)

i-o- under- water -deadlight

berth

berth

shelf

Profile plan labels (bottom):

hawse

sails

hawser locker

chain pipe

chain lkr

chain spurling pipe

bin

spare gear

shelf

berth

anchors

integral water tank

cameras

desk

files

shelf

underwater deadlight

mast support

shower & tub

spare chain & rigging

linen lkr

battery

outboard berth

settee

sole

diesel engine

heavy stowage

bosun's lkr

integral water tank

steel shoe

lkr

cockpit floor

vegetable drawer

berth

shelf locker

tubes for vane steering

waterline

CHAPTER 1

Hull design

A sailboat with an easily driven hull and clean and simple rigging will sail well on and off the wind. There is no reason to design a cruising boat that is not able to perform well on all points of sail.

The hull of a sea-going boat should be full and powerful, not skinny and slab-sided, nor fat and round. I favor a hull with a beam/waterline ratio of 1 : 3 or 1 : 3.5. A good hull should have an easy entry at the bow and an easy run aft where the water leaves the stern. "Easy" means shaped so that the hull moves the water aside and allows it to flow back together without an abrupt change of direction. As a displacement boat moves ahead, water parted by the bow is forced out and under the hull and then rises along the run to the stern.

Look at the underbody of a boat on a lines plan. The waterlines show the type of entry it has. In the vertical view they should be just about straight where they meet the stem. If the waterlines are curved or leave the stem at a wide angle, you are probably dealing with a bluff-bowed tub that will be hard to push through the water. A reverse curve at the bow or stern will make for suction and serious interference of flow.

At the stern, the buttock lines on the profile view will be long and relatively straight if the hull has an easy run. Curved buttock lines tell you that as the hull moves ahead the water must fill in around its shape, creating suction forces in the region of the stern. A long straight run lets the stern of a boat slip through the water with a minimum of drag. *Awahnee* actually makes less apparent wake than our Sabot dinghy, which we sometimes tow astern.

Closely related to easy entry and run is the location of the point of maximum beam on each waterline. Look carefully at the lines drawing, vertical view. At the waterline a good hull has its greatest beam close to halfway between bow and stern, with the maximum beam further aft in each successively higher longitudinal section. On *Awahnee* the deep underbody is widest under the shrouds, while at the sheer she is beamiest just forward of the cockpit. The aftward movement of maximum beam from waterline to sheer creates a more easily driven hull. The shape also contributes to the boat's steering, lending directional stability when moving forward with the hull heeled over. Remember that the shape in the water of a boat sailing well heeled is quite different from that at anchor. The performance of a boat on any point of sailing but a dead run is thus greatly influenced by hull shape above, as well as below, the designed waterline.

THE BOW

Above the waterline a hull should have ample sheer, with the bow curving out to a graceful shape. Plumb stems and slab-sided bows make for wet, dangerous boats; they lack the buoyancy necessary to rise in an ocean swell or a heavy sea. In extreme cases, these bows will plunge and ship green water, especially if the stern has proportionately greater buoyancy than the bow. Many boats are designed with the mainmast so far forward that a bowsprit is required to carry sufficient headsail area to balance the mainsail. Cost is usually the rationale, since it's cheaper to build a boat with the hull (the expensive part) small and the rig spilling over fore and aft. How much more seaworthy a hull could be if the bow were simply extended out to the end of the bowsprit! Then the boat would have a long, easy entry into the water. She would have reserve buoyancy forward with space below for a generous fo'c's'le. She would be faster because of longer waterline length, anchor rodes wouldn't foul the bobstay, sails could be handled on deck, and the most vulnerable appendage of the boat would be eliminated.

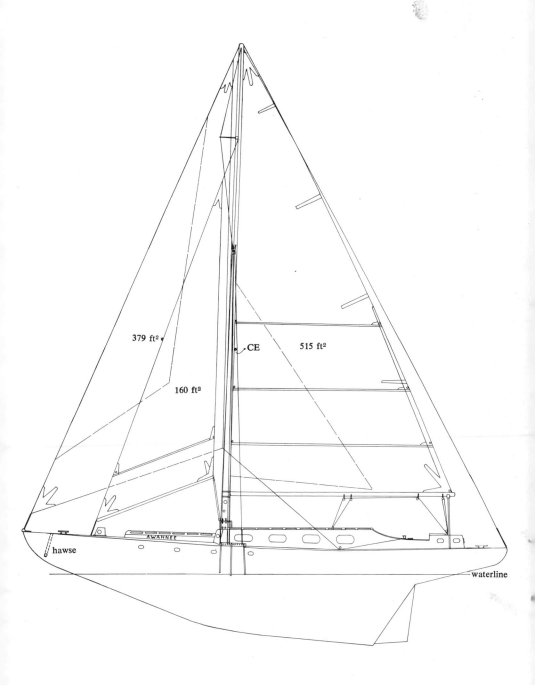

379 ft²

160 ft²

CE

515 ft²

AWAHNEE

hawse

waterline

Awahnee's sail plan

THE STERN

In my opinion, a boat designed to sail the ocean should have a pointed stern. Boats with transom sterns provide more space below and more stern buoyancy than double-ended boats of the same length, but a transom stern is fundamentally the result of a longer hull that has had its tapered stern cut off. The transomed hull has less space and flotation than if it had lines to please the forces of nature rather than the boat buyer's bank book. *Awahnee* is a 53-foot boat. Give or take a bit, a transomed 48-foot boat is a 53-foot boat that has been chopped off.

All displacement sailboats are double-ended below the waterline. In light air a boat does not immerse the transom (unless she is overloaded). But a boat heeling to 25 to 30 degrees or more in a seaway will suck water behind a dragging transom with a great loss of speed, control, and, ultimately, safety. Boats with especially wide transoms and rudders far astern can heel so sharply that all helm is lost, with the rudder rotated up near the surface. This is especially true of boats with relatively narrow bows. Such a combination of features explains many a spinnaker knockdown.

I consider a pointed stern the natural conclusion of a hull shape, allowing water to flow past with little turbulence on any course or condition of sea. A canoe stern, in addition, protects the rudder and provides reserve buoyancy. When paired with a bow of good proportion and easy entry, a canoe stern increases effective waterline length when heeled, resulting in greater hull speed. Sailing with her rail down, *Awahnee*'s waterline is about 50 feet, rather than 43 feet when she is moored. In ultimate conditions, when hove to by the "stern quarter," *Awahnee*'s canoe stern presents its easy curves and reserve buoyancy to outrageous seas and rides them well.

THE KEEL

The keel should descend with a long, sloping profile, reaching its deepest point just forward of the rudder. Besides the obvious protection this gives the rudder in the event of grounding, a sloping keel acts as a pivot point and enhances steering response. Once, working dead to windward in the narrow channel of Tomales Bay on a rising tide, I deliberately held each tack till *Awahnee* touched her keel on the hard sand bottom before coming about.

With this keel profile a boat can be safely placed on a marine railway in a nearly level position, or put on the hard and braced against a pier, where bottom work can be done at low tide without resort to a boatyard or carriage.

To my mind, this keel profile gives an inherent safety factor overlooked by many designers and sailing men. In extreme conditions the bow of a boat with a descending keel will yield and pay away before overwhelming seas, when another boat with a deeper forefront might capsize or pitchpole.

THE RUDDER

For me, a protected rudder is one of the prime requirements of a cruising boat. It should be mounted on the after edge of the keel and deadwood, but not extending as deep as the keel shoe. I have a personal fear of incorporating the gudgeon in the keel shoe or skeg. Gudgeons should be fastened strongly and separately. Otherwise, in a severe grounding, losing the keel shoe could unnecessarily disable the rudder. Rudders separately mounted at the stern are vulnerable to damage and fouling. Here I think it wise to rig a strap or cable extending from the keel to the foot of the rudderpost to provide a shedding surface in chance encounters with lines, cables, or logs.

Spade rudders do not have the strength of a rudder mounted in a gudgeon at the bottom of the rudderpost; I have seen them folded sideways against the hull from the lateral pressure of a broaching sea.

A triangular rudder shape, widest at the bottom where the water is least turbulent, gives the most effective steering area. Its bottom should not be parallel to the waterline, but should rise a bit to make a shedding surface. I have drilled a hole near the bottom of the trailing edge of *Awahnee*'s rudder where a shackle can be fixed for control lines if the tiller becomes inoperative. I keep the hole filled with putty and painted over.

I prefer to have the propellor aperture cut from the deadwood so that all of the water passing the hull bears on the rudder, and so that the propellor wash will increase the helm's responsiveness under power.

For steering, I favor a tiller over a wheel in any well-balanced boat up to about *Awahnee*'s size, 53 feet. Tillers, besides being simple, inexpensive, dependable, and fast-acting, allow the helmsman a better feel for the boat's responsiveness to wind and waves.

An observant sailor, with a sensitive helm, can learn things about sail trim and balance that a teacher cannot put in words.

One difficulty with wheel steering is its vulnerability to stresses in a heavy seaway or when grounding. Damaging forces cannot always be as promptly absorbed as they can with a tiller; as a result, castings, gears, wire splices, and other parts of a wheel system are more prone to failure. In the grueling 1961 Transtasman Race, *Awahnee* and four other tiller-steered boats finished without damage, while three of five wheel-equipped entries finished under jury steering rigs.

There is seldom opportunity to compare the performance of different cruising boats in ultimate conditions. Accurate storm data is almost impossible to gather from small-boat equipment, and two boats offshore rarely experience the same storm conditions. However, in February 1966, *Awahnee* was less than ten miles away from Jean Gau's Tahiti ketch *Atom* in a blow off the south coast of Africa. This storm ranked as the most ferocious we had known until our Antarctic voyage of 1970–71.

We had left Durban with a favorable weather forecast four afternoons before, enroute to Capetown more than 1,000 miles away. We expected easy going and a boost of two and a half to five knots from the southerly Agulhas Current for the first part of the passage. At midnight there was an eerie calm; then came the ominous cold breath of Antarctic wind. The "southerly buster" steadily and quickly increased to at least 80 knots against the Agulhas Current. By late morning we were lying under bare poles to three stern drogues in absolutely monstrous seas. Every now and then a huge wave would come quartering in on a diagonal from the Indian Ocean. The breaking seas were so high that they blotted out the sun at three o'clock in the afternoon. Three of them broke over *Awahnee*—knocking her down, spreaders in the water—during the 72 hours we spent lying to drogues. Our 12-foot skiff was lashed on the cabin top in a cradle, and held a sailing dinghy and a wet canvas jib under its boatcover. The seas washed the cradle from under the skiff. We never saw it again.

Awahnee withstood this weather without complaint. Time and again she would pivot through 50 or 60 degrees of arc without rolling over as the bow yielded to overwhelming beam seas. By comparison, *Atom* was washed by waves that rolled her over, sweeping away her bowsprit, masts, booms, dinghy, and everything else on deck. Jean was able to bail her out, remove saltwater from the engine, and motor 50 miles on his remaining fuel capacity of 55 miles to Knysna Heads, a village behind a slit in the cliff.

When we sailed into the river port of East London, South Africa, for refuge, the meteorological station at the entrance was registering gusts to 71 knots. A local coastal ship of 12,000 tons moored upriver from us shortly after we arrived. Her stanchions were twisted and her steel bulwarks crumpled; she had struggled 24 hours on what was normally an eight-hour run.

I am convinced that *Awahnee*'s hull, with its easy lines, lack of windage, and simple, strong rig, has been a major factor in her performance year after year, from the Bering Sea to Antarctica, without trouble or disabling damage where other boats have been stove in or rolled over by heavy seas. She is better able to perform in winds and seas of hurricane force than any other boat I have known.

CHAPTER 2

Deck structures

There are several basic structures and items of equipment which distinguish a sea-going boat from a drinking platform: the working space on deck, and the size and construction of the cockpit, hatches, deckboxes, ports, gallows, lifelines, and pulpits.

A clear, unobstructed deck wide enough for a person to walk easily and safely from the bow to the stern makes all anchoring, sailhandling, dinghy launching, fish landing, and loading and unloading easier. As a dividend, there is room to sleep under the stars, say, in an exotic tropical bay with a cool spicy breeze wafting down on you and the smell at dawn of woodsmoke from a cooking fire ashore. On *Awahnee*'s deck a couple can sleep just forward of the house, port and starboard; there is also room for one person farther forward. The cabin top provides sleeping area under the awning for several more.

High bulwarks make for topside weight and windage. Furthermore, they are vulnerable when lying alongside. A sea-going boat is better off with a simple toerail. Ours, of two-by-one-inch hardwood glued and screwed to the rubrail, contains loose items on deck quite satisfactorily and marks the edge of the deck nicely. It is low enough so you can lie on deck and touch the water, and gives a good handhold after a swim or when getting on board from the dinghy. The toerail has scuppers located about seven feet apart from the shrouds to the afterdeck to drain off water. The aftermost scupper is only five feet forward of the stern to carry off fish blood and scraps aft of the cockpit, minimizing fishy footprints on board.

When designing *Awahnee,* I thought that if collecting rainwater were ever necessary (and it has been, twice), I wanted to be able to collect it from the full area of the deck and the vertical area of the sails without major sailhandling, and without having to rig a special awning. Awnings are a favorite scheme for collecting water, but they are ungainly at sea in a squall—they get in the way of the running gear, and in a big wind you're lucky to get them rigged at all. I put a water intake fitting through the deck at the widest part of the boat, port and starboard, leading to a short nipple with a hose thread on it below deck. In a heavy rain, after the deckboxes and spinnaker poles have been checked and cleared of flying fish and squid, and after the sails, house, and deck have been rinsed free of salt, I plug the leeward toerail scuppers with clean cloth. Then all water striking the boat is available for collection. However, my three-quarter-inch fittings are not large enough to drain it all off the deck in a bountiful downpour.

The rubrail should be substantial to protect the hull from contact with a pier or other vessels. Rubrails are expendable fittings, and should be designed to be easily replaced if damaged. They should be strongly attached to prevent being displaced up or down in use. I accomplished this by laminating the rail, throughbolting the inner laminations and screwing the sacrificial outer piece to them.

THE COCKPIT

A cockpit should be strong enough to withstand the force and weight of a breaking sea, and should drain quickly. This means, of course, that it should not be too large, that the floor should slant to generous drains, and that the companionway sill should rise above the cockpit coaming or have washboards. Cockpit seats that serve as lockers are out of place in a sea-going boat, unless the lockers are watertight and drain elsewhere than the bilge. I once bought the handsome English ketch *America* in Tahiti, and sailed her to New Zealand in early winter. She obviously had been designed for day sailing; she had a beautiful teak cockpit nearly ten feet long which drained through the cabin door into the bilge. Before casting off, I put in beams and a cambered half-inch plywood cover over the cockpit, leaving a narrow space for the helmsman to stand. I was thankful that I had when we ran into a gale and heavy breaking seas south of Tonga. In this weather we held to runs of only 40 to 60 miles a day out of concern for the cockpit drainage system on the 67-year-old boat.

A cockpit should be comfortable, utilitarian, and protected. Many boats have center cockpits these days, and they can be very wet. One of the pleasures of sailing a large boat from a cockpit well aft is seeing spray blow across the cabin top while you stay dry at the helm. Some center cockpits are applied onto the deck structure rather than let into the deck. High coamings between main and aft cabins form the cockpit, with seats higher than deck level and the cockpit floors flush with the deck. In my opinion, such a cockpit is a dangerous place to be in heavy weather. If the boat, heeling heavily, gets tossed by a big wave, the helmsman is so far above the center of gravity that he is liable to be thrown off his feet or even out of the boat. In addition, center-cockpit boats usually have a punishing amount of windage in the long, high cabin trunks. Large boats absorb this configuration much more easily than small ones.

Most cockpit seats are at deck level and are a continuation of the deck construction. Seats should be wide and long enough for sleeping so the watch can be seconded without undue discomfort, but close enough together to brace your legs on the leeward side when heeled over. To relieve the cause of "helmsman's rear end," a drain should be put at the low point of the cockpit seat so that accumulated rainwater and spray drain off the seat. Another solution is to install raised slat seats; the effect is something like two park benches mounted in the cockpit.

Our cockpit coaming is continuous with the main cabin trunk and the after cabin. It is double-walled and narrower at the top than the bottom to form comfortable backrests for the cockpit seats. There is space between the inboard and outboard walls to store all manner of essential small deck items. The tunnel-like space also connects the inside of the main cabin with the aft cabin, providing good ventilation. In it we stow sail gaskets, winch handles, sponges, deck brushes, fishing gear, odd small lines, a knife, shackles and pliers, reefing lines, the leadline, the heaving line, the fog horn, and a waterproof flashlight. I hate to think how difficult life at sea would be without all these things stowed close at hand. Small tubes drain water overboard. Five-inch lips at the cabin ends of the stowage space usually keep water from finding its way below. But off South Africa during our knockdowns, water cascaded through the hollow coaming into the cabins. Now we are careful to put the storm covers over each opening in good time when the seas get rough.

HATCHES

Anyone who has slept under a leaky hatch or portlight has no doubt acquired a sincere appreciation of dry quarters. Forward hatches proofed against heavy spray and boarding waves are worth every effort of preventive maintenance; the alternative is sodden bedding and provisions. We designed hatches for the second *Awahnee* which remain the best I have seen or slept under, with the exception of metal-framed hatches that dog into gaskets. There are two forward hatches on *Awahnee*'s long foredeck, one over the fo'c's'le and a larger one over the forward cabin. Continuous coamings run from the cabin trunk forward to form two hatch trunks and three deckboxes (**see drawing**). These coamings form an extra lip

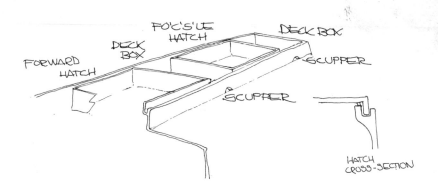

AWAHNEE'S HATCH PLAN

running fore and aft outside the hatches, protecting them from direct assault by heavy spray and forming a channel for drainage. The hatch cover seals on a gasket against the top of the hatch trunk, but not to the bottom, so that water drains forward or aft but not inside the boat. Under severe conditions, the hatches are secured by lashings from ringbolts below, and a storm cover is tied across the coamings on deck.

In my opinion, all hatches should be on the centerline of a ballasted boat. An open off-center hatch makes a boat vulnerable to swamping and sinking in a knockdown. Hatch openings from the cockpit should be above the cockpit coaming level, or should be equipped with solid washboards so a filled cockpit cannot flood below.

Sliding companionway hatches are difficult to make absolutely watertight. I built a fine one of standard design on *Awahnee* that was deeply protected on all sides by the hatch cover and a raised inner coaming with a heavy brass slide mounted atop it. It looked virtually airtight, but the water ran under its forward edge when a big green wave came across the cabin top. The problem was cured by bolting a watertight housing to the cabin top to receive the hatch cover in the open position and to protect the forward end when it is closed. The housing interferes with space on the cabin top, but a dry galley and chart table are well worth the slight inconvenience.

A well-designed collapsible dodger with windows is an excellent addition to a cruising boat. It is there when you need it and can be folded away when it gets too hot below, or when windage must be reduced in heavy weather. Permanently constructed doghouses offer nice shade, but they also present the problems of permanent windage and antiballast. Because dodgers or doghouses can at times interfere with the helmsman's vision, the collapsible versions are superior.

DECKBOXES

Having a place on deck for neat, safe stowage is an enormous convenience. Many boats don't even have a place for a pair of pliers on the foredeck. A simple job like shackling an extra length of chain to an anchor becomes maddeningly difficult when one must go below, lift up a bunk cushion, and rummage around for the proper shackle or tool. *Awahnee*'s three deckboxes accommodate not only tools, but also a wet headsail or two, a ready anchor, sail gaskets, seizing lines, shackles, quantities of fruit—and on occasion, a 55-gallon fuel drum.

I built my deckboxes by incorporating them into the spaces between two forward hatches and the fore-and-aft coamings that run from the cabin almost to the staysail tack fitting. Scuppers drain each deckbox. Handrails bolted to the coamings provide places for lashing in gear. The aftermost deckbox, just forward of the house, is quite spacious, about three and a half square feet; it accommodates the big loads. Sometimes we clean it out, plug the scuppers, and pipe in warm engine-cooling water for baths. The middle deckbox between the two hatches is about ten inches long and holds gaskets, a small assortment of shackles, and a pair of pliers. Forward of the fo'c's'le hatch is the third deckbox, where we stow odd pieces of gear, some lashing line, gaskets, or the ready anchor and chain. Its forward end, just aft of the anchor windlass, is designed to provide an alternative fastening point for the bitter end of an anchor rode.

PORTS AND VENTILATORS

Since I have never been able to keep opening portholes absolutely watertight in all conditions, I designed the second *Awahnee* without any lateral openings. Ventilation is a fore-and-aft affair anyway. Large fixed portlights are a common feature on cruising boats now, and they are one of the most vulnerable parts of a sea-going boat. They should be small, heavily glassed and equipped with storm shutters.

In the 75,000 miles the second *Awahnee* sailed before I built storm shutters—around Good Hope, around the Horn, and from Japan through the Bering Sea to the Aleutian Islands—three of her three-eighth-inch plate glass cabin portlights were smashed by the force of the sea. Since then I sailed *Awahnee* with storm shutters on a short circumnavigation of the world in Antarctic waters, and although we weathered far heavier blows than any we'd known, our portlights held.

Our storm shutters are simple to make and install. Heavy grooved battens are bolted on a taper to the cabin sides above and below the portlights. These receive the quarter-inch marine plywood storm shutters, which jam into the grooves. No hardware is necessary. Into each shutter we cut two holes four inches in diameter, which bathe

the cabin in dim but adequate light in heavy weather.

There are only three opening portholes on *Awahnee,* two on the forward end of the main cabin and one in the after end of the aft cabin. They give minimal but adequate ventilation when the hatches must remain closed.

At sea, those who sleep under the hatches are assigned to tend them. *Awahnee* has a good open airway below deck and is well ventilated by the forward hatches, which can be propped open on any side since they are not hinged to the hatch trunk. When we are taking spray on the foredeck, we usually open the hatch a crack on the lee or after side. Other times we rig the fo'c's'le hatch storm cover and open the hatch under it. Even a small amount of air pleasantly refreshes the entire boat.

Dorade ventilators, which duct air through a drain box and a standpipe, do the most successful job of delivering air below deck. But they have also been known to deliver a sizable dollop of H_2O, and to hide rats or rotting flying fish. It is important to keep an air current flowing continuously through the cabin. See to it that some ventilators are turned downwind to evacuate air from below. And keep the scuppers clear.

Awahnee's two dorade ventilators are recessed into the forward end of the cabin. Their structure gives broad support to the mast step and at the same time provides two storage places for small items like winch handles and a snatch block or two.

Many boats at anchor rig canvas windscoops at the forward hatch, but I have found that a dinghy sail hoisted over the hatch, its tack and clew made fast on deck port and starboard, creates a delightful draft through the boat. In hot, rainy weather a small awning over the forward hatch will allow you to let the air in, but keep the rain out.

We have never needed to rig insect screens because mosquito coil punks have always been sufficient. We no longer even carry screens.

THE GALLOWS

A permanent sturdy gallows is essential for safe handling of the boom. Taking down the main in a squall is dangerous business, and a dropped boom can be lethal to anyone beneath it. My gallows, mounted on the aft cabin trunk, holds the boom five feet above deck level, which in the cockpit provides full standing headroom under the mainsheet blocks. Gallows mounted by the main hatch may work into the design of a doghouse or dodger, but their position may also rob a sailor of sufficient leverage to wrestle the boom safely in during rough weather.

PULPITS, LIFELINES, AND HANDRAILS

Pulpits and lifelines are now fitted to practically every boat of moderate size and larger, and they should be designed to withstand heavy treatment. The force of a man falling against a lifeline is terrific. The legs of pulpits and stanchion sockets should end in generous-sized flanges that are bolted through both the toerail and deck (**see drawing**). Triangulating braces from the flanges to the sockets greatly strengthen them and provide excellent lashing points for deck gear.

Some lifelines are so low they can trip a crewman who has lost his balance, and cause him to fall overboard. In my opinion they should be a minimum of 30 inches high and have two strands of wire. The pulpits, being more subject to damage, should overlap the lifelines at the same height, but should stand separate. If the pulpits are torn off, the stanchions and lifelines will likely remain intact. Aboard

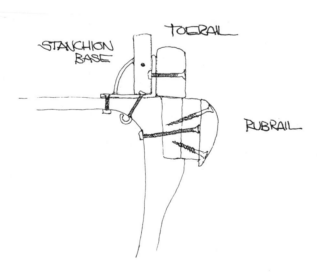

Awahnee no one lounges against the lifelines or uses them to pull themselves aboard because I don't want them exposed to wear that might result in failure at a time of vital need. Twice I have seen my lifelines prevent a falling man from going overboard.

When my two youngest children were two and a half and three and a half years old, I laced fishnet with one-inch-square mesh from the toerail to the top lifeline, making it safe for them to roam the decks.

We maintain a watch on deck aboard *Awahnee* at all times. Three or four stout lines rigged at different heights on the gallows supports to the ends of the handrails on the main cabin safely contain the helmsman and anyone else in the cockpit. More than once this web of lines has strained me from an engulfing sea.

CHAPTER 3

Standing rigging

Through the years I have come to realize that in day-in-day-out cruising, sailboat gear must be heavy enough not only to do the immediate job, but to do it safely even after signs of wear and age have started to appear. One ought to be able to detect these signs well before failure, rather than have a piece of hardware give way without prior warning. Reliability is the greatest need in standing rigging, yet many boats are outfitted by designers and builders who stint on strength to reduce weight and windage aloft. The frequent dismastings seen in day sailing, cruising, and racing are often due to this preference, which places a fraction of a knot of boatspeed before reliability. A fast rig is fast only if it stays on board. On the other hand, grossly overstrength rigging unnecessarily penalizes the performance of a boat with excess windage and weight aloft.

A rig is only as strong as its weakest part. I once stood on Marsden Wharf in Auckland, New Zealand, admiring a rerigged Bristol trawler about 80 feet long. Since it was low tide the spreaders were just above eye level, and I noticed that the three-quarter-inch-diameter main shrouds were attached to mast tangs by ridiculously small shackles. The apparent splendor of this classic boat only disguised her unseaworthiness. If dismasted in mid-ocean, she might take months to make port.

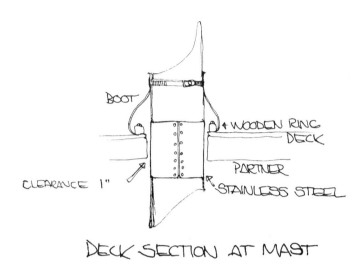

BOOT

WOODEN RING

DECK

PARTNER

CLEARANCE 1"

STAINLESS STEEL

DECK SECTION AT MAST

THE MAST

On the first *Awahnee,* the mast was stepped below deck on the keelson. It passed through an oversized hole in the partners with about an inch of clearance all around. Stainless steel bands on the mast and the partners guarded against possible chafe, while a Dacron boot coated with boiled linseed oil and kerosene kept water out. From my observations, a mast stepped on the keel is less likely to break if it is not wedged tightly at the deck. Under extraordinary loads it should be able to bend from foot to head. Ideally, a mast should be rigged to act as a column, but this is difficult to achieve since loads are so variable. Wedged masts often fracture right at deck level and in so doing often spring the deck, creating two major repair jobs. I have seen a wedged aluminum mast break so cleanly at the deck that it appeared to have been cut. Rubber wedges, though they tend to crawl under pressure, are better than wooden ones, but in my opinion, a free-standing mast with no wedges is best (**see drawing**).

On the other hand, a mast stepped on deck or on the cabin top, as with the present *Awahnee,* allows more room below, is shorter, and therefore is less expensive. Still, the downward thrust of the mast must be transmitted to the keel by a post or bearing bulkhead. Its chief advantage is that if a shroud or stay parts, a deck-stepped mast will probably go overboard in one piece, and can be recovered and stepped again.

Awahnee has a wooden mast with a single-spreader rig. There are two pairs of lower shrouds, an intermediate shroud, and a topmast shroud. She has twin headstays, which I highly recommend, a jackstay opposed by jumper struts on the mast (rather than running backstays), and a permanent backstay. Only on very severe passages do we rig the running backstays, which are usually stowed below deck.

Round or oval masts must be firmly fixed to prevent rotation. The butt of a mast should be cut at the proper angle, considering its rake, to rest squarely on the maststep.

STAYS, SHROUDS, AND FITTINGS

Bowsprits and bumkins are easily damaged in collisions with piers or other boats. In rigging a bowsprit, you must be sure that the shrouds and bobstay are at a sufficient angle to support the spar well, as lateral pull generated by a jib full of wind is considerable. Twelve degrees is acceptable, fifteen degrees is preferred. If the angle is too acute, whiskers (spreaders) must be rigged to increase it. The same angles also apply to the intersection of shrouds and mast.

One-by-nineteen stainless steel wire rope is much favored for standing rigging because it has the greatest strength per size and the least stretch of any commonly used shroud and stay material, except rod rigging. However, stainless steel wire rope is more brittle than galvanized wire. I have been disappointed many times by stainless wire breaking both along its length and at pressed or swaged fittings. One-by-nineteen wire, especially stainless, cannot satisfactorily be bent around a thimble without disturbing its lay, thereby putting an unequal strain on its strands. Individual wires often fail at a swaged terminal fitting from slight flexing. The swaging process itself often creates stresses that can lead to failure. Examining the lays of a three-eighth-inch 1×19 stainless steel headstay that once failed, I noticed dark, discolored inner strands that had broken long before, and bright, newly parted breaks on the outer strands. Despite the evidence of internal breakage, I continue to use 1 × 19 stainless steel for my headstays and staysail stay, since this wire best resists abrasion from jib hanks. I am wary of rod rigging because of the difficulty of replacing it, and because I have witnessed many failures.

For all my standing rigging, except the stays which carry sails, I have reverted from stainless steel to galvanized wire. Galvanized standing rigging served well for ten years on the first *Awahnee.* In fact, no galvanized standing rigging has ever failed aboard my boats. In general, galvanized wire has tensile strength comparable to stainless steel of the same size and lay. It can be found anywhere in the world, and, for the same money, you can buy four times as much galvanized as stainless steel. Also, galvanized wire provides signs of deterioration when rust and "fishhooks" (individual broken wires) appear. The fishhooks do not appreciably weaken wire rope laid finer than 1 × 19, although they do indicate that it is time for replacement.

On *Awahnee* the shrouds on each side have a computed breaking strength of one and a half times her displacement, and they have supported the mast through weather more ferocious than I care to see again. However, I have discarded two half-inch-diameter 1 × 19 stainless shrouds in the past eight years when several strands parted next to the swages. I suspect the damage resulted not from the working load but from countless lateral strains near the swage —crew members grasping shrouds when climbing aboard, for example, or lying alongside a wharf where high fenders press against them. For the shrouds and backstays, therefore, I prefer 6 × 7 or 7 × 7 wire rope. All strands of 7 × 7 wire rope are wire, but in 6 × 7 the center core is oil-impregnated hemp, which lubricates and prevents deterioration inside the wire rope. When splices are used, the center core is usually cut out, reducing the strength of a given diameter 7 × 7 wire to about that of the same diameter 6 × 7. Therefore 7 × 7 is preferable with swages where the center core is retained, but with poured sockets or splices 6 × 7 should be the choice. Stretch is small enough in these lays of wire rope to be taken up by the turnbuckles.

On *Awahnee,* I have always used galvanized turnbuckles. Stainless steel or bronze are prohibitively expensive in the sizes *Awahnee* uses. When the first *Awahnee* was lost on a Tuamotu reef in 1964, we salvaged the turnbuckles, chainplates, tangs, and some of the shrouds and stays, with which we rigged the new *Awahnee.* In

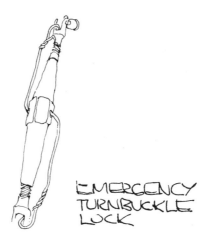

EMERGENCY
TURNBUCKLE
LOCK

1970, just before our Antarctic circumnavigation, we finally replaced the turnbuckles after 20 years and some 150,000 miles of
sailing, not because the threads were worn, but because the forks
had become too thin to entrust with the job of supporting the mast.
Threads can be adequately protected by dressing them with waterproof grease inside and outside the barrel, and taping from bottom
to top.

A locking device is needed to keep turnbuckles from turning
loose under the variable loads they bear. If the turnbuckle lacks
right-and-left-handed locking nuts or some other strong locking device, a length of heavy galvanized wire run from fork to fork
through the barrel of the turnbuckle and served will do the trick.
The wire should lead tight against the turnbuckle with the ends
securely twisted (**see drawing**).

A fine but rare piece of rigging hardware is the solid cast thimble. The cast thimble can withstand the compression on the eye of
a shroud, stay, or halyard better than pressed metal thimbles, which
can become misshapen or cracked, putting damaging strain on the
wire.

Chainplates should extend well below the rail along reinforced
frames or hull sections. *Awahnee*'s three chainplates reach slightly
below the waterline. These hold a bar at deck level which is drilled

to take the turnbuckle forks and variously canted to give fair leads to all shrouds. The center leads for upper and intermediate shrouds are almost vertical, pointing directly to the outboard end of the spreader, and the lower shroud leads are inclined more inward. It is an excellent system, as stress on any shroud is distributed to all three chainplates. Through knockdowns and standing jibes, no chainplate bolt has ever failed or even started or leaked. I have not seen this kind of rig on any other modern boat. The equalizer bars could provide the attachment for support legs with *Awahnee* standing on her keel while work is done below the waterline.

Awahnee displayed the strength of her equalizer bar, chainplates, and rigging at the end of the first and only Gladstone-to-Bowen race through the Great Barrier Reef of Australia. After the finish we were taken in tow by the committee boat and accidentally dragged along the high town wharf. Structural steel projecting 18 feet above the water broke our $7/_{16}$-inch intermediate shroud and damaged the topmost shroud. No chainplate or tang fitting gave enough to crack the paint on the hull or mast. In another boat we might well have had the whole rig down around our ears.

The tangs and chainplates salvaged from the wreck of our first *Awahnee* taught us an unforgettable lesson. These fittings, badly twisted in the wreck, were hammered into shape before reuse. The backstay chainplate was overstraightened, and had to be bent back toward the mast on installation. Six thousand miles later, in the middle of the Indian Ocean, we discovered it had torn halfway across at the bend. Immediate jury rigging prevented loss of the mast, but it was very close. We later had a similar problem with the backstay tang at the masthead. I can only advise that salvaged gear be used with caution. Make sure it is annealed to relieve internal stresses and prevent hardening. Above all, give it a fair lead.

Mast fittings taking the strain of the shrouds should be well engineered. I feel it is best to use long tangs screwed, riveted, or welded into place and throughbolted. Another option is bands that encompass the mast and are throughbolted. Numerous bolts should be avoided because of the weakening effect of multiple holes close together in a spar. My pear-shaped Scottish spruce mast has two clamped, fenestrated ten-inch-wide metal collars with only one five-eighth-inch bolt through the mast at the shroud tangs. Cracked paint is the first indication that a fitting is starting to give;

it is a danger sign that cannot in safety be overlooked. Rather than peening bolts aloft, which virtually prevents their removal and re-use, I secure them by distorting a single thread with a screwdriver and hammer. This prevents the nut from turning except under the force of a wrench.

The angle of tangs and chainplates is critical to sound standing rigging. They must be set at the same angle as the shrouds, or else strain will cause flexing, most often at the swaged fitting, until either the tang or the wires break. Many sailors use toggles to pro-vide a fair lead. I prefer to avoid the expense and weight of addi-tional parts by seeing to it that the gear itself is led fair. This way stainless steel bolts can be used to attach shrouds directly to the turnbuckles and to attach turnbuckles to chainplates. *Awahnee*'s headstays are attached by $\frac{7}{16}$-inch stainless shackles which allow them to move. This arrangement accommodates the varying lead angles induced by headsails straining the stays without forcing a lateral pull on the fittings.

The problem of attaching rigging at the masthead is crucial to the seaworthiness of a boat. All the forces are downward, com-pressing the mast. Mounting the stay and shroud tangs on a metal masthead box that fits over the top of the spar is the best solution I have seen. This design distributes the load of the rigging through-out the total area of the mast top, and maintains maximum strength in the mast because no bolt holes are drilled, except for one small keeper. In addition, the box prevents water from getting inside the mast and acts as a radar reflector high above the water.

Awahnee's masthead box is constructed of welded steel, galva-nized after fabrication. It rests atop the mast on a horizontal parti-tion six inches from its bottom, and the box extends ten inches higher. The upper section contains the main halyard and the two jib halyard sheaves. Welded across the top fore and aft is the one-piece headstay and backstay tang; another steel strap athwartships forms the upper shroud tangs. A $\frac{3}{16}$-inch stainless steel work halyard sheave is mounted on the extended main halyard sheave bolt. The work halyard provides the means for a crewmember to go aloft in the bosun's chair at sea with full working sail hoisted to steady the boat, and it also serves as a flag halyard. It could serve in a pinch as the main halyard. The masthead light is mounted on top of the box.

LIGHTNING

One of the great imponderables a sailor faces at sea is the threat of lightning. He is all too aware that his mast, with its metal fixtures, is the highest thing around. A common device to provide an avenue for electricity to pass from masthead to the ground is heavy copper wire or woven battery straps trailed in the sea from the lee shrouds. But this certainly is a lot of fuss and bother when you tack. One would think a steel boat has the best possible ground, but we met one in the West Indies so magnetized when struck by lightning that her compass had a deviation of 50 degrees.

It has always been a comfort to me, perhaps a false comfort, to know that our chainplates, bolted on the outside of the hull, reach the water and provide a ground for the mast. But one can never be completely sure with lightning. After our Antarctic circumnavigation, *Awahnee* was dismasted on the New Zealand coast on a night of raging black thundersqualls and stiff winds. My son was at the helm and I was in the cockpit. For some time we had been surrounded by lightning, and it was impossible for either one of us to adjust our eyes to the blinding flashes. The sails had been up and down a dozen times since sunset. As the force of another squall hurtled us through the turmoil of water, rain, spray, and islands, I went forward to let go the jib halyard. It was cleated on the windward side of the mast. The next thing I knew I was standing in the cockpit, and there was nothing higher on the boat than the dinghy stowed on the cabin top.

Neither of us can say for sure if the mast was struck by lightning, but I am convinced it was. The bottom half lay intact, close alongside the hull, held by the lower shrouds, with the torn mainsail floating amid a tangle of boom, sheet, and rigging. The top half of the mast had disintegrated above the spreaders. None of the four lower shrouds had parted, but the mast butt had jumped out of the steel mast step on the cabin top. Though I was on the foredeck when we were hit, I had no recollection of crawling aft over the rigging. I must have been stunned. The only sure evidence we found that lightning struck was a bit of charred wood where a wire to the masthead light had burned and melted; the light had not been on. I believe the chainplates bled most of the electrical charge harmlessly into the water. On further thought, I must consider the possibility that the metal masthead box attracted the lightning in the first place. Nonetheless, I installed the masthead box on the new mast. And use it still.

TUNING THE RIGGING

Properly tuned rigging will optimally distribute forces to mast supports designed for the load. Overstressed rigging and a loaded mast put great strain on the hull, the fittings, the mast step, and even the garboard. If rigging is slack, excessive flexing and movement of the parts may reduce support throughout its length.

The mast of a cruising boat is basically a column and should be held straight under load. Most masts rake aft. They should, however, be perpendicular to the waterline when viewed from forward or aft. To accomplish this, trim the boat carefully to eliminate any list and hang a plumb bob from some distance up the mast track. If the mast leans one way or the other, the plumb will reveal it.

The only way to tune a mast satisfactorily, according to my experience, is while the boat is sailing in a breeze with full working sail up. Sight up the sailtrack on one tack and then the other— whatever curve there is will be apparent. Check to see that each pair of shrouds is equally tight. Feel the tension on the lee shrouds through a series of quick tacks. The leeward shrouds should slacken a bit when the boat is on the wind. Remove no more than half the excess slack from a leeward shroud, then tack and check the other side. If you have two lower shrouds on each side, they should be under equal tension. A well-tuned mast under load may have a slight fair curve throughout its length.

Jumper struts and shrouds are required to support the upper portion of masts without masthead headstays, and on mizzen masts they can take the place of forestays. They put a thrust aft against the mast and counter its forward movement by stiffening the upper portion of the mast as a whole. Jumpers are particularly effective when they are paired and when intermediate shrouds attach at the same place. If the mast bows forward at the staysail tang when the staysail is drawing, the jumper shrouds should be tightened. Before a passage where very heavy winds are expected, tangs where running backstays can be rigged if necessary should be fitted at the jumpers. This gave me great comfort on *Awahnee*'s passages south of Australia, around the Horn, and around Antarctica.

Tuning a headstay tight enough to attain a straight jib luff is practically impossible in a long headstay. It would place excessive tension on the rig and all its parts. I have never seen the luff on a large jib held straight in a good breeze. Just the same, headstays and backstays should be very firm—as a general rule, tuned at rest to the same tension they would sustain in a force-six wind with the working jib up.

Rigging should be retuned after a hard passage or long sailing on the same tack. Any slackness is cause for concern and requires close examination of the mast, rigging, and fittings for signs of failure: cracked paint, bent or warped parts, cracked swages, elongated openings, worn pins, and loose or drifted screws.

CHAPTER 4

Running rigging

The various components of running rigging—sheets, blocks, halyards, shackles, lifts, vangs, and guys—must all be sufficiently strong to control sails and spars under all conditions. Wherever possible, strength should be combined with simplicity. Simple running rigging allows easy use and repair and less possibility of failure. In some respects, simplified gear may prove more efficient than the complex gear on racing boats, and will likely perform longer.

Adjusting the sails and running gear is the essence of the pleasure I get out of sailing. It is a challenge to spend an afternoon at sea in a brisk wind, changing combinations of sails to get the best performance from your boat. You can fly a headsail higher off the deck to keep it from shipping water; sailing downwind you can rig a small jib below the spinnaker pole or the main boom to catch more air; or the jib sheet can be led through a snatch block on the main boom to gain more draft on the headsail and avoid backwinding the main. In heavier weather you can discover for yourself what jib best balances a double-reefed main. Perhaps the #3 jib flying on the staysail stay gives an easier ride than it does on the headstay, since it operates closer to the hull's center of lateral resistance.

I don't expect ever to know all there is to know about sailing.

RIGGING A BOOM

In sheeting a mainsail, realize that the wind exerts an upward and leeward stress along the length of the boom. If a sheet is rigged to a bail at the after end, a common arrangement, the stress in heavy wind can flex the spar enough to distort the sail and even break the boom. Boom vangs are rigged to counteract this. In my opinion it is simpler and better when dealing with large sails and long booms to have sheet blocks on several bails to distribute a compensating downward pull on the spar. This also provides support near the clew of a reefed main, a factor often overlooked in sheeting arrangements.

Bails should be bolted through the boom and supported by metal straps over it. *Awahnee*'s 24-foot boom has four bails with the mainsheet rigged as a six-power tackle. By running the sheet along the boom over the cockpit, we keep it clear of the standing helmsman and others in the cockpit. This rig has withstood many—too many—full standing jibes without damage in over 200,000 miles of sailing. As a matter of fact, on *Awahnee*'s record-breaking 1963 Atlantic crossing one fellow jibed five times without equipment failure. I marvel now that I did not relieve him of his watch, but he was cheerful, pleasant, and earnest.

When the helmsman heads off too far before the wind, the boat staggers, rolling without an identifiable heel to leeward. She is sailing "by the lee" without the full press of wind in the sails. It doesn't take an experienced sailor to know there has been a change, and to know there will soon be another. Usually I can get to the cockpit in time to prevent the impending jibe. One time when I got to the cockpit too late, there was nothing to be seen to leeward. For an awful instant I thought the backstay was broken and the mast gone. As it turned out, the three-quarter-inch manila preventer had parted, and the boom, instead of jibing clear across, had lifted and hung up overhead against the backstay.

I have not yet fully resolved some problems in the use of a preventer on the main boom. Long elastic preventers have been known to stretch enough for a complete jibe, while a tight and inelastic preventer puts a tremendous strain on the gooseneck and boom— especially if the boom dips in the sea. I now use a permanently rigged three-quarter-inch-diameter Dacron preventer made fast at the end of *Awahnee*'s main boom. I rig it with a snatch block to a two-power nylon preventer tackle on the foredeck, thereby gaining a degree of spring with sufficient mechanical advantage for control. I once saw a beautiful 36-foot "T" section boom destroyed when its end dragged in the sea and the boom was too inflexibly prevented at a midlength point. Preventers on the main boom should be rigged whenever needed, and removed as soon as they are not.

I find it a great benefit when jibing in severe conditions to throw the preventer completely into the water from the foredeck. Then as a controlled jibe is executed, the drag of the preventer in the water and against the stern pulpit and backstay cushions the jibe's impact. A much greater cushioning effect is gained by taking the mainsheet in hand over hand as the boom comes across, and then stopping the sheet gradually as it runs through the blocks, absorbing the impact of the jibe. After the jibe, the preventer is led forward and made fast, and rope burns treated if necessary.

Clew outhaul tackle should be rigged along the boom where it can be handled from a secure position on any point of sail. On *Awahnee* this is done with a six-power tackle. The clew car travels on a short, heavy track and is moved by a quarter-inch stainless steel cable with a two-power arrangement at the end of the boom to a three-power cheek block tackle on a track fixed to the side of the boom a few feet from the gooseneck. However, with synthetic sails in cruising conditions, there is little need to make frequent adjustments to the outhaul.

The topping lift can also be handled from the inboard end of the boom. A three-power cheek block tackle on track should be rigged on the same side of the boom as the main halyard so that one man can conveniently work them both.

By lifting the outer end of the boom, the topping lift greatly influences the set of the sail. Too tight a topping lift impairs windward ability by allowing too much twist in the sail and spilling wind out of the leech. However, deliberately done, this adjustment to the lift gives a fine control over drive in the main and is a great help in balancing headsails and main. On the wind, the sail should bear nearly the full weight of the boom, with the topping lift slightly taut (if slack it will chafe the leech of the sail). Off the wind in light air, raising the boom slightly will allow the sail to work better by deepening the draft. Topping up the boom to form a bag in the sail during rainsqualls makes a good water-collecting rig. Water can flow off the sail into an upright dinghy or bucket under the gooseneck.

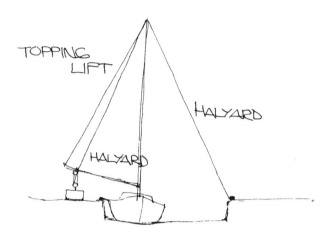

TOPPING LIFT

HALYARD

HALYARD

USING A HALYARD FOR LOADING

By rigging a halyard as an auxiliary single- or double-power topping lift, you can use the boom to hoist heavy loads (**see drawing**). Staysail or spinnaker booms can be used to do the same. In either case the topping lift should be directly above the tackle bearing the load. When a heavy weight, such as an engine, is swung aboard on the boom, it will heel the boat a great deal. Another halyard can guy the mast against this force, or a short strong mooring line can be run from an inboard chainplate up to the pier.

The heeling effect of a heavy load on the boom, supported by its topping lift and swung outboard, is useful in getting a boat off a grounding. Once in a race off the Great Barrier Reef, the entire crew sat out on the boom, lessening *Awahnee*'s draft enough to sail off a sandbank. In more serious groundings, anchors, chain, movable ballast, or other gear can be hung off the boom to heel the boat.

Goosenecks take a great thrust from the boom. They should be sturdy and allow the boom to rotate and lift as well as pivot. We have a sliding gooseneck mounted on two bands around the mast, an excellent arrangement. I keep the luff of the main tight enough to hold the boom at its highest position while sailing. This means sweating up a bit on the halyard as necessary underway.

Most boats are regularly rigged with vangs to stress the boom down in heavy wind. *Awahnee*'s main boom, however, is heavy and is stressed downward against the sail by the mainsheet tackle at four points. I have never found it necessary to use a vang except to flatten the sail in light airs on the wind, in which case it is rigged from the forward mainsheet bail to the ringbolt of the jibsheet block. Then it keeps the boom from beating the wind out of the sail as the boat rolls.

Travelers should be as wide as practical in order to provide a downward rather than an inward pull on the boom when close-reaching. The traveler assembly should come up against shock-absorbing padding to reduce wear on gear and nerves. In fact, every block that can flop on deck in light airs should be silenced. A flattened "Turk's head" around the ringbolt or pad eye of a block helps eliminate this most maddening of sounds and prevents damage.

HALYARDS, WINCHES, AND SAILTRACK

For halyards, I prefer flexible stainless steel wire spliced to rope tails. This gives the advantages of rope's ease of handling and wire's resistance to chafe and lesser windage and stretch. A splice will pass over the masthead sheaves, which are double-grooved on *Awahnee* to take both wire and rope. I have used full-length half-inch Dacron line for halyards, but chafe at the masthead makes it unreliable for permanent use.

Reel halyard winches with their ability to house long wire halyards have become very popular, yet I still prefer the simplicity of the rope–wire marriage on an open drum winch. I enjoy seeing *Awahnee*'s sails go up faster than those of other boats her size. An experienced man on the halyard can haul at full arm's length until three turns are thrown on the winch to pull the sail up the last few inches.

To make the halyard fast we keep three turns on the winch, pass the line under the deckhook, and make fast on the pinrail. With only three turns on the drum, some of the halyard tension is transferred to the deckhook. This simple, old-fashioned rig relieves the winch and its fastenings of some of the strain and braces it. I never put too many turns on winches when making lines fast; synthetic lines are so strong that deck hardware can be pulled out before a line breaks. For this reason I distrust winches with cleats built into their tops, since they absorb all the tension on a line from one direction. I feel that all winches should have separate cleats mounted on the side opposite the direction of pull to provide support.

In analyzing multiple gear failure, I am sometimes surprised by the basic cause. One breezy afternoon in the early days of my cruising, I was sitting on the leeward deck seizing hanks on a Yankee jib. We were charging along comfortably but somewhat pressed in moderate seas on a close reach. Suddenly all hell broke loose. There was a tremendous crash on deck inches from my foot, the jib halyard fell around me, and the jib dropped into the water, held only by its tack. It took some time to piece together what had happened. The winch had been taking the full load of the jib halyard, with four or five turns on its drum. The winch had then torn off the mast and, as the turns spun off the drum, whirled to the deck, cutting a groove an inch deep. The jib halyard had suddenly become slack and then, just as suddenly, snapped tight as the sail took up hard against the bitter end still made fast. The metal of the hanks had sheared in quick succession from top to bottom like an opening zipper, leaving the wire-luffed jib suddenly flying free, held only by the tack, the jib halyard, and the sheet. The pressure had been so great that the halyard had parted at the masthead and the sail had dropped into the sea while the halyard snaked down to the deck. Hence, my "three turns on the winch" rule. No winch aboard *Awahnee* has pulled off its base since.

On lowering the sail, you can keep accurate control with a turn or two left on a drum winch. When handling a large headsail, I often blanket it behind the eased-out main and lower rapidly in stages when it is inboard so it will drop on the foredeck dry. I might also mention here that the bitter ends of all our halyards are fast at the pinrail to prevent accidental loss when dousing a sail.

Awahnee's 542-square-foot mainsail does not require a downhaul because I take great care to keep the sailtrack firmly in place, fair all joints accurately, keep the slides in good condition, and oil the track with a small wick attached to the top slide. In heavy weather I will often haul the main down hand over hand without coming into the wind to save wear and tear on the sail. Before the wind, the main can be lowered by this method without coming up.

I have a separate track mounted on the mast for the main trysail. When it is required, we bend the trysail on and leave it lashed to the lower part of the mast or to the shrouds. Then we can set it without trouble, and without interfering with the working main. The tack is made fast to the gooseneck on a lead long enough to let it fly above the furled mainsail. Sheets (one for each tack) lead aft around mooring cleats to a jibsheet winch at the cockpit.

The sheet winches in *Awahnee*'s cockpit are mounted on the coaming, with their cleats aft and cocked from the line of pull so turns can be put on without binding against the line coming off the winch. The main, jib, and staysail sheets should be cleated within reach of the helmsman. For shorthanded sailing, the topping lift as well can be led to the cockpit.

In handling running rigging, keep in mind that small-diameter synthetic line may be adequately strong, but it is too small to haul your whole weight on. (See FINGER CUTS in Chapter 15, "Health.") Half-inch-diameter line is the smallest practical size for hauling, and even that is uncomfortable if it's heavily loaded. I use three-quarter-inch line for jibsheets and spinnaker afterguys.

SPINNAKER POLES

In my experience in races, spinnaker poles have failed more frequently than any other item of running rigging. I believe that the spinnaker pole, with its fittings, is the most fully loaded piece of equipment on the boat in long distance sailing. The tension transmitted to the pole from an afterguy can be tremendous. I don't trust interchangeable bell fittings nearly as much as I used to, and on *Awahnee* I now make the afterguy fast completely around the outboard end fitting with a clove hitch and bowline (**see drawing**). This balances the tension and eliminates twist on the pole. At the mast fitting I rig a safety line on the pole to prevent its jumping from the bell fitting. I also find it best to rig the spinnaker pole topping lift three-quarters of the way out, as it provides better control and support of the pole.

I carry two spinnaker poles, one of which is three feet longer than the base of the foretriangle. The long pole gives added power before the wind by holding more of the spinnaker out in clean air. Also, since this pole is longer, it can pole out an overlapping jib. As I once discovered, the longer solid pole makes a better jury-rigged mast than the hollow, but heavier, shorter pole. My poles are

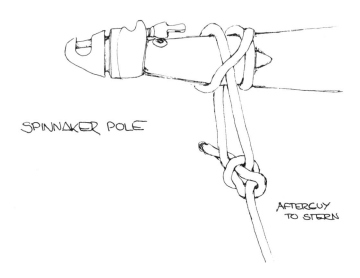

SPINNAKER POLE

AFTERGUY
TO STERN

stowed on deck, port and starboard, secured to the stanchion bases, usually with the ends outboard unless we are lying alongside a pier. This arrangement keeps more deck space clear and braces a crewman sleeping under the stars. On deck, the poles provide much less antiballast, windage, and general interference with sailing ability than if they were mounted vertically at the base of the mast.

In the 1969 Transpacific Race, the ends broke off both spinnaker poles aboard the 83-foot *Pursuit*. As watch captain, I rerigged each pole with a crown knot tied in three-quarter-inch Dacron line, slipped over the broken ends and seized in place. The four loops of the knot took, successively, the clew of the 3,600-square-foot heavy kite, the afterguy, the foreguy, and the topping lift—and we drove on at speeds that reached 16 and 17 knots.

CHAFE

Chafe works against gear all the time a sailboat is rigged. Wherever sails or lines move, chafe is doing damage. Mindful as I am of chafe, I prefer not to rig baggywrinkles. (Use of baggywrinkles and other excessive chafing gear, unnecessary spars and gear stowed up the mast or on deck, double ratlines, dodgers, wind screens, lazy jacks, multiple purchase halyards, and too many ropes aloft all do their continuous and cumulative part to hinder windward performance.)

Instead of baggywrinkles, when sailing broad before the wind, I wrap a large-diameter mooring line around the after leeward shroud ten or twelve times in a long spiral to give increased contact area to the mainsail. Continuous attention to the set of the sail and prevention of hard contact can greatly reduce chafe. Plastic hose or wooden tubes rigged over shrouds prevent chafing jib sheets, and hose on running backstays reduces wear on the mainsail. Wire will chafe wire, as in the case of stainless steel lifelines wearing the larger shrouds if they aren't led clear. Synthetic lines suffer from wear when led around corners or small radius turns, as their tendency to stretch causes an abrasive or sawing action. Halyards must be closely watched and listened to; you can hear them chafe when you're hoisting a sail. A foul lead across a stay, across another line, or around the hauling part can wear through in a few hours. Split plastic hose can be put around lines or solid hose slipped over their ends. The eyes of mooring lines can be spliced with chafe-preventing hose in place. A piece of leather with punched holes and laces is handy and versatile as chafing gear.

DECK FITTINGS

I prefer to keep deck fittings and gear to a minimum. The work of many deck-mounted toe-breakers can be done as well with various pendants and snatch blocks. Unencumbered decks are safe to walk on, good to sleep on, and neat to look at. (I recommend bare feet for safety, health, quiet, and simplicity aboard *Awahnee,* and for the welcome absence of deck shoe aroma.) Snatch blocks can be made fast to the shroud equalizing bar, deckhooks, jibsheet block ringbolt, jibsheet cleat, and several other spots that ingenuity finds. Thus I have only one jib sheet block ringbolt on the port and starboard decks. Strangely, half-inch bronze ringbolts have served longer than any of several five-eighth-inch stainless steel ones, which crystallized and broke under load.

I set all jib tacks except the genoa and storm jib at a height where the sheets lead fair through the deck block. As a general rule, jibsheets should angle down about ten degrees from the miter of the sail. Storm-jib sheets are led through snatch blocks on pendants at the mast step deckhooks to the jib deck blocks and then to the cockpit winches. The genoa sheets go through snatch blocks to a #7 Merriman winch mounted on the afterdeck. This winch doubles as a stern anchor windlass and as a mooring winch.

RIGGING STRENGTH

Most cruising boats, except ones that are especially tender, can take an ordinary squall all standing, although it may be necessary to reduce effective sail quickly by easing the main and falling off dead before the wind with the jib blanketed in the lee of the main. The last time we sailed from Hawaii to New Zealand, we were hit by terrifically heavy squalls in the doldrums. Instead of lasting their usual 20 minutes or half-hour, they blew for several hours at forces up to 50 knots. In the doldrums there is rarely any wind at all outside a squall; you ride zephyrs right up to a squall's relatively stationary black wall before the blast hits.

When one caught us at two in the morning with all plain sail up, we were suddenly driving hard with the whole lee deck buried and a heavy wash coming in over the cockpit coaming. Nancy pinched up to ease the force on the sails, as the wind was far too strong to risk bringing it abeam while falling off to sail before it. Once we had reduced to staysail alone and established an acceptable course, we realized that had there been an off-center hatch, we might have actually sailed *Awahnee* under. In the old days, before synthetic fibers and swaged rigging, sails would blow out or halyards, sheets, or splices would part before a knockdown occurred. As we learned on this occasion, it is possible for everything to hold while the boat is pinned down on her beam ends.

Some people might think there is no excuse for being caught in such a situation. They may be right. But on a dark night without moon or stars to see by, there is nothing to differentiate an ordinary squall from a super squall. My own experience has persuaded me to sail the boat at night in light airs with enough sail to move well and comfortably. I have always felt a boat should be sailed to use the wind she has to make the most productive course.

CHAPTER 5

Sails

Working sails drive a boat day in and day out through fair wind and foul for thousands of miles into unknown and changing conditions. For a boat that will embark on a voyage beyond the horizon, sails should be made to measure by an experienced sailmaker. Stormsails and supplementary sails for light air can be inexpensively obtained second-hand. Realize the simple fact that a boat in passage sails longer in one month that a boat underway for 12 hours every weekend for a year.

SAIL MATERIALS

Sails of Dacron, Terylene, and Tetoron (materials that are all chemically the same but manufactured in different countries) are generally strong and lasting, but I have learned from hard experience that some of them are not. Synthetic material seems to vary greatly in quality without apparent differences. I once commissioned a suit of sails from a sailmaker in New Zealand. At the time I was confused by the broad selection of available materials. I made my choice: 11-ounce imported Dacron. The main blew out in less than a year. Within two years, no less than 14 heartbreaking and sometimes heart-stopping failures had occurred in the cloth itself. The material was just plain rotten. I had to throw away the whole suit of sails.

I have since learned that the New Zealand government imposes an annual monetary limit on fabrics and all other products bought overseas. I now suppose that the Dacron I bought was low-priced and less than first quality at the outset. I am only glad I didn't lose my boat because of it.

On the other hand, I still use a Dacron Ratsey and Lapthorn #2 genoa that I bought second-hand in 1963. My #3 jib, which has flown on all three of *Awahnee*'s circumnavigations, is British-made Terelyne cloth sewn in New Zealand.

Weak thread has also been the cause of failure in some of my newer sails. Whether due to the sailmaker's poor choice of thread or faulty manufacture I do not know, but the strength was gone before the cloth failed. Chafe was not a factor; the seams simply fell apart from normal use.

Working sails for a cruising boat will cost in the neighborhood of two dollars per square foot. Most cruising skippers cannot afford to order additional sails custom-made for their boat, which might include a genoa or two, two or three smaller jibs, a genoa staysail, a mizzen staysail, a spinnaker, and stormsails. For hard-pressed sailors, Bacon and Associates at 528-SD6 Second Street, Annapolis, Maryland 21403 save the day with their lists of hundreds of used sails at favorable prices. They will ship by Railway Express to any address in the U.S. or Canada. In addition to the four suits of working sails I have commissioned since 1959 from Denmark, New Zealand, and Hong Kong, I have bought sixteen extra sails from Bacon and have never failed to be completely satisfied with them.

As a veterinarian I well know the futility of beating a dead horse, but I do want to mention that I have had great pleasure and excellent service from flax and cotton sails. The first *Awahnee* was fitted out with two suits of flax sails in 1951. Flax, which when bleached and combed becomes linen, has the highest oil content of any natural fiber, making it highly resistant to rot. Before synthetic material was developed, flax was favored for cruising sails even though it presented serious stretch problems. The era of synthetic working sails overtook *Awahnee* in 1961, except for one flax Yankee we carried three more years until it was retired to replace the lining of a sleeping bag.

I continued to buy occasional sails of cotton and flax, though, because the price was right and I was beginning to appreciate the convenience of having sails for all seasons. I was once chagrined to notice that a 750-square-foot cotton genoa, for which I had just paid $75, was stamped "1942—mold treated." The sail was 24 years old. We flew it for four years; true to claim, it did not mold even though it was not extensively cared for. However, it was more weight than two men could handle when wet.

No one can forget the warmth of rolling up in a soft, fragrant flax jib on the foredeck, or dozing in the trough of the flax main along the boom. Nor can one forget the small secret pleasure of hurriedly cutting two feet of hoist off and reshaping the head of the stretched flax main the night before a club race and romping along near the lead, surprising the competition with a decently setting sail that could be tacked without having to lift the boom over the gallows.

WORKING SAILS

In general, I favor heavy or moderately heavy working sails to allow for the occasional heavy gust or squall. *Awahnee*'s are made of ten-and-three-quarter-ounce Tetoron, the Japanese equivalent of Dacron. Moderate roach and battens are necessary for full performance of the main, but battens below the highest reefing cringle should be parallel to the foot of the sail for easier reefing. All working sails should be triple-stitched and leathered at tack, clew, head, and at each slide or hank. Synthetic substitutes for leather are entirely satisfactory and sometimes an improvement. Tabling should extend generously from each corner of every sail and from the reefing cringles of the main, jib, and staysail. The cringles should be set into the fabric of the sail rather than standing externally, where the roping around them will be chafed. Roping should extend full strength for some distance above the highest reefing cringle before tapering into a rattail.

Choice of the reefing method is crucial to ordering your mainsail. I favor slab reefing for two reasons: it gives unquestionably the best reefed sailfoil, and, just as importantly, it doesn't interfere with the normal placement of mainsheet blocks along the boom where they support the spar.

Lacing in a reef may sound like a tedious process compared with cranking up a few turns on a roller-reefing main, but the choice is not that simple. Roller-reefing systems commonly place so little tension aft along the foot of the sail that the leech creeps forward as the boom is rolled, making a baggy sail that won't drive the boat to windward well. This is true even when the boom is shaped. While rolling the sail, the luff piles up. Each successive turn of the boom rolls up more luff while the leech spirals forward along the boom, where the diameter is increased only by the sail material with each roll. A deeply roller-reefed sail will make the boom droop, sometimes so low that the boat cannot come about or the sail cannot be reduced farther. In addition, a long or light boom is insufficiently braced in heavy weather with the sheet attached only at the outer end.

The thought of a luff-furling mainsail on a large cruising boat is disturbing to me because of the complicated gear and arrangements necessary. A seaman is always cautious about changing a reliable procedure; a gale in the Bay of Biscay is a long way from a boat-show display or a Sunday demonstration sail.

Originally, I used reef points on *Awahnee*'s mainsail, but after experiencing the various problems inherent with them—ties of unequal tension, mismatched ties, knots coming undone, loose reef-points spinning and cutting themselves off—I changed to lacing and now consider it undoubtedly the best method.

The first row of reefing grommets is five feet above the foot of *Awahnee*'s main, the second is six feet above the first, and the third reef tucks in seven feet more of the sail, reducing it to half its full size. The reefing grommets are set in a slight downward curve to give a relatively flat sail for good windward performance. In all but extreme weather conditions, the reefed *Awahnee* can continue sailing the preferred course instead of falling off to leeward. She is maneuverable and capable enough to come about for a man overboard, should that extreme situation present itself.

The working jib should have the clew cut high. Genoas and low-cut jibs often ship water from the bow wave when sailing hard, putting enormous strain on sail and gear. It is not uncommon for this reason to blow a jib and/or rip off several hanks. Extending the tack pendant helps, but may require moving the sheet block farther aft.

In order to fly any sail properly, but especially a jib, the halyard must be tight enough to set up the luff. Thus tension is distributed evenly to all the hanks, and the sail can develop maximum power. If the luff is scalloped, the airfoil of the sail is inefficient and wear on the hanks is increased, as is the possibility of a seam giving way under the concentrated tension at each hank. When the lowest and uppermost hanks are some distance from the corners of the sail, they are subjected to much more tension than usual because the luff wire tends to sag away from the headstay. By seizing extra hanks or slides at the head and tack of a sail, you can assure a straight luff and greatly improve its set. Hardware thus located is the mark of a carefully designed sail. An extra hank at the miter of a jib will also give added support at the point where maximum tension results if the halyard is accidentally released with the sail drawing heavily.

I favor wire luffs in jibs. Once I was talked into a tape luff on a Yankee jib when the sailmaker assured me that it was as strong as wire and, because of less handwork, cheaper. I suppose it was cheaper, but stronger it was not. The head tore right out of the tape-luffed Yankee a couple of years after it was built; a wire-luffed sail of exactly the same dimensions and weight and three years older is still flying. (I do, however, subscribe to the idea that a sailboat doesn't go anywhere unless the sails are up—that is, I didn't baby that jib. I used it pretty hard, as I do all my sails.)

Roller-furling jibs have become popular in recent years. Many cruising men see them as effortlessly providing the whole spectrum of jib sizes on a single sail, free from the expense and bother of acquiring, bending on, taking in, and stowing several different head-sails. This might be so if furling jibs really worked in all conditions of furl. But in heavy weather when it is furled way in, the luff of a roller-furling jib disturbs the airflow, making the sail inefficient to weather and increasing the boat's windage. When the sheet is trimmed in hard, the bulky luff tends to sag no matter how tight the roll. Sometimes the swivels jam and it will not furl properly. And, flying at the bow of the boat when used as a stormsail, a roller-furled jib is far less desirable and beneficial than a stormsail closer to the center of lateral resistance of the hull. Even when furled and not in use, the sail will age and weather at the clew and along the exposed spirals of the leech and foot. Mounted in the usual place just aft of the headstay, the roller-furling jib seriously hinders use of a second jib, since it will interfere with tacking. For anyone who does rig a furling jib, I recommend one that can be lowered to the deck without anyone going aloft; at anchor or un-derway in storm conditions its windage can be eliminated, and it will be more accessible when repairs are necessary.

Under no conditions should a furling jib be a boat's only headstay. Twin headstays and several jibs are simpler and more efficient at sea, and give flexibility and control on the foredeck.

STORMSAILS

Stormsails are critical, and their balance is critical. The ability to claw off a lee shore in 50 knots of wind is basically a matter of hull design and rig, but the principle bears repeating here, for stormsails in those conditions are the most reliable means of getting underway and continuing to move. In a real blow with a steep bay chop one must be cautious about performance expectations. Simply reducing sail area in inverse proportion to wind strength does not give equivalent sailing performance. *Awahnee* will come about under mainsail alone in fair weather, but she couldn't come about in a heavy blow without a headsail in addition to the reefed main.

In order to have real ability in heavy weather, a boat needs a balance of sails working forward and aft of the mainmast. This means, ideally, a storm main and a storm staysail, though a storm jib will do if there is no staysail stay. Sails that work on the ends of a boat like the jib and jigger of a ketch do not drive the boat to weather efficiently. On my 45-foot ketch *America* with jib and jigger flying we made good mostly sideways in a 40-knot blow off the Kermadec Islands. We had plenty of sea room, so it didn't really matter—that time. All we lost was a day and a half of progress. The closer the stormsails are to the center of lateral resistance of the hull, the more efficient they are driving the boat to windward and giving ability to come about. This is essentially why I have been unafraid to sail *Awahnee* on voyages around the Horn, in the Bering Sea, and on a circumnavigation of the Antarctic.

I like well-sewn and reinforced synthetic material in stormsails. It need not be heavier than the working sails since the material is strong and the total area small. Stormsails can even be sewn of material a little lighter than heavy working sails. Stormsails should have hand-sewn grommets and be roped on all sides. Heavy hand-stitched canvas or flax is acceptable, too, as long as the material has its full strength. The storm main and staysail should be cut full for big wind, but not so baggy that the boat won't sail to windward under them. As the result of terrifying experience, I recommend that the storm main fly with the head no higher than the lower spreaders. Then if the track pulls off the mast, the sail can be laced around the mast and flown anyway.

Awahnee's storm main is a second-hand heavy Dacron mizzen sail with a Dacron rope luff supported by a stainless steel luff adjustment wire. We roped this sail on its leech after buying it in order to make it strong enough to serve as the storm main. Still, I can't bring myself to discard my noble old hand-sewn canvas trysail cut with its panels parallel to the leech. It has endured amazing blows. The storm staysail is roped on all sides. Because its area is less than 50 square feet I call it the "handkerchief staysail." It alone has driven the 25-ton *Awahnee* at more than six knots downwind.

ADDITIONAL SAILS

One spends 90 percent of passage-making looking for wind, so sails for light airs are the most useful additions to the required working sails and stormsails. A ghoster jib the weight of a heavy spinnaker will fly when the swell rolls the wind out of a heavier sail. You'll have to hand the ghoster when the wind picks up, of course, as it is relatively delicate. It should have only a modest overlap, or none if the base of the foretriangle is relatively long, to ease handling and to minimize contact with the spreader. The clew should be low. But the important thing is that the luff be as long as possible.

Sailing to Japan from Hawaii in 1967, *Awahnee* was becalmed or in the lightest breaths of air for 18 consecutive days of the 4,300-mile, 35-day passage. We motored and motorsailed for six days and still did not find wind. I removed the prop to reduce drag. Two days later in exasperation I replaced it, and we burned our reserve fuel and what stove kerosene we could spare, then I took the prop off again. One thoroughly demoralizing morning we fitted a papaya skin with a splinter for a mast and a paper sail and watched it sail away from us. Sometimes we steered an outlandish course in order to be able to sail at all. We experimented using a light jib in place of the working mainsail. This gave us the idea that a very light main with a wire luff, set without slides or hanks and sheeted to the afterdeck, would be a splendid addition to the inventory of sails aboard a cruising boat. It would work like a giant fair-weather trysail, and being unattached to the boom, it would have only its own weight to lift before supplying power to the boat. We have since acquired a ghoster main, and with the ghoster jib we now sail zephyrs that would have left us becalmed, floating with last night's orange peels and this morning's egg shells still in sight.

Jibs drive a boat, and a well-suited yacht will have several. A big genoa will give many miles more than a Yankee in light steady going. A genoa staysail also is a good light weather sail on the wind in combination with the genny or Yankee and off the wind when it captures the air that escapes under the spinnaker. A jib about two-thirds the size of the working jib is very handy as well; with the reefed main one can take full advantage of strong winds for comfortable, fast sailing. Another smaller jib will give greater choice and reserve in heavier going.

In a light following wind the only sail that will fly is a spinnaker, and I recommend that a cruising boat carry the largest one possible. The alternatives are to motor or to wait for stronger wind. In a fresh breeze the best arrangement is to have twin headstays and pole one jib out to windward and another set to leeward. Under this rig it is possible to sail a course that would normally cause the main to blanket the leeward jib; the poled-out windward jib solves the problem by effectively scooping air into the leeward jib. Many trade-wind routes are on this point of sail. With three or four different-sized headsails you can sail comfortably before as much wind as you care to. In augmented trades or the westerlies, the double-jib rig with smaller headsails is the one that will give easiest handling and maximum miles made good. (See discussions at greater length in Chapter 13, "Sailhandling.")

SAIL REPAIR

When sail repairs become necessary at sea, the best course of action is to go ahead and stitch away. Practice makes perfect. A palm, sailmaker's needles, spare material, and waxed twine are all you need to make strong, lasting repairs. A household sewing machine is not really capable of sewing anything but the very lightest sails, so don't regret not having one aboard.

The simplest repair is stitching a torn seam. Although a sailmaker's is one of the longest apprenticeships, anyone who can sew a button on can put a seam back together. Sewing a small patch comes next on the scale of difficulty. Rebuilding a tack or clew is more demanding; open up the tabling of the damaged sail, insert and align the spare part, stitch heavily through the whole lot, and splice or seize the boltropes together. I keep a mainsail headboard and the tacks and clews of a couple of long-gone sails for emergency repairs.

Just north of the Tres Evangelistas Islands off the coast of Chile at the western end of the Strait of Magellan, we managed to blow seven sails, including the working main, in two and a half days of storm that threatened to drive us back around the Horn. Only the stormsails, the ghoster, and the spinnaker remained intact. Stitching up the heaviest ones first, we succeeded in keeping pace with the wind as it eased and larger sails were needed. By the time the wind had dropped to force six, the main was repaired and flying with a single reef tucked in it.

Boltropes or tape along the edges of sails take a great deal of strain, and their stitching has to be inspected and maintained continually. Restitching a boltrope is not really difficult, but it does require careful work. Stitches should pass around one of the strands of the rope rather than through it to avoid weakening it.

Every needle hole weakens synthetic material. To avoid making unnecessarily large holes, small needles should be used. Stitches should be rather large and not too close to the edges of the material. A #16 needle is a good all-purpose size, though larger ones will be needed on very heavy material. Patching material should be close to the same weight as the sail being patched, or chafe can result. The edges of synthetic patches can be melted over a stove burner or kerosene lamp to eliminate the need for folding under a hem.

Restitching a few seams and closing and patching a tear or two will give you the confidence to rebuild a torn-out grommet. For this, use copper or stainless steel wire bent at least twice around the desired circumference to form the enlarged grommet. Lay it in place and sew it to the tabling with radiating stitches all the way around, covering the metal completely. To end off, cut the thread and tie its two ends together at the surface of the material. The knot won't pull through unless too large a needle has been used.

Don't waste time. As soon as damage is detected in a sail, take it down. A seam open six inches can rip out to 20 feet in a matter of seconds. If luffs are permitted to scallop, the strain on each slide lashing increases and eventually a grommet may pull out or a tabling seam rip—weaknesses that herald a sail blowing out completely. If you use point or lace reefing, keep a weather eye on the reef patches where seams are under severe strain.

Slides and hanks that have come loose can be seized with sail twine, wet rawhide or soft braided waxed Dacron cord with a braided core. The braided Dacron has worked best for me. Hard-twist marline is usable for jib hanks, but it tends to cut and wear rapidly on slides. Copper wire and tiny stainless shackles wear the boltrope leathers and grommets of a mainsail. I haven't tried the nylon-bushed sail shackles, although I have heard that they are satisfactory and strong.

Wear gradually appears on jib hanks even when they are used on large-diameter 1 × 19 stays—a thousand-mile windward leg takes its toll, as do all the hours of work a sail performs. Extra hanks in abundance are a must for the cruising sail kit. For some years now I have successfully brazed new metal on worn jib hanks without removing them from the sail, safeguarding the piston spring from the heat with a wet rag. This may sound picayune, but I have found it helpful. Also, I have seen brand new hanks wear much faster than repaired ones ever have. I can only conclude that though it looks substantial on the surface, some bronze must be adulterated with pot metal. And bubbles can occur in any casting.

CHAPTER 6

Engines and electricity

Sailboats are designed to rely on the wind, but only the real purists—and the truly destitute—turn their backs on auxiliary forms of energy. Choosing which engine and what kind of electrical gear to install on a cruising boat is an important decision.

ENGINES

Engines are available for a wide range of conditions and preferences, so the choice must be made carefully.

One consideration must be the relative safety of gasoline and diesel fuel. The crux of the matter: gas explodes and diesel fuel doesn't. I carried a 58-horsepower gasoline marine engine in my first years of cruising, and I now feel fortunate not to have been blown out of the water by it. The fuel tanks were mounted up under the cockpit seats in order to gravity-feed the carburetor. When we were motorsailing and the wind came up enough to heel *Awahnee*, the fuel float valve would stick against the side of the carburetor. This would keep the valve open after the engine had been shut down, and the fuel would overflow into the bilge. I became more and more afraid to press the starter button, and I recall my relief when I did it for the last time: to motor over to a work dock for the installation of a diesel.

Gasoline engines are comparatively inexpensive and give high-speed performance with a small prop. Diesels are of two types: the low-r.p.m. engine that is easily started, turns a big prop, and burns little fuel, and the high-speed models that perform like gas engines. I prefer the reliability and the long-range capability of a slow engine. A slow-turning diesel engine that can be hand-started is a most reliable and undemanding piece of propulsive machinery. My choice was a 30-horsepower Yanmar marine diesel. It turns a 23-inch-diameter by 19-inch-pitch three-bladed propellor through a 2:1 reduction and reverse gear. It can be started by hand or electric starter, or jump-started under sail. *Awahnee* has a very easily driven hull, and in flat conditions the Yanmar engine will push her at seven knots. At three or four knots she will power 600 miles on the 120 gallons of fuel in our tanks. The Yanmar also is equipped with a three-quarter-inch constant-action bilge pump that operates whenever the engine is running. The water-cooling pump is piston driven, one and a half inches in diameter, and can quickly be valved to take water from the bilge. The Yanmar is cooled by saltwater, but three sacrificial zincs protect it from electrolysis.

More boat owners should consider mounting their engines farther forward in the boat, moving the center of gravity lower and nearer the center of lateral resistance. More space is available forward, and the engine is more accessible to the mechanic. Also it will be farther from the weather and the shaft closer to horizontal. I know a cruising ketch that has the engine mounted in the forward cabin with a 22-foot shaft to the prop. Hydraulic-drive main engines are also available. These can be mounted just about anywhere, with hydraulic pipes delivering the power to a short shaft at the stern. Another device that has long been used in Europe but seldom in the Western Hemisphere on small boats is a variable-pitch propellor. Forward speed, reverse, and neutral are controlled by changing the pitch of the prop while the engine turns at a constant speed, thus eliminating the expense and weight of reduction gear.

Few things about boats are as frustrating as a perfectly good engine that won't start because the batteries are flat. My Yanmar can be started by sailing the boat through the water at five knots or above. In neutral, with the decompression levers engaged, the thrust of the prop turning in the water turns the gears. I open the throttle, then I shift to forward to start the engine moving. As soon as it reaches a good speed, I put down the decompression levers and she fires right off. A spray can of starting ether is helpful in cold climates but not necessary since the propellor gives enough power to turn the engine over many times.

Once, just as we arrived at a favorable position to tack into the entrance of a harbor at the southern tip of Baja California, the crews of anchored tuna clippers and yachts saw us fall off on a reach. They thought we were nuts and later told us so, but of course they didn't know we were just cranking up the engine.

In most sailboats the engine is installed below the waterline, which makes it vulnerable to water damage. Exhaust-cooling water jackets are under constant hydrostatic pressure and can leak through cracks and pinholes into the exhaust system, the engine cylinders, or into the bilge. In a following sea, when swells push water into the hull fitting of a stern exhaust, backflow prevention devices such as loops or vertical silencers minimize flooding, but they become increasingly ineffective the more the boat heels. When you are sailing hard with an exhaust fitting that is far off center to leeward, the exhaust pipe can actually siphon the ocean into your bilge or fill the engine with saltwater. All exhausts should have hull valves and external flapper valves. Water-cooled systems should have a drain cock at the low point of the exhaust line so that the cooling system can be completely drained.

A dry exhaust eliminates most exhaust problems, but it must have a high enough lead or a valve to prevent flooding in heavy seas. A boat with a steel mast can have the best engine exhaust of all: out the top of the mast, no water, no smell, no smoke.

On *Awahnee,* having run the full gamut of variations on the water-cooled exhaust theme, I installed a dry exhaust that leads out to the afterdeck. When the engine is not in use, we cap the pipe-fitting. Before we start the engine we replace the cap with a shaped copper pipe that delivers the fumes over the side close to water level. It is as silent as our quietest wet exhaust was. On our Antarctic trip we removed most of the lagging and ran a loop of exhaust pipe forward through the boat to the fo'c's'le bulkhead and back, thereby making a very effective radiator. We became the world's only 53-foot boat with a 65-foot exhaust pipe.

The most common problem with diesel engines is clogged fuel lines. I have found that a gravity-feed tank or daytank is the most practical and trouble-free arrangement. Be very careful to filter all fuel coming aboard, especially when taking it out of drums, and to have a large sedimentation filter in the fuel line. My filter has a two-gallon capacity, and I drain the gunk from its bottom every few months.

ELECTRICITY

I have lost all patience with electricity. It requires far too much time to keep an extensive electrical system operating. Over many years and many oceans we have gradually eliminated or disconnected electrical devices on *Awahnee* until now only the navigation lights, fathometer, and engine starter remain wired to the batteries. My only generator is the 30-ampere one that came with the engine. Alternators generate more power at low operating speeds than generators, but under marine conditions of humidity and salt spray their diodes tend to short out faster. A good protected generator in my opinion is more practical.

When I first cast off, I thought that a refrigerator and a deep-freeze were musts. Then came repeated losses of full loads of fine frozen meat and other prime food, with more and more effort going into a losing battle trying to maintain the gear. I hated the daily hour or two of generator bark, and after a final indignity in the Indian Ocean, I made the decision for simplicity and freedom. I threw the generator overboard, salted the meat, and used the freezer for dry stores. We then learned the true value of the corned beef tub and beef jerky—delicious a dozen ways, inexpensive, and simple. We also found that we had never before appreciated the full flavor of many foods. Try a bit of cheese or a cantaloupe at room temperature. No doubt some foods are preserved by refrigeration, but the flavors fail at the same time.

Similarly, although I have a small generator, a big battery, and basic electrical gear aboard, including electric cabin lights, we truly prefer kerosene lamps. A lamp can be turned down to give the merest glow at night if desired, and it can be adjusted immediately to give full illumination. You can read, write, or take out splinters by it, and you are not totally blinded when leaving the lighted cabin for the deck. Kerosene lamps are warm, friendly, intimate, and available the world over. Time and time again, the cost in both money and time for repairs and replacements have convinced me that it is best to simplify wherever possible.

All in all, electrical equipment mixes poorly with saltwater and oxidation. A boat used for light cruising and weekend sailing can have all manner of electrical gadgets, but the farther she sails from a yachting center, the less certain is the assistance of Reddy Kilowatt. The most miserable man in the world is the owner of a $200,000 electrical miscarriage who can't get a drink, flush the head, raise the anchor, hoist the sails, or even see what he is doing because his batteries are flat and he can't start his generator. My answer is to eliminate nonessentials, have large batteries, and isolate them completely by opening a knife switch in the circuit when they are not in use.

I admit that I do admire some men's abilities with electricity. Don Gillum, an electrical engineer, and his wife have cruised for a dozen years in a relaxed and seamanly manner. We were talking about the relative practicality of trying to sail through the hot, windless doldrums or giving up and motoring when Don said, "Aw, when it gets too blamed hot and calm, we toss a can of evaporated milk in the fridge. After a couple of hours Dottie plugs in the blender and we have chocolate milkshakes under the cockpit awning." I don't know how many dozen times this remark has come tantalizingly to mind when *Awahnee* was lying becalmed in the ocean swell.

ELECTRONIC GEAR

Sensitive instrumentation is undoubtedly a great aid to a racing sailor, but on a cruising vessel the value of sophisticated electronics is harder to evaluate. Apparent-wind indicators, close-hauled indicators, anemometers, speedometers, and such are helpful when they work, but if they don't, they make for some pretty expensive ballast. Once when we were sailing hard in bright sunshine, I saw saltwater mist blow through a tiny crack around the hatch as if it were mist out of a spraygun. When atomized spray invades your boat like that, it is practically impossible to protect electronic instruments, radios, typewriters, and cameras. I do not necessarily scorn needles and dials, but it is my experience that the unadorned powers of human observation combined with the computer of our minds are sensitive enough to get excellent performance from a boat. And they only seldom go on the fritz.

The only electronic gear required aboard a cruising boat is a short-wave receiver, used for checking the chronometer. Everything additional is at the option of the boatowner.

A radio direction finder is the first optional piece of gear I would buy. A good one with a null indicator can guide you safely to land almost anywhere in the world. Hull metal and rigging can cause inaccurate readings, so these instruments must be given a deviation check before departure. My transistor RDF can be used on deck, and has short-wave and marine receiving bands in addition to the RDF band. Aerobeacons are generally located inland and are weaker than the powerful and strategically located coastal RDF sending stations. It is important in some areas to have a list of AM stations and their locations, as they sometimes provide many more bearings than the rather sparse RDF beacons. Beware of AM networks where all stations broadcast the same program and are hard to identify.

The second most useful electronic contribution to a cruising boat is a depthmeter. They tend to be somewhat distracting to the helmsman, though, and I prefer to have another man monitor the depthmeter in close situations.

Third is a short-wave transceiver. It provides ready contact with boats close by, amateur shore stations, and commercial marine operators of the telephone company. But their use is limited or nonexistent for long-distance messages or away from the U.S., where language, regulations, and ship-to-shore, ship-to-ship, and even distress frequencies may be different. It is a fact that the merchant ship distress frequency, 500 KC, is monitored many places instead of 2182 MHz. A license is required for operating 500 MHz. (See further remarks on communication and signalling in Chapter 18, "Emergencies.")

Some boats have luck with radio communication, but *Awahnee* is not one of them. I haven't successfully sent more than a half dozen radio messages during my 18 years of cruising, and long ago I quit trying. Though I still carry my transceiver aboard, it is stowed away in a locker to protect it from corrosion.

For reliable long-range communication, a single-sideband radio is required. The single-sideband necessitates a licensed operator and a sizable investment.

At the beginning of our 1970–71 Antarctic circumnavigation, we met a U.S. Coast Guard icebreaker, the *Staten Island,* which was navigated by satellites. This sophisticated system can print out accurately the ship's position within 200 feet at the press of a button. The *Staten Island*'s captain visited *Awahnee* and, with the idea of setting up an Antarctic rendezvous, asked what navigational equipment we used. "Sextant and chronometer," I replied. There was a long pause.

"Well . . . it can be done," he said. Sure it can be done, and it was. Ships have been navigated by sextant, chronometer, and lead-line for centuries. (Ironically, we completed our circumnavigation, but the *Staten Island* found an uncharted pinnacle of rock near Mawson Station on the coast of Antarctica below the Indian Ocean, ripped open her hull, and flooded five compartments. She had to abort her voyage and sail to South Africa for repairs.)

Remember, there is no electronic navigational gear that cannot be replaced by manual instruments and human assimilation of observed data—and sometimes to better effect. I would love to have radar, especially the hand-held kind that doesn't put weight and windage aloft; it would be a comfort approaching a coast in thick weather. But it would never replace a pair of sharp eyes. Twice when I was sailingmaster on the 100-foot school ship *Westward,* ships in the Gulf Stream approached us on a danger bearing without having appeared on the radar screen due to atmospheric conditions. Both times they were seen first by the apprentice on lookout.

CHAPTER 7

Equipment and gear

No matter how spacious your boat, for every item carried aboard many must be left ashore. Nevertheless, a cruising boat should have a properly equipped galley, a seaworthy dinghy, and tools and parts for every eventuality.

HARDWARE

The rigging locker, the bosun's locker, the sail kit, electrical kit, carpenter's box, and pump repair kit should each provide capability for major repairs. Engine spares and tools, pipe and hose fittings, stove fittings, lamp parts, the paint locker, and the abandon-ship locker should all be well stocked. I carry many tools and supplies in addition:

- an old-fashioned non-electric soldering iron that we heat on the stove (I do *not* carry a propane torch, as I won't have propane or butane aboard)
- underwater-setting epoxy paste
- a pipe wrench large enough to use on the exhaust fittings and through-hull fittings
- an open end wrench to fit the main engine flywheel nut
- a ring wrench that fits the nut on the propellor

- a sturdy, full-sized, round-pointed shovel for clams and incidental digging

- a wrecking bar and sledge hammer, regretfully employed in salvaging the wreck of the first *Awahnee*

- a two-and-a-half-inch slick (wood chisel), a hatchet, and a drawknife for spar building and wood shaping

- bronze and copper bar stock of quarter-inch, three-eighths-inch, and half-inch diameters with dies for cutting threads, and nuts and washers to make bolts

- a bundle of assorted pieces of wood ranging in size from small battens to two-by-fours

- offcuts of quarter-inch and half-inch plywood for emergency patching of hull or ports

- flexible halyard wire, and stainless steel and galvanized seizing wire

- a few long lengths of $3/16$-inch galvanized telephone wire for any situation requiring extra strong emergency repairs. From it I have made grommets in sails, quick rigging attachments, and even fish spears.

These items and more (corks, sheet metal screws, a spare key for the clock, buckets, springs for winch pawls, wing nuts, and such too numerous to mention) are part of our routine sailing supplies. All at one time or another have been used on our boat or others.

Bilge pumps. I favor a hand-operated bilge pump, and keep two of them aboard *Awahnee*. My principal bilge pump is an old-fashioned self-priming piston hand pump, four inches in diameter. With a strainer on the intake it does not clog, and can move 20 gallons of water a minute. In addition, I carry a portable hand-operated bilge pump with a two-inch intake and exhaust hoses. Diaphragm pumps are the best hand pumps in my opinion as they can pump small bits of debris and are easily cleared if they clog. I recently installed one in the engine compartment. I shy away from electric pumps because they are useless in a critical situation when the power has failed. Some engines, like my Yanmar, are equipped with a constant-action bilge pump and a water-cooling pump. I used to have an impeller pump on a clutch belted off the main engine. It was excellent when it worked, but when it burned out a bearing overseas, I was unable to get it running again. Finally it seized up from disuse, and I did away with it.

In an emergency, more water can be bailed by buckets than by hand pumps. It has been said that the best bilge pump is a bucket in the hands of a frightened man. Three or four buckets, passed hand to hand from the most accessible bilge into the cockpit or over the rail, can move water at a rate close to 2,000 gallons an hour. A major bailing job is best done with a two- or three-man crew using a large bucket on a halyard or whip tackle. One man guides the bucket, another fills it, and the third hauls the trace and dumps the bucket on the deck or over the side. One awful night an Egyptian frogman, Nancy, and I bailed 650 buckets (each holding five imperial gallons, equal to six and a quarter U.S. gallons) from the first *Awahnee* after we had sailed her off a reef in the Red Sea. We barely managed to keep the water level below the settees in the main cabin until we beached her in a sheltered sandy cove.

Handy billy. A handy billy, or watch tackle, is a versatile piece of gear and should be aboard every offshore cruiser. It provides portable power in many applications. It can be clapped on a working line with a rolling hitch to give additional purchase on a sheet or halyard if a winch goes bad. It can hoist an anchor, lift the engine off its bed, hoist a boat aboard, or haul the yacht down by the mast in order to accomplish work below the waterline.

Firearms. Unless you have to put down a mutiny, heavy handguns and large rifles are of little value aboard. However, small-caliber weapons have their place on a cruising boat. With them one can bag an occasional sheep, goat, or bird on a deserted island. I carry a 12-gauge shotgun, a .22 rifle, and a .22 pistol. They have served well in getting game and even coconuts. I also have a box of one-ounce solid-ball shotgun slugs stowed away for moral support. Although I've never had to use them, it has reassured me to think one of these whizzing projectiles fired across a bow would go a long way toward discouraging a modern-day pirate.

THE GALLEY

Except for the mast, there is no single item of cruising equipment put to greater use than a stove. In fair weather or foul, the ship's company must be fed, and the more easily the task is accomplished, the better for both morale and, ultimately, the safety of the ship. Selecting a stove is a decision of lasting effect.

Elegant electric stoves powered by large generators strike me as an unreasonable expense of money, space, and complex machinery, even if the appliances work faultlessly. What one asks of a stove is safe heat, and it can be had at much less cost in both money and noise.

All things considered, kerosene is the best, simplest, and most commonly used system internationally, even though it is not popular in the United States. Millions of meals have been prepared at sea on Primus stoves like *Awahnee*'s without fuss or muss. In many countries, Primus stoves are popular ashore as well. Parts and fuel can always be found, even in remote areas. Only in the U.S., where kerosene has almost become a thing of the past, might you have to substitute light diesel oil. A replacement burner that sells for $2.50 in Egypt might cost you $12.00 in the States, if you are lucky enough to find one. It well behooves the stove mechanic to obtain the two special wrenches and an assortment of parts with which Primus burners can be rebuilt for pennies.

The major criticism of pressure kerosene stoves is that they take time and care in lighting and sometimes flare up with a smoky yellow flame. Clean burners and good kerosene free of rust particles and water go a long way to prevent trouble. Kerosene stoves flare up only when the fuel is not hot enough to vaporize. When lighting a cold burner, you must be sure that there is no draft on the stove, that the air holes in the burner cap are open, and that no old coffee grounds or other spilled food occupies space in the preheating cup. Completely fill the cup with alcohol and light it, clean the orifice with the pricker before pumping up pressure, and light the burner as the alcohol burns away. If the stove flares up, close the fuel valve and preheat the burner again, preferably before it cools off. The end result should be a strong ring of hot blue flames with orange tips.

Butane stoves with fuel tanks stowed on deck are favored by many boatowners and are undoubtedly the easiest stoves to use. However, butane is heavier than air, and leaking gas can lie in the bilge liquid-like for days until a spark ignites it. Too frequently it does; every year boats are blown up by butane. Two valves on the fuel line, one at the stove and the other in the pipe on deck, will reduce the chance of leaks. For safety's sake, both valves should be closed when the stove is not in use, even though opening and closing them might be a hassle when making a cup of hot chocolate in the middle of a stormy night after coming off watch. In my opinion, mounting a butane stove on gimbals is too dangerous to consider because of the probability of wear and leakage in the flexible fuel line. Filling butane tanks can be a problem away from home. The well-equipped butane-burning yacht from the U.S. should carry filling-pipe adapters for European threads. Many a cruising boat in a foreign port has had to have an adapter machined before refueling.

Gravity-fed alcohol stoves are easy to light, the fuel burns evenly and without pressure, and alcohol fires, though fast and spectacular, can be extinguished with water. Even pressurized alcohol systems are relatively safe, although prone to flare-up. These stoves burn up large quantities of alcohol, which costs about five times as much as kerosene, and is sometimes impossible to find. Also, cooking is a long process on an alcohol stove, because alcohol simply doesn't generate the heat of other fuels. Another objection is that fumes from an alcohol stove burn the eyes and nostrils when ventilation is restricted below deck.

For cooking under sail, the stove should lie fore and aft and be gimballed. The axis of the gimbal should be two or three inches above the burner surface so the contents of the pots remain at the center of motion. That way the soup, at or below the point of rotation, won't make a top-heavy load in the pot. We prefer a three-burner stove, though we rarely cook with all three at once. The extra burner serves as a reserve gimballed surface to hold bowls when serving, or to safely hold the teapot while the tea steeps.

Sheet metal folding ovens, made more efficient by fixing asbestos sheeting around them, are a tolerable substitute for the real thing, and can cook roasts, baked potatoes, and even birthday cakes quite well. Skewers to pierce bulky items conduct heat to the center, reducing oven time considerably. Ovens that are not gimballed are impossible to use in a seaway. And though gimballed stoves with ovens take up a lot of swinging room, fortunate is the crew whose cook has one.

Kerosene burners cannot be turned down very low or they will burn with a smoky yellow flame. Because of the intense heat, the cook must watch his pots closely. An asbestos pad will distribute heat over the bottom of the pan and allow slow cooking. For cooking utensils, cast iron, heavy aluminum, or very heavy stainless steel are best. We carry two iron skillets, which allow the cook to produce hotcakes almost as fast as the crew can eat them, a Dutch oven, two six-quart saucepans, and a small double-boiler. Our pressure cooker is a great help in preparing vegetables, beans, fresh meat, or fish. We have also used it to distill seawater in an emergency. The Norgroves in *White Squall* used their pressure cooker to can tuna whenever they caught a big one. We find that pots with "ears" for handles are far more seaworthy than ones with long handles, since on a gimballed stove they are less likely to catch on the sinkshelf or a passerby.

Dishes and cups should stack in custom-made compartments so they don't bang back and forth. A shallow spice cabinet mounted above the stove is a great aid for tasty meals.

The sink should be deep enough to use heeled over, and should have pumps for both salt and fresh water. Nancy prefers one sink and the extra counter space to two sinks, though the latter has become customary on many new yachts. The counter should be of welded stainless steel to allow a hot pan to rest on it and to avoid cracks where cockroach fodder inevitably accumulates. (If this doesn't strike you as a significant problem, read Chapter 16, "Vermin.") A rail high enough to brace dishes against heeling is a must, or they will forever be clattering to the cabin sole. Lastly, a built-in cutting board is a great convenience, but not if it also acts as the top of the ice chest and must be cleared off to get out the butter.

In a seaway, we serve all meals in plasticized wooden bowls and eat with a single utensil, which is all that one can handle on a pitching, heeling boat. The beverage follows the meal when you can put the bowl down and hang onto the cup. This is not an arbitrary whim—it's the neatest way to get the food to the desired destination. For state affairs at anchor, we break out our glasses and plates. Our cups are of unbreakable plastic, stackable, generously sized, and have a wide base. Double-layer insulated cups may keep their contents hot or cold longer, but they eventually will lose their seal and often become unsanitary.

CLOTH AND CLOTHING

Foul weather gear. Nothing except a wet bunk causes more misery at sea than leaky, inadequate foul weather gear. Anyone who has stood for hours steering in the rain with a wet spot growing beneath a tear in his rainjacket will attest to this. Therefore, we buy the very best rain gear we can find, and for us the best is Canor Plarex. Because it is stifling to wear a pullover jacket in warm weather, we prefer the open-fronted ones that have a flap to keep water out, fastened with stainless steel snaps, not zippers or plated snaps. One of our crew had a jacket that fastened with Velcro, which worked very well.

On your head, a sou'wester hat is far better than a hood. When you face to windward the brim keeps you from being blinded and stung by driving rain, you can turn your head freely without impeding your vision, and you can hear much better than with a hood on.

Foul weather trousers should be high-waisted with suspenders, since jackets invariably blow up when one bends over. In the tropics, foul weather trousers are too hot. Besides, rain feels good on bare legs and feet if your torso is dry and warm. We use "tin shorts" (cut off waterproof trousers) in the islands. A jacket long enough to sit on will save you a wet bottom if you skip putting on foul weather pants.

Deck shoes. In any kind of reasonable temperatures we go barefoot. In the cold, we wear deck boots on deck but only socks below. Bare feet are best, for you can actually feel how much of a grip you have on a wet deck. Many people are able to cure chronic athlete's foot with sunshine and air. A man becomes aware of the forces and twisting movements he puts on his feet when he starts going barefoot and soon walks quietly and smoothly on deck. (And *Awahnee* isn't cluttered with foul-smelling deck shoes that never seem to dry.) When the crew is barefoot, no one hesitates to step out of the dinghy into the shallow water to avoid grinding it on the beach.

Linen. Sleeping bags are almost always too hot, they get very ripe from receiving an unwashed body (or a washed but salt-encrusted one) every night for a month or two, and they can't be laundered readily. I like to sleep between sheets. But white sheets, and especially white pillowcases, are a tactical error. We use colorful Tahitian *pareu* cloth for pillowcases and sheets, the brighter the better. Two or three fresh pillowcases during a voyage does a lot for morale. Feather pillows, like feather quilts and down sleeping bags and jackets, get damp in the sea air and stay damp. They may mold even if aired periodically. Polyester fiber is much better. For bedcovering, a "Tahiti blanket," made by stitching *pareu* cloth over a sheet with the excess sheet width forming a border around the *pareu* design, is cheerful, bright, and all you usually need for comfortable tropical sleeping. However, blankets should be carried. We have made quilts by sandwiching quarter-inch sheets of foam in *pareu* cloth, and find them light, very warm, washable, and non-mildewing.

After observing the effect of many large, wet towels on below-deck smell and humidity, Nancy one day tore all our bath towels in half. We found them a perfectly adequate size, with twice the number to use, and each had a better chance to dry out at sea. Few of those towels are still with us, for now we buy only hand towels in dark colors.

Clothes. The apparel worn on *Awahnee* consists of shirts and shorts. We tell crew members to bring two pairs of decent shorts for ashore, and quite a few "indecent" ones for on board. Half a dozen should be enough. It is always a pleasure coming off watch to change into dry clothes. Cut-off Levi's are best because they hold up against the rough non-skid deck the longest. There are no work-clothes in the world equal to Levi's. It is not surprising that a black market has cropped up for them in most places. Beware of sending them to be laundered—they don't always come back.

A couple of pairs of jeans, a watch cap, and a sweater or two worn under foul weather gear will answer any weather condition short of real winter, when a suit of long johns is needed. There is no substitute for wool in socks, long johns, sweaters, mittens, and caps. Even wet wool is warm.

In addition to foul weather gear, clothes, and sleeping gear, I require each of our crew members to have a hat, a pair of sun-glasses, a flashlight, batteries, and a knife.

THE DINGHY

The dinghy is contact with the shore, a work boat, and a ve-hicle for sounding and exploring. It could become your lifeboat.

On a cruising boat, the availability of a dinghy can become a serious matter. Nothing is more frustrating than to be marooned aboard a yacht gazing across at your dinghy drawn up on the beach while someone lingers ashore. The best solution is to have two dinghies aboard. This gives everyone free access to land or boat, and contributes to the pleasure of visiting and the ease of life at anchor. Stowing two dinghies need not be twice the trouble of stowing one. Two can be nested with the thwarts of the outside boat removed, or the second can be inflatable or foldable.

The best dinghy I have ever had is made of riveted aluminum, an eight-and-a-half-foot Grumman "Yacht Tender." This small craft has two rowing positions—amidships and forward—assuring good trim when two adults are aboard. When two pairs of oars are used we have power enough to make way against wind and chop. Capable of carrying up to five persons, it is also the lightest and strongest dinghy I have ever had. Large flotation tanks riveted in bow and stern make it virtually unsinkable. This dinghy is now 25 years old and still going strong. After it was crushed several years ago when *Awahnee* was dismasted, it was restored to perfect condition by a body-and-fender man. Someday I hope to win the first dinghy race around Cape Horn in it.

Dinghies are relatively delicate, and considering the indispensable tasks they perform, they should be selected with care. Stability is the most important consideration. A dinghy should be stable enough for a person to stand on the middle of the center thwart while getting in or out. Other considerations are ease of handling, ample freeboard forward to get safely through rough water, loading capacity, and adaptability for sailing, motoring, and rowing. A dinghy should have integral flotation so it can be bailed out after a capsize without beaching.

Dinghies do very heavy work in proportion to their size, and they must be used with care. Constant grounding on rocky beaches, for instance, is bound to take its toll on material and strength. A dinghy should be given the same attention to wear as the yacht it tends.

An inflatable boat with floorboards for stiffness and a motor for power is a handy arrangement. However, it is easily damaged, expensive, and often wet, and it is hard—sometimes impossible—to row. Molded rubber fittings are difficult to repair. Although you can tie an inflatable dinghy alongside without hurting your topsides, the dinghy's seams, corners, and even the float fabric may wear thin. I keep a ten-foot inflatable dinghy for a lifeboat, which I do not subject to regular use.

Fiberglass is the most popular hull material for a dinghy, as it is strong, light, and readily repaired. I use a fiberglass Sabot as my second dinghy, and I have found it stable and easily rowed, sailed, or motored. It is serviceable for two or three persons. I have beefed it up considerably with an extra layer of fiberglass inside and out and a bronze rubbing strip on its keel. Wooden dinghies are heavier, their seams are apt to open, and clinker-built ones are practically impossible to maintain leak-free in hard use.

It is always fun to poke around an anchorage in your dinghy, and a small outboard gives great mobility. It's also a decided advantage in rough water. A dinghy with outboard can be made fast alongside the quarter, tug-style, to propel a yacht. Steerage is gained by means of the yacht's rudder, the outboard merely supplying forward motion. However an outboard is by no means essential. The ancient and honorable "Norwegian steam" is a far more reliable power source and one that eliminates storing gasoline aboard. In quiet water it is quite possible to tow a displacement yacht behind a rowed dinghy if it is on a long line; I have done so many times.

A sailing dinghy is the thing to have for long exploratory jaunts inside a reef, say, or to a nearby village for fresh bread. A gunter or lug rig for the sail will stow inside the dinghy's hull. A leeboard is better than a centerboard since centerboard trunks often leak and are especially hard to repair. (But I must put in another word for my aluminum Grumman dinghy, for it still has a tight centerboard trunk after all its years of work.) If towed in rough water or at high speed, a dinghy can be swamped by water welling over the top of a trunk. It must be taken aboard, or the trunk closed.

The dinghy should have two ringbolts through its stem: one for a painter high enough so the person in the dinghy can recover it from the water without a capsize, and one low for towing. I prefer a rather long painter on the dinghy to let it ride just in front of *Awahnee*'s sternwave, allowing it to tow more lightly.

Tying the dinghy to a boat at anchor can become a real nuisance. If it bangs against the hull, both yacht and dinghy are likely to suffer. When a light wind is blowing against the current, the dinghy will work around the yacht continuously. The wind blows it to leeward, and once in the lee the current pushes it out into the wind. A boat pole longer than the dinghy—many skippers use a spinnaker pole—rigged with a block and endless line will satisfactorily hold the dinghy clear while letting it swing, but this is awkward for a small yacht. Fore-and-aft painters and a spring line will often hold the dinghy quietly against a fender where the water is smooth. At times a sunken bucket tied to the dinghy's stern will act as a sea anchor to keep it clear.

If the yacht is firmly secured in a position by double or triple anchoring so it will not swing, a small anchor set 30 to 40 feet abeam will give the dinghy swinging room but keep it close enough to be brought alongside by a tag line when needed. On occasion I have tied a small block to *Awahnee*'s anchor line about 30 feet from the hull and pulled the dinghy away on an endless line rove through the block. In very severe conditions where you are concerned about dragging your anchors, you must take the dinghy aboard to reduce windage. At anchor in a blizzard in Antarctica our dinghy repeatedly became airborne and overturned at the end of its painter off *Awahnee*'s stern. We had to take it aboard and lash it to the foredeck to keep it safe while at the same time trying not to raise *Awahnee*'s profile to the wind.

Standard daytime equipment for a dinghy should include strong oars and oarlocks (paddles are not sufficient), a bailer, an anchor and line, fore-and-aft painters of strong three-eighth-inch to half-inch line, and a whistle and lifejackets, especially if there is no integral flotation. At night a flashlight is needed.

For a lifeboat the experts usually favor uncapsizable rubber rafts over rigid dinghies. This, however, seems to contradict the experience of the Dougal Robertson family. The Robertsons spent 38 days in dinghies after their yacht was stove in by a whale a few miles leeward of the Galapagos. Their rubber raft sank beneath them on the seventeenth day adrift, and their nine-foot dinghy, which had been rigged with a square sail to tow the raft, thereafter carried all six of them 700 miles toward the coast of Central America before they were picked up by a Japanese tuna boat.

If your dinghy is to serve as the yacht's lifeboat, a survival kit should be stowed handy to it. (See ABANDONING SHIP in Chapter 18, "Emergencies.")

CHAPTER 8

Accommodations and stowage

Compressed into a space about equal to a studio apartment, the accommodations on a cruising boat must be well ventilated and carefully laid out for the needs of the ship's company. There is little excess room to provide much in the way of gracious living. The crew will live a simple, even elemental life for months at a time.

Yet despite limited space, even with as many as eight aboard, *Awahnee* never seems crowded on a passage. Someone is always on watch and others are napping after standing their watches. There is ample space for lounging on deck and in the cockpit. The main cabin is reserved for those who are awake. (In port, where the tempo of life aboard is not so regulated, five persons can live comfortably.)

Personal accommodations may be simple, but they must provide some privacy. It is a terrible imposition to assign someone to sleep in a convertible dinette, because he or she won't be able to turn in until cabin work or socializing is done for the day. This might be tolerable on a summer vacation spent gunkholing down a coast, but not on a long passage. On *Awahnee*, besides a permanently mounted table, there are two settees, a bunk, and a quarter berth in the main cabin, but I rarely take so many aboard that these must be assigned for sleeping. This is where we read, talk, sing, sew sails, and eat. Separate cabins give valuable insulation from too much togetherness, even if the separation is only a curtain or louvered door.

Many accommodation plans have a spacious forward cabin adjoining a tiny forepeak cubby labeled "chain locker." That, to me, is a poor use of space. Where are the lines, anchors, storm and light-weather sails, fenders, extra blocks, extension cords, hoses, spare lamp chimneys, hand tools, oars, shackles, and paint to be stowed? There may even be a bicycle, an outboard motor, a sewing machine, skin diving gear, and fishnets.

The fo'c's'le on *Awahnee* is 14 feet long. There are bunks port and starboard over sail and line bins, and cubbies for small gear. Forward and level with the bunks, the fo'c's'le is floored-over completely, providing plenty of room for tires (which we use in making drogues), fenders, and large gear. Beneath this shelf is a partitioned bin where I stow my long lines at the ready (about a quarter-mile in three lengths). Outboard, port and starboard, a wide shelf runs the full length of the overhead for such bulky light stowage as kerosene lamps, toilet paper, and floats. Oars, a fender board, and dinghy spars lie along the hull forward of the bunks. Anchors are stowed under the floor.

The fo'c's'le bulkhead is designed to withstand serious flooding forward without letting water into the rest of the boat—the opening is above *Awahnee's* designed waterline and can be closed by a plywood door. The master's cabin extends aft to the mast-bearing bulkhead. A shoe locker forms a seat and a step just aft of the fo'c's'le bulkhead. On one side is a high double bunk with dry stowage beneath it. Bins with oval hand holes line the port side of the cabin above the bunk. On the starboard side is a small hanging locker and single bunk settee with writing desk and cabinets outboard.

It is a mistake to rely on sleeping two to a double bunk. In heavy weather or if the boat is rolling badly in a calm, you are apt to spend the whole night crashing into each other or else wakefully trying to defy gravity. Hence, we have an additional single bunk in the master's cabin. At the after end of our double bunk is a small locker with clothes hooks. Free ventilation is necessary for all clothes lockers (and especially shoe lockers) to prevent mildew. Outboard of the clothes locker are three tiers of bookshelves.

Next aft comes a small double cabin, with a bunk that extends partially under the main cabin settee on the port side. The space under the head of the bunk and the lockers against the hull are ample stowage for the occupants of this cabin. The paint locker is located under the foot of the bunk close to amidships. The cabin is partitioned from the passageway by a curtain on sailtrack.

Opposite is the head, fitted with a louvered door which swings across the passageway and closes off the sleeping cabins from the main salon. There is another louvered door between the master's cabin and the middle cabin, providing ventilation without sacrificing privacy.

Awahnee's large main cabin also houses the navigator's station and the galley, which are separated by partial bulkheads from the cabin proper. Vinyl upholstered settees impervious to wet bottoms are on either side of the table. A spare berth is outboard above the starboard settee; bookshelves and stowage for the radio, sextant, and chronometer are outboard the port settee. The table off center to port allows a clear passageway to the forward cabins, head, and fo'c's'le. At the after end of the main cabin starboard of the ladder are oilskin stowage and a kerosene locker, which doubles as a seat. Farther aft on the starboard side is a full-sized watchberth which is continuous with the full-length after-cabin berth. This provides a foul weather crawlway between the after and main cabins and has the added advantage of berthing an extra tall crewman, who can sleep there foot to foot with a shorter person. On the port side aft of the galley is a four-by-five-foot bulk dry food stowage space, with the port after-cabin berth farther aft.

The galley should be located just inside the after companionway, and the table close forward of it. Then, whether you eat in the cockpit (as one usually does in the tropics) or below, food can be served within easy reach of where it is prepared. In the days of paid hands, galleys were forward and the cook fed two tables, the owners' dining table and the crew's mess in the fo'c's'le. Large charter boats sometimes have this arrangement.

Our after cabin was designed with the idea of chartering *Awahnee* in mind. We could live aft and reach the deck and galley without passing through anyone's sleeping quarters. The after cabin is quite small and has only sitting headroom; if you want to tuck in your shirt you have to stand up in the hatch. If two people live back there, it must be true love, and sometimes it has been.

DRAWERS AND BINS

In the main cabin outboard the table are four drawers, which are assigned to crew who occupy the fo'c's'le bunks or the after cabin. This allows them to keep a toothbrush, a camera, a sweatshirt, dark glasses, and other small gear close at hand. These drawers stay closed at all angles of heel because the sides are notched at the bottom. Fingerholes cut through the drawer facings are knobless "handles" that don't poke you in the back when you are sitting on the settee and at the same time ventilate the contents. In the galley we use this design on the drawers for cutlery, pots, and pans. The knife drawer and the bottle drawers beneath it slide fore and aft and do not require a drop-lock.

Bins over the bunks and in other handy places about the boat provide maximum stowage space since they conform to the shape of the hull. Gear is more accessible at sea from these bins than from drawers, and they never fall open when the boat heels. Hand holes (no hardware is required) should be at the top of the facing board.

TABLES

Our table is not gimballed. In my opinion, gimballed tables are unhandy and accident-provoking. Ours swivels on a central axis and will lock into five possible angles. When the helmsman calls, "Ready about!" the cook stands by to tack the table.

Fiddles with short dowels projecting from them peg into place around the table's perimeter and divide its surface into three sections. This system works without a hitch in all reasonable weather. In heavy going we put all our condiments and seasonings in a small box that fits snugly into one of the table compartments.

LAMPS

Gimballed lamps are not without a certain fascination as they pivot in a dark cabin. However, I have found that in bad weather they are a hazard to off-balance crew. We have four old brass ship's lamps, rectangular in shape, permanently mounted along the cabin trunk. As long as the wicks are kept in a fore and aft direction, the bowl of the chimney will rotate around the flame when the boat heels without getting a hot spot and cracking. These lamps have worked well in all seas. A mirror behind the chimney greatly increases the light given.

STOWAGE

Stowage, though one of the lesser arts of the cruising sailor, deserves attention, as it critically influences the balance of the boat as well as the condition of supplies. An unoccupied berth stuffed with sails, foul weather gear, bottles, and fresh fruit does not measure up to my idea of stowage.

Keeping weight centered, low, and out of the ends of the boat increases stability, reduces pitching in a heavy sea, and "hobbyhorsing" in light choppy conditions. This principle applies as well to a racing yacht. But in a cruising boat there is far more bulk and weight to be carried. *Awahnee*'s engine is under the main cabin sole and the gravity-feed fuel tanks are under the settees, port and starboard. The main water tank (110 gallons) is integral with the hull aft of the engine space and below the cabin sole. Forward water tanks originally built into the hull on each side of the mast-bearing bulkhead became foul, and now that space is used for the heaviest stowage: spare chainplates, wire rope, an anchor or two, chains, pipefittings, nuts and bolts, and two scuba tanks. Canned goods and dry stores that are not stowed in the galley are stowed under the main cabin settees and other bunks. Sometimes before a long trip we fill the space between the bunks in the master's cabin up to the level of the single bunk with cases of food. We also stow case goods in the head. Light dry stores are put higher and farther away from the center of the boat. Sails and rope are forward in the fo'c's'le.

For heavy weather stowage, I move all high weight to the level of the forward cabin sole—bosun's supplies, tools, and even canned goods. I was stimulated to form this plan by seeing our spreaders in the water three times off South Africa. I have not yet gone to the extreme of moving books and charts, but I always keep in mind the placement of heavy weight when stowing gear. The weight of the crew, for example, can become important in a very heavy blow. A thousand pounds of crew used to advantage in the windward bunks or amidships has a noticeable stabilizing effect on the boat.

PART TWO

Voyaging

There are essential differences between sailing the ocean and living ashore: ashore we are constantly faced with the pressures of social living, limited choices, and directed decisions; at sea the sailor has his boat, himself, the elements—and no more. His responsibility is clear and total, and the effect of his decisions immediately visible. He knows what he is capable of doing in the world of his vessel and, more importantly, what is beyond his capability. That which he cannot control—the weather—he had best not worry too much about, for it is utterly beyond his influence though it rules his life and the outcome of his voyage. He studies it, he adapts himself to it. He uses it to advantage when he can. When he can't, he either waits for a change, selects another course, or takes his chances.

Preparing for the forces of wind and sea can be a challenging experience. Risks must be calculated, danger must be recognized and faced. Let me apologize here for repeatedly pointing out danger in the pages that follow, but realize that when anyone goes to sea in a small boat he carries potential danger as a passenger. In cruising as in no other common endeavor, a man is isolated from outside help for long periods. He can't quit and go home when he's in the middle of an ocean or off a lee shore, no matter how badly he wants to. A sailor is committed to finish every voyage he begins. But even in the worst of times, he has the pleasure of living in the full force of nature, self-reliant, using those forces with greater or lesser success to take him across the sea. A voyage completed well is a satisfaction for life.

When does a trip start? It can start with a reading of someone else's experiences. Maybe a trip is beginning now as these words are read. When can a voyage fail? It can fail before your boat is ready to cast off. You can get into hellish difficulties before you even launch a boat, if you build. It is my opinion that many fine voyages are never completed because of too much planning too soon, and too little experience too late. Some people make an abstract thing of cruising, based on a dream, nurtured by selective reading, and expanded by euphoria. In many ports of the world I have met would-be ocean voyagers who made the vast number of choices and decisions involved in selecting a design (ketch? gaffheaded? centerboard? double ender?) and building (strip planked? aluminum spars? diesel engine? dinette?) without ever having set foot on an ocean-going boat. By the time their boat is built they are too embarrassed to admit their inexperience in sailing. They may not learn how to handle a boat until they are half way around the world. Others, at a sudden turning point in their lives, buy a boat.

Courageously these romantics cast off, committing themselves to the open sea without benefit of the knowledge, experience, or training that could easily be gained from coastal boating in home waters, and not necessarily in their own boat. Some find the fulfillment of their dreams. But some experience unexpected discomfort, inconvenience and danger; these put their boat up for sale at the first port, or work frantically as they try to get their ship off the rocks.

In the world of small boats, there seem to be the talkers and the doers. You rarely find a blue-water sailor running around telling landlubbers how to do it. Just as you can't learn to ride a bicycle by reading a book about it, sailing has to be learned by doing. Knowledge, beyond the very fundamental principles, comes slowly and as the result of accumulated observations and thought. Many cruising people simply don't know how to sail. Some figure it out. Some never learn.

Keep in mind that togetherness at sea is inescapable. In a house or an automobile it may get on your nerves; at sea it can become a serious thing. I like sailing with crew aboard because the interaction of people makes a trip eventful, easier, and often happier. Some cruising men reject this and sail alone. These I do not admire. Their courage is not in question—only their responsibility to themselves, their boat, and to others at sea. All maritime nations subscribe to the International Conference of Safety of Life at Sea. These regulations require a vessel to keep a proper lookout at all times, exhibit prescribed lights and shapes, and be handled in a seamanlike manner. All the time a vessel is underway the skipper and crew are responsible for maintaining a proper lookout. Pat-

Top: *Awahnee* under sail in a light breeze, leaving virtually no wake, thanks to her hull design. Note the multiple boom support.
Above: A masthead view of double-ended *Awahnee* with a poled-out jib ready to be hoisted.

Preceding page: Approaching Almirante Brown, the Argentinian scientific station in Antarctica. (Photo by Bill Curtsinger.)

Left: After a storm off the Columbia River in Oregon, the clew cringle of our storm trysail was crushed and its lashings stretched. The same blow smashed two of *Awahnee*'s portlights, stove in the side of her cabin trunk, and blew the anemometer right off the deck of a nearby tugboat after it had registered 80 knots.

Above: The Chamber of Horrors—a pile of assorted cracked, bent, collapsed, and otherwise broken rigging hardware.

Right: One of the problems of sailing in the Great Southern Ocean: as on Captain Cook's voyage of 1772–1775, the sheaves froze in the blocks.

Overleaf: *Awahnee* motoring in the Gerlach Strait off the coast of Antarctica, 600 miles south of the Horn. The arch in the background, formed while submerged, was brought above the surface when the iceberg capsized.

Below: Planting a Northill in a small patch of sand, sometimes the best solution to anchoring in tricky ground.

Bottom left: There are dangers one can encounter that don't appear on charts. Here a breaker reveals shallow bottom—the peak of a developing volcano in the Bering Sea off the coast of Alaska. We may have been the first to see it.

Bottom right: Using coordinate information from the Antarctic Pilot, we extended this chart of the strait between Anvers Island and the Antarctic continent to show the island's western coastline. Good weather had enabled us to approach the Antarctic landmass at 65° south, farther south than I had planned.

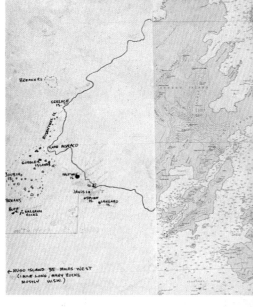

I used the salon mirror to signal for help when *Awahnee* was severely grounded in the Red Sea in 1962. We had signalled for four days with flares, smoke, the spinnaker streaming aloft, and fires hoisted to the masthead at night while 200 ships passed within five miles of us. But it was our mirror that finally worked, stopping a 35,000-ton tanker. Her officer on watch told us the light from the mirror "burned onto the bridge," making an unmistakable signal.

After our portlights were smashed by heavy seas in a storm off the coast of Oregon, we immediately covered the holes and fractured cabin side with our genoa. Later that morning in quieter seas we bolted plywood in place on top of gaskets cut from our rug, giving a secure repair until the end of the passage.

ently, this is impossible for a single sailor. A man has to sleep sometime.

The confidence of a hard-headed businessman is not necessarily the best preparation for an ocean voyage. Credentials and cash don't impress the sea, nor does cool, youthful arrogance. The preparation necessary above all others is competence in handling a boat in all weather, at anchor and at sea. I value more highly the person who has been in charge of his own El Toro or Dyer Dink, alone in wind and wave, than someone who has spent months casually crewing on a large boat. This is because dinghy sailing puts a man in a position to make decisions. He recognizes that if you fall off the wind the boat drives harder; if you pinch up, you kill forward motion; that you must have good way on to come about; that it's more comfortable with eased sheets; that the wind seems lighter sailing before it than against it. These are elemental facts that, if overlooked, may put a boat in danger. Everyone who contemplates cruising the ocean should know the exhilaration of sailing and the misery of being cold and wet, late and lost, before making the final decision.

CHAPTER 9

Planning a voyage

The principal consideration in deciding when and where you sail on a long voyage is the weather you expect to encounter. Prevailing winds, currents, or an impending hurricane season may require the selection of a route thousands of miles longer than the straight-line distance between two ports. It would be unwise, for example, to attempt to cruise south along the coast of Chile breasting the Humboldt Current; far better to strike the coast in the south and follow the current northward. From the West Indies you don't sail east against the trade winds to the Canary Islands, but north to winds more favorable for an eastward passage across the Atlantic.

I don't recommend downwind sailing exclusively, as do many cruising "experts." As long as you travel with the wind and current, you could sail around the world in anything that floats. You could drift around on a log if you held on long enough. It is great fun to run before the trades, but a well-designed yacht can make good passages to windward and gain a far greater choice of ports of call. I have made several unprecedented voyages with routes and times of the year selected on the basis of information provided by the Pilot Charts.

In 1961, for instance, we sailed 4,000 miles against the trade winds from the Great Barrier Reef to Hawaii via New Caledonia, the New Hebrides, Fiji, and Samoa. We took it on the starboard tack. South of the equator where the southeast trade blows, we sailed easily, making all the easting we could. When we found the doldrums, we motorsailed and tacked once to remain in the equatorial counter-current, which gave us an eastward boost of between 12 and 20 miles a day. Across the Line in the northeast trades we sailed a close reach, making good a course of true north. We made it to the Ala Wai Yacht Harbor in Honolulu in 42 sailing days after having gone about 5,500 actual miles on the wind.

Another time, in 1962, *Awahnee* was the first boat in recent history to sail against the westerlies in the Roaring Forties from Tasmania across the Great Australian Bight to Perth on the Australian west coast, although Charles Darwin in *Beagle* made the same passage in 1836 as undoubtedly did other square-riggers. When we arrived we were searched by incredulous customs agents in Perth who suspected us of bringing contraband south from Singapore. The passage had taken 16 days, sailing north from Tasmania to 40 degrees south latitude, then across to Cape Leeuwin at the southwest corner of Australia and north to Perth. We had expected to take 19 days. Although westerly winds prevailed most of the way, we were able to tack on advantageous wind shifts as each low-pressure area passed. Each weather cycle lasted about four days. The experience gave us a more realistic sense of the weather we would later encounter in a series of high latitude passages north and south, in the Roaring Forties, Furious Fifties, and Screaming Sixties (which don't always scream).

CHARTS AND REFERENCE BOOKS

The stuff that cruising dreams are made of is all put down on the Pilot Charts of the U.S. Hydrographic Office. These charts are compilations of weather and sea data over the years for each body of water in the world. No other single sheet of paper contains so much of interest and value to a blue-water sailor. Pilot Charts mark off the ocean into ten-degree squares of longitude and latitude. The percentage of wind that blows from each direction and its average strength is shown by a wind rose in every square, along with the percentage of calms. The set of surface currents is also shown, as are the percentages of fog and gales, average temperature and barometric pressure, magnetic variation, the extent of sea ice, and a discussion of seasonal weather for the area. The tracks of hurricanes and major storms are plotted, accompanied by a table of the dates each occurred. Major shipping routes are shown, and if you are fortunate enough to get an old Pilot Chart, sailing-ship routes are plotted. On the back of each Chart is an article on some aspect of oceanography, weather, seamanship, or piloting.

In May, 1966, a close study of Pilot Charts and weather reports in the appendices of the Sailing Directions, Volumes I and II for South America, led me to the decision to sail from Montevideo, Uruguay, around the Horn to Hawaii. I obtained corroboration of the information from the Russian whale fleet and the Uruguayan Navy at Montevideo. We decided to round Tierra del Fuego in early winter because the average wind velocity was five or ten knots less at all three weather stations in the region of Cape Horn during that season. Our passage through the Le Maire Strait to Buen Suceso Bay was actually made in good weather, but it took us a week of hard sailing to make the next 65 miles to windward.

Our 1970–71 voyage around Antarctica was closely studied before we decided to go. Although the Pilot Charts do not include the Southern Ocean, the Antarctic Sailing Directions and the logs and journals of whalers and explorers—Captain Cook's second voyage in particular (1772–1775)—made it possible for us to appraise accurately the weather conditions and determine whether *Awahnee* and her crew were up to the task.

A ship's chart room alone often has more space in it than that available on an entire yacht, yet the smaller boat sails the same oceans, approaches the same dangers, and relies on the same aids to navigation to negotiate the seas and find safe harbors. Since it is impossible to carry a full supply of charts and printed directions, the skipper of a small sailboat must pick and choose them carefully.

First he will want the appropriate volumes of Sailing Directions, or Pilots, as they are called by the British, which cover all the coasts and oceans of the world. They discuss all local conditions of interest to the mariner: weather and storm cycles, the coast and off-lying dangers, harbors, and facilities ashore. The British and U.S. versions are identical in content. Because they are bound as a standard-sized book, the British editions are far handier to carry on a small boat. However, the U.S. Hydrographic Office Sailing Directions come in a heavy loose-leaf ring binder which simplifies making corrections. The choice is yours.

A word of warning, though. The information contained in these volumes is oriented to ships; much of interest to small-boat sailors is lacking. Reliable information about shallow water soundings, fishing boat harbors, and marine railroads, for example, must be gathered from local sources or detailed charts. Nonetheless, coast and harbor approaches are so clearly described and hazards to navigation so carefully enumerated that, in the absence of an official chart, you can safely pilot a boat on these facts alone, drawing your own chart from them.

I have done so several times. I lay out a grid (or use graph paper), assign it a scale, and draw on a compass rose showing both true and magnetic north. Then I put down the features as described in the Sailing Directions. These are given within fractions of a mile, and thus can be accurately hand-drawn. Often I sketch in my approach to a landfall on my navigation plotting sheet because it is almost always on a smaller scale than the charts I carry. When you use such a constructed chart, however, you must not cut shoreward of any hazards, but keep to the recommended route for ships.

We carry general coastal charts, island group charts, and approach charts to major harbors. A large number of detailed harbor charts is usually unnecessary for a small, slow-moving boat. Berthing in big-ship harbors away from home where there are few marinas, we have found it easy to strike up friendships with men from large vessels. Before we had a transistor radio for time signals, we used to go aboard these ships during the second officer's watch (0800 to 1200) and ask to compare chronometers, an ancient but honored courtesy. The second officer is the navigation officer, and it is his duty to replace out-of-date charts with new ones as he receives them. He is supposed to destroy the old ones, but it often happens that they get stuck away somewhere and a lucky yachtsman just might find himself spending a lovely morning deciding how many more charts he has room for.

On our 1967 passage to Japan, we were given a full set of charts showing everything down to the smallest harbor detail. It was a great convenience and made piloting in that island-strewn, current-washed archipelago much easier than it otherwise would have been. The pile, however, weighed 200 pounds, and the only place to stow it was under the double-bunk mattress, which it raised five inches. That many charts usually cost hundreds of dollars.

One way of extending your supply of charts, especially detailed charts of places you might visit once you have entered an unfamiliar area, is with tracing paper. A few hours of work with borrowed charts can provide you with quite reliable tracings for piloting. We sailed some 1,000 miles of the Aleutian Islands on charts we traced at the Coast Guard Station on Attu. We had been unable to buy them in Japan. In tracing charts, you don't need to put down every detail. Study the chart and the Sailing Directions and lay in major features and coastlines as needed. Concentrate the fine work on those areas that are either hazardous or particularly confusing, then double-check for completeness and accuracy. The vital information for several separate harbors may be included on a single sheet of tracing paper, as on the British Admiralty detail plan sheets.

But of course, charts and Pilots are not all you need to make a safe approach to an unknown coast. You must also be able to identify lighthouses, calculate the tides, and find out the frequencies and signals of radio direction beacons. Thus, three additional volumes are required: a world light list, world tide tables (instructions are included in the preface), and *Radio Aids to Navigation*. A navigational reference book is extremely valuable and instructive as well. *The American Practical Navigator* by Nathaniel Bowditch is so encyclopedic in scope that it is sometimes confusing, so we also carry the more readable *Dutton's Navigation and Piloting,* the textbook of the U.S. Naval Academy. *The Mariner's Notebook* by William R. Crawford is knowledgeable and practical in discussing all aspects of piloting and seamanship, and is a clear, concise source of information on modern electronic aids to navigation. Also, don't overlook the excellent material, usually local in application, available free from the U.S. Coast Guard.

You will also need navigational sight-reduction tables, a copy of the Nautical Almanac, plotting sheets, navigation instruments, and a star finder. All navigational materials are available from a chart-agent who is licensed to sell charts and publications at the government-subsidized price. It is a heady experience to visit a chart agent's store—a pleasant relief from the mounting humdrum of drydock, painting, purchasing, stowing, and the odd carpentry that always precedes a voyage. A yacht chandlery that stocks only a few charts and Bowditch just doesn't have the same voyaging aura.

MAIL

As the result of varied experience, in my opinion the surest way to receive your mail promptly is through the public postal service.

Few people realize how important the first mail in three or four months is to a yachtsman. Your mail-receiving friends may be out of town, the consular service may have sent all your letters somewhere else, or the bank may be closed when you arrive in port. Handling mail is the primary concern of the post office, which in a port of entry is always centrally located and punctilious in handling the letters of transients.

Prior to our arrival at a major port, we always write to the postmaster stating the name of our boat, the name of each crew member, and our estimated week of arrival, and ask that he hold all mail for us. I always allow a generous time for the passage, but if we linger along the way I write again giving the new estimated time of arrival. Post offices will hold mail for months as long as they know you are still coming. In addition, they are very reliable about forwarding it.

Everyone aboard my boat receives his letters in care of *Awahnee*. This way one of the crew can collect all our mail rather than everyone having to go on his own. However, some postal officials are very particular. To avoid confusion, those not going to the post office should write a note authorizing the "mail clerk" to pick up his mail and send his passport along for positive identification.

The best way for a traveling boat to have satisfactory contact with home is to choose major mail stops where the address will be good for at least six to eight weeks. Many people don't write if they think you may have moved on, and they often expect letters to take weeks to arrive at a foreign destination, not realizing how fast international airmail is to major seaports.

MONEY

Letters of credit, certified checks, credit cards, cashier's checks, traveler's checks—I have been refused cash or credit upon presentation of all of these at one time or another. It is a chilling experience to arrive in a new country, sea-weary and hungry for shoreside amenities, only to be forced to wait for a cashier's check to clear before you can get any cash. Clearance is a matter of two weeks in a modern country like New Zealand; the time and treatment would be the same for a personal check. Short of finding someone to guarantee your check, the only alternative is to telegraph for funds, which is a matter of three to seven days and can easily nick you eight dollars each way.

I used to think cashier's checks were the best way to carry money. But I changed my mind after presenting a limp, but perfectly good four-month-old cashier's check to the foreign exchange manager of the biggest bank in Heraklion, Crete. First, he didn't like it because it was "old." Then he noticed that it had been sent to me in Egypt. Why hadn't I cashed it there? Because the Egyptian authorities refused to cash even part of it in dollars or English pounds, insisting that I take all $500 in Egyptian pounds, which could not be converted to any other currency. I had refused because I wasn't going to spend that much money in Egypt. Our man in Crete accepted this with great reserve (Greek money also was inconvertible). He began leafing through an ancient register of official bank signatures while I stood shifting from foot to foot in the heavy silence. My total liquid assets amounted to $1.50, not even enough to wire for money. Eventually, the banker demonstrated that the signature on my check (issued by the Bank of America in Point Reyes Station, California, population 350, where I had banked for 20 years) was absent from the tome. Result: no money. We walked out, dejected. It was November and we intended to move on through the Mediterranean and across the Atlantic to the West Indies rather than spend the winter there. We had no time to spare.

Down the street a couple of blocks we tried again in a Dutch import-export bank. The foreign exchange officer looked carefully at the check, at me, and at my passport. Without another word, and without consulting the thick book of signatures we could see behind him, he asked if I would prefer English sterling or American dollars.

Many foreign storekeepers in out-of-the-way places, and even in distant parts of the United States, have been burned by extending credit on the basis of bad checks, stolen credit cards, or counterfeit bills. The result is that they will not deal in anything except cash or traveler's checks. If you can plan ahead sufficiently, bank transfers to major ports along your route are satisfactory.

Letters of credit are no longer issued by some banks. Certified checks don't travel well, being more for domestic than international use. Credit cards are limited to goods and services that tourists are interested in, for the most part; it might be impossible to finance testing the injectors on your diesel engine with one, for example. But you could buy a plane ticket home.

I have concluded that traveler's checks issued by a major bank or American Express are the safest and simplest way to carry money with you. However, since they can be honored only by a bank or someone who has a bank account, they are not always negotiable. Many an isolated town or far-away island does all its business without benefit of banking service, and in these places only cash or barter has value.

As I stated earlier, the best protection is to carry a reserve of $1,000 in cash aboard while sailing away from home. I start out with at least $300 of it in one-dollar bills, and the rest in fives or tens. Then if I hire men to work for me, I can pay each one the exact amount rather than give all the money to one of them to convert, and take the chance that he might not distribute it equitably to his co-workers. This type of misappropriation has happened in my experience, and leaves those who get short-changed without any recourse—and perhaps with a misdirected anger.

SELECTING A CREW

The most important single factor in enjoying a satisfying cruise is the crew. The weather may be bad, the boat may not be able to sail well, the drinking water may become foul, or you may run out of sugar, but the crew that accepts the situation as it is and makes the best of it will have a good trip. On the other hand, a self-centered, callous person or group can destroy a wonderful cruise in the loveliest chain of islands in the world.

I enjoy the comings and goings of a changing crew, the development of sailors and their adaptation to the ship and sea. Anyone who chooses to cast off from the predictable, protected ways of land-locked existence is to some degree a freethinker, and having several independent spirits aboard makes life interesting. I enjoy the conversation, good company, and opinions they bring. A cruising family can become too one-sidedly self-reliant and lose some of the habits of easy sociability. The presence of a crew alleviates this.

On a boat big enough to carry four or five persons aboard, you can get mad at one fellow and still have someone else to talk to. With only two or three aboard, you live mercilessly close to each other, unless you're lovers and enjoy it. Nancy rightly judged it when she came on deck the morning after we had embarked across the Atlantic with three new crewmen aboard. We had been sailing for two months with the same company. She heard three different conversations going on, and had a hard time deciding which one to join. "It's going to be a good passage to Antigua," she predicted.

In Tahiti, the major crew-swapping stop in the South Pacific, I saw a beautiful 120-foot cruiser enter the harbor one morning. As soon as the immigration authorities had been satisfied, the gangplank was crowded with people and their duffel: the guests and their children, the schoolteacher and doctor, their wives and the owner's wife all left within minutes. We never heard the whole story, but when the yacht was scheduled to sail a week later, there wasn't enough crew to man her, and the port captain refused to clear her for departure. Eventually this vehicle of a shattered dream voyage around the world was delivered to the United States by hired hands.

As a group the crew should have an eager vested interest in the success of the voyage, a realization of the cost and effort involved in providing a seaworthy craft and sailing her well, and a helpful desire to do their part in full. I try to instill in my crew the feeling that we are undertaking a joint venture: without their presence and good work I would not be able to make my anticipated voyage, and without my experience and boat they would not be able to make it either.

A full crew does much to assure attentive sailing and enough manpower to make light work of many hard jobs. It provides good fellowship, leisure and the opportunity for each person to pursue his interests. We have seen experts develop in the fields of meteorology, navigation, piloting, fishing, reading, fancy ropework, and, almost invariably, chess.

When I am looking for crew, I let the word circulate around the waterfront, and I never fail to mention this if I give a departure story to a newspaper. Sometimes I hang "crew wanted" signs in the rigging, as was done on the old ships. Usually there are many applicants for each berth available. There is no sure way to choose a good crewman, but I have developed a reliable sense for eliminating poor prospects. I believe in personal impressions. The characteristics a person will show at sea can be discerned on land. Nancy and I talk informally with a prospective crewman for 20 minutes or a half-hour, but it is more than casual conversation. We are actually observing his or her attitudes, interests, discipline, and willingness to participate. Then we ask ourselves simply, "Do we want to live ten feet away from this person for a couple of months?" If he wants to smuggle something or live on a deserted island, if he is merely looking for cheap transportation, or if he has an illogical history, I steer clear of him.

What I require is financial self-sufficiency and the willingness to do one's best. Previous sailing experience doesn't matter to me nearly as much as interest and a sense of responsibility. I want to be able to rely on my crew.

I sign crew on from one major port to the next, avoiding long commitments. Then, anytime they don't love me or I don't love them, they can get off with no hard feelings. There is only one place for someone who is not enjoying a sailboat trip, and that is off the boat. Remember that a vessel bringing someone to a foreign country is legally responsible for taking them out of that country, so be sure your crew members can pay their way home by commercial carrier if it becomes necessary. I usually hold their return passage money myself for safekeeping. In Aden we had to wait five miserable days for a New Zealander who had caroused away his passage money to receive a ticket from home before the port captain would give permission for *Awahnee* to sail.

Everyone shares all duties by the roster, be it cooking, standing watch, sweeping the floor of the main cabin, or pumping the bilge. The inequities in duties benefit or burden each in turn, and it all evens out in the end. I like to form a crew well before departure so they can help in drydock and in preparing and stowing the boat for a trip. Everyone then becomes acquainted with each other, the boat, and her provisions and equipment before casting off.

I like to hear the thoughts and desires of each member of my crew before common decisions are made. Virtually every day a meeting is held to discuss, instruct, question, and decide all manner of things. I do not ordinarily allow a crew meeting to decide policy or course, for a ship is not a democracy; I honor and consider opinions, but I make the final decision on the basis of my greater experience and responsibility.

Mild physical disability in a person keen to sail does not cause me to turn a chap down. One fellow with an immovable hip joint and a woman with both ankles immobilized after a case of polio made long voyages aboard and were excellent crew. They did their best. I would not, however, by choice take along someone who has boils, ringworm, lice, or venereal disease.

In 18 years we have had a total of 219 persons as crew, ranging from 5 to 73 years old. Many have sailed with us as long as six months, and one fellow was with us a year and a half. The old-timer was Bill Parker, who in the years before World War I had sailed before the mast in a square rigger. He signed aboard from Napier, New Zealand, to Tasmania across the Tasman Sea. "There's only one reason I want to sail with you, Cap," he told me. "I've never sailed in a fore-and-aft rig, and I want to see how she goes."

Well, she did just fine, and so did Bill Parker. He tacked us into Wellington Harbor at night against an outgoing tide, loving every minute of it and marvelling at how easy *Awahnee* is to handle. Fourteen hundred miles farther on when we were approaching our destination, he admitted, "It's been 50 years since I last sailed up the Derwent River to Hobart, and it was a spanking good day just like this!" He told us lots of sea stories on that passage, increasing the kinship we already felt with the men who sailed in the glorious days of sail. I remember he was shocked at Nancy when we hit a calm spot in Cook Strait and she whistled for wind facing forward. "You *never* do that," he said, "You'll get a headwind. You must face the direction you want the wind to come from!" He never missed a watch. I know that now and then Bill takes a noon sight of the sun from his front porch, using the stringer on his picket fence as a horizon, just to make sure that God's in His heaven and all's right with the world.

EARNING MONEY WITH A YACHT

Many would-be voyagers put their last dime into a boat and set out with the idea that they will be able to turn a dollar by chartering, trading, or working ashore. It is a romantic notion, and would that it were true—but, for the most part, it is not. In our travels we have met penniless captains and crews, portbound and hard-pressed to provide basic needs for themselves, let alone to purchase materials necessary to maintain their boats.

There is no way to earn money with a yacht legally in the U.S., since a yacht by definition is a pleasure craft. She must be listed as a passenger-carrying, fishing, or research vessel or as some other category of working boat for her owner to use her for generating income.

Furthermore, "share-expense" crews are illegal in the U.S. It is unfortunate for cruising sailors that the United States Coast Guard, in an effort to protect the public, has taken a stand that virtually prevents a man of moderate means from doing extensive cruising within the law in U.S. waters or on a U.S. vessel. For an owner not licensed to carry passengers, regulations make it illegal to accept anything at all of value in exchange for a boat trip. Money, an outboard motor, even a bottle of whiskey or a box of sandwiches— any of these change a guest into a passenger who has bought his trip with the contribution. It doesn't matter how many watches a person stands or trips to the foredeck he takes; those who receive pay for sailing aboard are crewmen, those who give something of value directly or indirectly are passengers, and those who neither give nor receive are guests. That's the law (paragraph 175.10–28, *Rules and Regulations for Small Passenger Vessels,* U.S. Coast Guard).

A further drawback of this regulation is that guests do not always make the best crew, as I found in my early cruises. A person who shares the cost will be more likely to do his part to make the voyage successful.

With no such thing as share-expense crew in U.S. waters or aboard a U.S. vessel in foreign or international waters, another yachting myth is dispelled: that "crew" on a documented U.S. vessel are entitled to medical care by the U.S. Public Health Service at home and, under USPHS authority and through the consular service, by arrangement abroad. Only bona fide paid crew qualify, and owners of commercial fishing boats who perform the duties of a seaman.

In order to receive income by carrying passengers in a boat equipped with a motor, the skipper must be licensed by the U.S. Coast Guard, and the boat must be listed as a passenger-carrying vessel. A boat less than 65 feet need not be inspected by the Coast Guard to carry six passengers, but with a larger boat or more passengers the involvement of the bureaucracy increases. Penalties for violating these codes are nothing to sniff at: they range up to imprisonment and fines of $1000.

Perhaps the only practical way to earn money legally in the U.S. with a pleasure boat is the bare-boat charter. An owner may charter his boat for a fee with the charterer assuming sole control of the boat for a specified time. The charterer in turn may hire someone to operate the vessel for him, and that person may be the boat's owner. From the point of view of the law, under such circumstances the owner is not considered to be taking passengers for hire because the charterer is legally in command—the owner has become hired crew. However, the two agreements must be separate to be legal: one for chartering the boat and the other for hiring the crew.

In foreign waters, a vessel must be operated according to the law of that country. In general, governments (including the USA) prohibit foreign-built or foreign-owned vessels from engaging in local trade, thus reserving all commerce for its citizens. A Hong Kong–built yacht may not charter in American waters. The French government allows only French vessels to charter between two ports in French Polynesia. A boat may, however, take on passengers anywhere if she is bound for a foreign port or discharge them if she has arrived from another country.

Cruising yachts, unlike commercial vessels, are generally required to pay little or no port fees. These may amount to a few dollars, and probably include a fee for taking on water. Similarly, yacht crews are usually classified as tourists rather than seamen by immigration officials, and as tourists they may not take jobs ashore.

However, in places where particular skills (usually professional) or nautical services are needed, opportunity for work does exist. Often yachties quietly but illegally work on the waterfront in one capacity or another, or in a small town away from ports of entry and officialdom. In general, though, a job is hard for a cruising yachtsman to find.

TRADING

Carrying cargo in a small boat is impractical because of lack of cargo space, even if it is done with government sanction. Wherever you go you will find more than enough local boats trading and carrying cargo, and they usually work very hard for little return. There are exceptions, though. Once we saw the *Annette,* a beautiful Tasman fishing ketch, carrying oranges in the Cook Islands. She was about 45 feet long with a ten-ton hold between the cabin and the fo'c's'le. The two trading schooners that bring the orange crop from the far-flung outer Cook Islands to Rarotonga for shipment to New Zealand were both unavailable; one had sunk, and the other was hundreds of miles away in Fiji for repairs. The capable little *Annette* saved the day and turned oranges into cash for the islanders, who have precious little opportunity to earn money, by busily plying between Rarotonga and the outer islands for six weeks, carrying her capacity each trip. By the time a cargo ship arrived (there are from one to five per year), *Annette* had carried 165 tons of oranges to Rarotonga. She turned a tidy profit for her owners, but it was well-earned with hard work in dangerous waters.

(In the South Pacific Islands trade vessels are always called "schooners," though most of them now are 500- to 3,000-ton motor vessels, some quite new and handsome. Only one or two very tired sailing vessels still operate, and they rarely put up any canvas.)

On the other hand, in isolated groups of islands throughout the world, all yachtsmen carry many things that people value, even though trading is not their object. We have exchanged galvanized nails for exquisite shells, shirts for pearls, a face mask for a beautiful fine-woven hat. Once we delighted the entire female population of Uvéa in the Wallis Islands by trading maternity bras and expandable maternity clothes—which they had never seen—for hats, tapa cloth, and carved coconuts and shells. Isolated people often value tools and clothes more than money, especially women's dresses and children's clothes, since their stores don't have them to sell. In the Marquesas Islands, where handsome woodcarvings are made, waterproof sandpaper used to be a hot item. So were deepsea tuna-fishing lures.

Barter is now prohibited in French Polynesia and some other places because the government fears it will interfere with normal commerce. But it is difficult to refrain from exchanging used but serviceable items which you have and the locals desperately want. Once we were formally called in to pay customs duty on a gift of clothing and blankets we presented an island man who had sailed aboard *Awahnee* for several months. No trade was involved, but the authorities were not convinced.

Where trading is allowed, native-crafted goods are always available in less than abundant quantity. The possibility of making a dollar or two buying and selling crafts diminishes to practically zero with the time and distance that must pass before a buyer can be found. The souvenirs must be stowed out of harm's way (difficult with delicate pearl-shell-inlaid outrigger canoes), protected from humidity (fine mats emerge from under a bunk covered with mold), safe from deterioration and bugs (feather leis almost always carry bird lice, and moths and silverfish love them; sleeping mats are often inhabited by bedbugs). And nothing stinks like rotting creatures in seashells.

When we do arrive in a port with items to sell, they must be declared and duty paid, if any. Then to find a buyer. I have walked the city streets with beautiful natural pearls unable to sell a one because they weren't absolutely uniform in size and color like Mikimoto cultured pearls, which come by the perfect thousand. I have sought a fair value on exquisite original woodcarvings and failed to compete with mass-produced items. The result is that we have given away many lovely island things, and have trunks full of treasure stored away for the time when we will live ashore.

I make it a practice, though, to keep exotic gifts aboard for those hospitable people sailors meet in every port. The most satisfactory—from the point of view of cost, stowage, durability, and beauty—are large mother-of-pearl shells. Before the age of plastics these shells were harvested and sold by the ton to make buttons. They now have little commercial value. They can be used as ash trays, bon-bon dishes, or handsome ornaments.

As for using a boat to deliver prohibited goods like drugs, duty-free liquor, or firearms and ammunition, the best advice is to forget it. The first action a government takes if a yachtsman is suspected of serious misbehavior is to seize his boat. If the sailor is found guilty, the authorities can fine him before releasing his boat to him. Or, if they feel the situation warrants it, they can simply confiscate his boat and tell him to leave, or even imprison him. It is my belief that honest, considerate behavior and a reasonable manner is the best way to be happy abroad in the world.

Rarely, the tables are turned and natives seek to buy things you have for cash. Arriving in Vavau, Tonga, after piloting through an incredible maze of islands, we tied up alongside the pier, which was just long enough for *Awahnee*. Two of our Hawaiian crewmen, who had been at the spreaders during the coral-infested approach, jumped in the water to cool off, and discovered ulua fish under the pier. They speared a couple for our dinner, but the Tongans that had gathered to greet us started bidding against each other for the fish. The Hawaiian lads ended up operating a brisk auction. Every fish they caught was sold before it stopped wiggling. That night we ate bully beef for dinner, but nobody minded: we had met and fulfilled a need of islanders from the Royal Family on down, and they entertained us generously in the following weeks. Sophisticated skin-diving gear was practically unknown in Tonga then.

One of the easiest sources of income to the cruising yachtsman is slide lectures and sea stories. Of course, you can't lecture until you have cruised. But you will find that small seacoast towns contain interested and uncritical audiences. Once you overcome stage fright, you will realize that people everywhere are interested in what happens to people like themselves who embark on an existence largely independent of the complexities of civilization.

With experience you will be able to select and plan photographs and stories to please your audience. Slides are much easier for lectures than movies are; you can hold a slide on the screen as long as you wish while describing what it illustrates. It is far simpler to take good slides than movies, and the cost of getting a slide show together is merely the cost of duplicating your best slides (reserve the originals in dry, cool storage). The costs of putting together a short movie can easily run into thousands of dollars.

Good photographs sell articles and books also—words alone aren't enough for an unestablished writer. Clear black-and-white pictures sell more easily than color because they are much less expensive to publish. First-rate camera equipment and plenty of film aboard a boat can provide the basis of income long after a cruise is finished.

CHAPTER 10

Preparing to navigate

In this day of electronic marvels that record and correlate subtle variations in wind, speed, and course, it is easy to overlook the wonderful reliability of human observation. Thousands of years ago men began to read in the stars and sun the pattern of seasons and their influences on prevailing winds, calms, and storms for their part of the world. Not tied to artificial light, they seem to have seen more in the night sky. Today we little realize the scrupulous care and frequency with which ancient observations were made. The stars were the ultimate regulating force in the uncertainties of life.

To avoid the searing heat of day, Arabs many centuries ago traveled the desert by night. They were the inventors of celestial navigation, and today 37 of the 57 navigational stars in the Nautical Almanac bear names given them by these Arab nomads.

Polynesians a thousand years ago sailed the Pacific to destinations thousands of miles distant, while Europeans were essentially shorebound. The Polynesians developed a system of navigation using over 200 stars, a system supported by their knowledge of wave patterns, weather, and bird and sea life.

Celestial navigation is the practice of locating one's geographical position from the observed positions of heavenly bodies. It is different from the method of position-fixing in coastal waters from bearings on lighthouses, headlands, buoys or radio beacons, which is known as piloting. Piloting is full of danger, while celestial navigation is not usually that critical. Rocks sink boats, not the open sea—ordinarily. Few slow-moving boats are lost through mistakes in navigation or piloting alone, however. Usually failure in seamanship is a major part of these accidents. Lack of cautious judgment and good sense, over-positive identification of doubtful landmarks and the feeling that "it couldn't happen to me" are factors involved in most wrecks.

One of the principal causes of wrecks is running into danger without knowing it. If you expect a landfall in the late afternoon and don't find it, you are on edge and alert all night. But if you expect the landfall an hour after dawn, your night watch might be too relaxed. A favoring wind and current can bring you to the danger sooner than you expect. In a night fog or heavy overcast, the unexpected can come on fast.

I lost my first *Awahnee* in the Tuamotus in 1964 due to a mistake in judgment. Having failed to locate the tiny atoll of Vahunga, two miles in diameter, around noon as I had expected, we searched all afternoon for it. The masthead lookout saw it in late afternoon, and we motored up and hove to just before dark in the lee. I assumed the coconut trees I was looking at were full-grown. Though *Awahnee* was a safe three miles from full-grown trees, these were on the windward rim of the tiny atoll, and I was looking at stunted 25-foot coconut trees on the leeward shore. *Awahnee* was a scant mile off the beach and much closer to the wide reef. Shortly after midnight, propelled by the reverse current leeward of the land, we drifted to windward into danger among outlying coral heads. . . .

THE COMPASS

The key piloting instrument is a good compass. I don't use a hand-bearing compass, and since *Awahnee*'s binnacle-mounted compass in the center of the cockpit is easy to sight over in any direction, I do not carry a pelorus. If I need a very accurate bearing, I direct *Awahnee* right at the object and call for one of the crew to give the reading. If, due to wind, sea, or danger, this is impractical, I direct the helmsman to call out "On, on, on" when he is on the assigned compass course, while I sight the bearing over the main or after cabin hatchcover, each of which carries a half-rose for that purpose.

I have a number of requirements for the compass of a cruising boat. It must be corrected for deviation. Metallic objects must be stowed with their possible effect on the compass in mind—three fish spears in *Awahnee*'s lazarette once induced a 15-degree deviation. The compass should be checked frequently. This is easily done at sea as well as around the buoys. Calculate the azimuth of a star and steer directly toward it, comparing the compass reading (corrected for variation) with the azimuth. If you use HO 249 Selected Stars navigation tables, you can read the azimuth of seven stars directly from the tables once you figure the LHA of Aries.

The compass card should be large and easy to read, and for this reason I prefer cards that are boldly marked with the traditional points in addition to degrees. Although I figure courses in degrees, we steer by points because it is easier in all respects and in my opinion leads to more accurate helmsmanship. A helmsman steering southeast by south has a broad, distinct mark on the compass rose to guide him rather than a number that is squeezed next to other numbers that probably can't easily be read from his station.

I do not have a binnacle light on *Awahnee* because I prefer not to have my night watch hypnotized by staring into the moving lighted circle. One night back when I used to "do it right" with a lighted binnacle, I stood undetected in the hatch for ten minutes without the helmsman once glancing up to look out. Ever since, I have used a flashlight to see the compass at night. On course, the helmsman notes the angle of our rigging against a bright star, the moon, or a distant shape in the clouds. His fingers held over the flashlight lens let him squirt a small beam on the compass card to check the course without dazzling his eyes, and he can also see the water, the press of wind in our sails, and perhaps the lights of a Japanese fishing boat or the loom of an island. Habits are hard to break. I sometimes cover the compass with a plastic bucket to stimulate a helmsman's awareness. It is surprising how capable a group of steersmen can become when trained over a dark binnacle. The results are reflected in the crew's evident sense of enjoyment and in the average runs of 150 to 208 miles per day posted on our passages.

CELESTIAL NAVIGATION

The one essential distinction between coastal and blue-water cruising is that a yacht offshore is guided by celestial navigation. A sextant and chronometer are the only added items, plus, of course, the navigator's knowledge. Today you can buy full-size plastic sextants for $20 to $50, or new metal sextants for $250 to $400. The plastic models usually work well enough, but to obtain tolerable accuracy the mirrors must be checked and adjusted frequently. Also, because their finest reading is two minutes of arc, closer readings can only be interpolated by eye. Their tiny mirrors are difficult to use, for if you wobble a bit when bringing down a star, or even the sun, you may lose the image in the mirror and have to start over again. After half a dozen attempts your arm will grow tired and your patience thin. Combination bubble-horizon sextants, such as those sold in military surplus stores, are also usable, though unsuited for small-boat star sights because of their very small mirrors.

A skipper who chooses to commit his boat, his life, and the lives of others to a sea voyage should not economize on a sextant. Except for perils of collision, fire, or storm, the safety of a seaworthy vessel depends largely on her crew's ability to fix her position. You should be able to use all the navigational bodies—stars, planets, moon, and sun—with your sextant. It need not be so exquisite as a Plath (over $800), but it should be accurate, easy to read, reliable, and ready to use without adjustment, and it should have a micrometer drum vernier and large mirrors and shades. It's a good idea to carry a plastic reserve sextant in the abandon-ship locker.

A cruising sailor *can* get around using only the sun for navigation; after all, Columbus, Magellan, and Drake did. But no matter what you do, you can get only one line of position from a single heavenly body. You will be somewhere on that line. If you take a second observation ten minutes later, the second line of position will be practically parallel to the first. Theoretically your position would be at the intersection of these two lines of position, but as they are virtually superimposed, there is no fix.

If you take one observation when the sun bears east and a second when the sun bears south, you will get two lines of position that intersect at right angles to each other. But you still do not have a fix because five or six hours have elapsed between the two sights and you must advance the first line of position on the chart as far as your boat has moved in the intervening time. This is no simple matter, for you could easily be dealing with a sailed distance of 36 or 42 miles or more, plus a current effect of perhaps 20 miles in any direction, plus leeway of several degrees and a steering variation of possibly five to ten degrees. The position you determine in this way is called a "running fix," and it includes many influences that cannot be checked. So it is easy to see that sun navigation alone is neither easy nor necessarily accurate.

On the other hand, if you look at the sky a short while after the sun has set or before it rises, you can see the brightest stars and planets while the horizon is clearly visible. Shooting three stars on different bearings will give three lines of position. These will intersect to form a small triangle indicating your position. Furthermore, by any method stars are easier to calculate than the sun since their declination never changes and doesn't need to be figured at all. With a three-star fix you can approach land (and all land is danger in a sense) from a known point.

The navigational stars are not difficult to identify. The stars never change their relationship with each other, and on a passage the same ones will appear each dawn and each dusk. We often use the same stars for sights from start to finish of an ocean crossing. The Rude Star Finder, half the bulk of the Nautical Almanac, is available at any chart agent. It is a mini-planetarium which can be set to portray all the navigational stars at any time from any location on earth.

In my opinion, HO 249 is superior to all other methods of celestial navigation because it is simplest. Traditionalists object because it is accurate to the nearest whole mile, while other methods locate a line of position in tenths of a mile. They are talking about a distance of 600 feet, and since observations from the deck of a small boat aren't that accurate, I see no point in calculations that fine. In addition, HO 249 is an excellent star finder, and leads to a comforting familiarity with the stars. It precomputes for any given time at any latitude and longitude the seven best navigational stars. Directly from the tables you can read their names, their true bearings (azimuths), their altitudes, and the three that form the most desirable lines of position. This gives you the invaluable capability of getting a fix in cloudy weather. You preset your sextant to the computed altitude, and aim it in the direction of your star. As the star appears you will see it in the sextant mirror close to the horizon. All you need do is make the final sextant adjustment. A three-star fix with HO 249 can be worked with no more fuss than doing a single sun sight by any other method.

In normal conditions, with accurate observations of stars and time, you can expect a fix on the plotting sheet within one to three miles of your actual location. Keep in mind that the fix is where you were when you shot the stars. If it takes an hour to work the sights out, you aren't there anymore; you might be closer to danger than your fix is. In fine weather even a sharp lookout can approach to within seven or eight miles of a large atoll island in a small boat before seeing it, and by no means is all land as high or as large as that.

Though I have always carried a chronometer or a hack watch, I think electronic or quartz-crystal watches are perfectly good for use as a chronometer, and certainly they are smaller and no more costly. Self-winding watches may have changeable rates. They must be worn to keep them going, and the easy-sailing man doesn't always move them around enough to wind them.

A short-wave receiver is necessary to check the chronometer's error. We have had two Zenith Trans-Oceanics and found them excellent. With them we have been able to hear the time signals put out by the U.S. government everywhere we have sailed, even in the middle of the Indian Ocean and off Cape Horn. Sometimes it has been necessary to take the time announcement by Morse code rather than voice transmission. The BBC and all British Commonwealth countries broadcast exact time signals, but they don't always announce the time. The BBC hourly signal is five short beeps, followed by a sixth which is slightly longer than the others to designate the exact beginning of the hour.

A stopwatch is needed to time and thereby identify lighthouses and buoy lights. It also allows one person to take navigational sights without someone below to read the chronometer. The navigator starts the watch at the moment of observation and stops it when taking the time off the chronometer. Chronometer time less the stopwatch time will be the observation time.

A stopwatch is also essential to figuring the speed of the boat. It makes our helmsmen sensitive observers of the way of a boat through the water and spares us pulling a taffrail log. A log—which slows a boat down, fouls the fish lines, and may end up in the stomach of an undiscriminating fish—only approximates travel through the water. It shows little relationship to distance over the bottom since it fails to record the effect of current or a helmsman's wanderings. In my early days of cruising I towed a log. One time in the doldrums it showed a day's run of 108 miles but my sights worked out to 204 miles that day. Confused and unsure of our position, I reworked the sights without finding an error. Since we were a thousand miles from anywhere there was no danger, but I was puzzled. Next morning the dawn sight confirmed the previous day's sights. I finally decided we had received a current boost of 96 miles that day, and I reeled in the log, never to trail one again in clear weather. (The Sailing Directions note currents up to 104 miles per day in the area.)

The time in seconds it takes a vessel to travel 100 feet, divided into 60, gives the speed in knots within one percent. This takes two people. One throws a floating object (a wad of paper or a tin can) ahead of the bow and signals just as it is exactly even with the stem. The other starts the watch at the signal and stops it when the object is opposite a point on the deck a known distance from the stem. On *Awahnee* we use a 50-foot distance, but 25 feet or 33 would do almost as well. If, for example, the watch shows four seconds, we multiply it by two to get the time it would take it to travel 100 feet. Dividing eight into sixty tells us that we are doing seven and a half knots.

Other tools of navigation are soft and hard pencils, a pencil sharpener, a good eraser, dividers (get ones with needle points so they won't slip on the chart), parallel rules, a right triangle, and plotting sheets. These last items are blank charts printed in one-degree rectangles of latitude and longitude, with only the lines of latitude identified. Select the plotting sheet for your particular latitude, label the longitudinal lines, and plot your fixes in pencil. When the plot reaches the edge, renumber the longitudes and go across again. Thus you need only one set of plotting sheets to cover all the longitudes of your voyage, and you could plot fixes all around the world. Universal plotting sheets on which you scribe the appropriate longitude lines are a little more difficult to use but are smaller and preferred by many.

CHAPTER 11

Provisions

Some people plan elaborately color-coordinated, balanced, and economical menus weeks in advance. Down to the last dill pickle, every item is painstakingly logged in and checked off as it is consumed. Not so on *Awahnee*. Not only do we hate paperwork, but we wouldn't dare predict what will sound good for dinner the twelfth day out. Will it be hot? Rough? Raining? Maddeningly calm? Will we have caught a fish? Will the cook have been pressed into hours of sewing on a crucial sail? On my boat the menu is the cook's choice.

On *Awahnee* we carry plenty of food, at least four months' supply. This is because if you lose your mast in the middle of the ocean you'll be a long time getting anywhere. Though on only six passages has *Awahnee* been at sea longer than 19 days, our basic supply is two months' provision of choice stores, one month's reserve of staples, and one month's emergency foods. The reserve consists of flour, sugar, cooking oil, tea, coffee, dried peas, beans, rice, rolled oats, and a case apiece (48 cans) of evaporated milk and corned beef. The emergency food is a 100-pound sack of seed wheat—it stows easily, costs about eight dollars, and will keep a full crew going for a month. If it happens to get damp and moldy, we donate it to a farmer for his chickens and buy a new one. These items are not separated from the other stores, but are a general level of supply that we lay in at the beginning of a passage and maintain aboard while on a voyage.

We purchase food in case lots from wholesale food suppliers. When a wholesale license is required to deal directly with these people, we arrange for a third party to make the purchase. Usually a sailing restaurateur or occasionally a yacht club manager will assist. Cash on the barrelhead satisfies everyone, and the savings are considerable.

The case lot method also applies to produce, which you can usually buy at the commercial market. Crated fresh produce will be just approaching ripeness, which suits the needs of a departing boat perfectly.

BUY BASICS

We buy basic ingredients for our meals—for example, canned meat instead of Irish stew, which may be over 50 percent potatoes and as expensive as meat. A case or two of dried soup for flavoring meat dishes, several dozen envelopes of dried sauces, favorite spices, and maple syrup flavoring are on the list of requirements. Specialty items that do not spoil we keep in good quantity. Freeze-dried peas, beans, carrots, and broccoli can be bought in some foreign ports at a fraction of their price in the U.S. Other items are sugar, flour (we mix whole wheat and white), canned milk, margarine, jam, pickles, mayonnaise, sardines, instant saimin (Japanese noodle soup), canned bacon, nuts, canned and dried mushrooms, pimentos, bell peppers, olives, capers, tomato paste, Parmesan cheese, tabasco, and anything else that might be used to flavor up the bully beef and canned hamburger. Our 25-pound tub of peanut butter always creates a stir among Americans in places far away from the U.S. Hard sausages and salamis hang from our gallows—they don't need refrigeration—and below we stow a wheel of cheese.

Starches we bring are rice, powdered potatoes and pasta. Rice is available the world over, stores easily, won't go bad, and can be used with almost anything. We use brown rice when it is available at a reasonable price. Commercial powdered potatoes come in one-gallon cans that hold up to 170 small servings; fresh potatoes don't grow in warm climates, and the imported ones tend to be old, soft, tasteless, and overpriced. Taro, cooking bananas (boil them with the skins on; some taste exactly like baked Irish potatoes), and kumara (sweet potatoes) are the tropical starches, aside from rice. They make fine substitutes for potatoes.

FRESH PRODUCE

As the days at sea pass and you are eating more and more soft canned food, you will discover that anything crunchy is relished. Fresh produce is the *pièce de résistance* of the meal. Vegetables will last a long time if they are stored with care; fruits not quite so long. The secret is to give them plenty of ventilation. If they are allowed to lie against a solid surface they will bruise, become moist, and rot. Dry, airy storage is the answer. We stow our ready supply of fresh produce in mesh baskets set in a long bottomless drawer under the cockpit. It keeps almost as well as in a refrigerator. We stow cabbage, lettuce, and potatoes or taro in the dinghy, covered and ventilated to keep them cool, or in the deckbox, where they must also be protected against spray.

Cabbage is the longest-lasting leafy vegetable, but it will get quite slimy and unpleasant after two or three weeks at sea. If this happens, don't throw the whole head away; the bad leaves can be pared off. Hold the cabbage over the side and cut away the rotten stem and outer leaves. Keep one hand uncontaminated so you can handle the cleaned head without fouling it. Store it in a clean, dry place. The cabbage saved in this manner is perfectly good. Corned beef with slightly steamed cabbage is a lovely meal two weeks out, and coleslaw then or later is food for the gods.

Leaving with a crew of six, we would carry two cases of fruit in season, ten large heads of lettuce, twenty pounds of carrots, ten pounds of tomatoes, a case of cabbage, a sack of potatoes, and a sack of onions. Onions will outlast all the rest. And when there is no other fresh thing on board, I am fond of eating onion and peanut butter sandwiches. Our supply of onions is intended to last a couple of months.

In the tropics you can get thick-skinned sweet grapefruit (*pamplemousse*), oranges, limes—which go well with rum—lychees, mangos, soursops, and bananas. And avocados almost by the sack, if you are in the right place at the right time. Native papaya are not always as good as cultivated varieties and are relatively delicate to carry for eating as fruit; however, they are like squash when cooked with chicken before they ripen. Husked coconuts split open in the sun's heat, but unhusked nuts will stay sweet for well over a month on deck. In Polynesia it is worthwhile to learn to husk coconuts the native way using a sharp hardwood stick braced on the ground as a pivot to peel off the husk, and to take the opportunity to help in a local cookhouse to see how coconut cream is used with fish, chicken, and vegetables quite like sour cream (but it tastes so much better).

Green bananas can be stored in the dark of the fo'c's'le to ripen as needed. Salt spray ruins bananas. When the fruit shows yellow, we hang the stalk from the gallows, where it is easy for everyone to help himself. One hand after another ripens over several days. A favorite *Awahnee* lunch is limeade and bananas split and filled with peanut butter, eaten like a sandwich.

Our meals are simple with clear leanings toward the Oriental style, such as rice with fried or steamed meat and vegetables with flavored juice. Ginger, garlic, and soy sauce play a big role in cooking aboard, and mung bean sprouts enhance many a meal. Sprout them in a jar by covering with fresh water for 24 hours, then rinsing with a small amount of fresh water two or three times daily, depending on the heat, and draining to keep them moist but not wet. They will be ready to eat in three or four days. (The drained water, of course, can be drunk or used in cooking.) Sprouts are crunchy and delicious raw in salads or sandwiches, or gently steamed, alone or with meat. They make lovely omelettes and jazz up canned sandwich spread. Barley, wheat, alfalfa, and other seeds can also be sprouted.

We managed to boost the spirits of Kashima-san, a Japanese singlehander, with *Awahnee*'s fresh stores when we met him at sea on his forty-second day out on a very long passage. We gave him two heads of lettuce, some bananas, onions, garlic, tomatoes, cabbage, fresh ginger, mangos, papaya, and limes and some meat, bread, and water. It was quite an assortment, and when we later read an account of his voyage in a Japanese magazine, he described sitting in his cockpit trying to decide which to sample first. He chose lettuce, and after tasting a leaf, he noted in his log, "Wonderful sensation between the teeth!" It took him 67 days more to reach his destination—his voyage was nonstop from Los Angeles to Kobe, Japan, 6000 miles.

BUYING IN FOREIGN PORTS

A little of the local language goes a long way in foreign countries. The first things to learn are "thank you," "good morning," and "good evening." Then learn to count to ten. Rounding up supplies for a boatload of people hungry for fresh provisions sometimes creates a sensation in a local market, and the local public market is the only place to buy in quantity. Once in Heraklion, Crete, Nancy returned to the boat followed by three taxi-loads of curious locals. They couldn't figure out what she was going to do with all the eggs, cheese, ropes of onions, garlic, salad greens, and oranges she had bought in her halting Greek. Seeing *Awahnee* in the ancient harbor, they understood, laughed, and helped get the stores aboard, and then came aboard themselves for tea or something stronger. We sailed that same morning for Sicily, but we know that when and if we return, we will be welcomed with friendship.

When you have provisioned in far-flung places of the world, your galley inventory takes on the look of a souvenir collection. When we arrived in the U.S. after our circumnavigation of Antarctica, these are some of the foods we were carrying aboard: Chilean condensed cream and canned smoked multona fish, Argentine jam, fruit, and marmalade, New Zealand corned beef, canned butter, oatmeal, dried string beans, dried peas and dried onions, Australian honey and dried fruit, French paté, English canned breakfast sausage rolls that we found in good shape at an abandoned whaling station, Samoan tuna fish, South African dried figs, and Japanese long rice and dried squid.

We once listened to a cruising wife tell of her search in Tahiti for apples and potatoes to stock her boat for the return to California. After not finding them in the one-block-square open market full of local produce, she eventually succeeded at a specialty grocery store. She returned triumphantly to her boat with apples that had been picked weeks before in Washington state, and *pommes de terre* that were dug halfway around the world in France. Potatoes were about 50¢ a pound in Tahiti. Not only did she supply a voyage that would take a month, at least, with old produce, but she had paid far too much for it. The same bulk of taro would have cost between one-eighth and one-tenth of what her potatoes cost, and probably would have been as nourishing and longer lasting. There is no Tahitian equivalent for apples, but then there is no European equivalent for mangos.

DRY STORES

If you plan to sail out of the Western Hemisphere, take a good supply of yellow corn meal with you. It is hard to find elsewhere, except in South Africa. Besides baking it in cornbread and eating it as mush or polenta with stew, it is perfect for breading fish and chicken and for adding to hotcake batter. It doesn't spoil.

Flour and grain items bought outside the U.S. and such supplies as navy beans, split peas, lentils, and rice often develop weevils. Baking for ten minutes in shallow pans at 200 degrees kills them. However, if you can't arrange this, weevils will float off beans, rice, peas, and lentils when you wash them, and they can be largely sifted out of flour. A bay leaf in each storage cannister is said to prevent them.

Dry stores of all types often come in packages too flimsy for sea stowage: light cardboard cartons crumple, paper bags absorb moisture, thin plastic bags puncture, and loose bulk items soil and spoil easily. I recommend using large-mouth airtight tins and plastic containers. Items that will pour, such as rice and beans, can be stored in plastic jerry-cans, with the galley supply in smaller plastic pouring containers. Be careful that bulk sugar is stored dry, for it easily absorbs moisture and bursts a paper wrapping. It is satisfactorily kept in cloth sacks that are lined with plastic or sealed in heavy, multiple-layered paper sacks.

BREAD

We usually try to arrange a special order of double-baked whole wheat bread to be ready on our sailing day, up to 40 loaves for a crew of six or eight. We ask that it be unsliced and unwrapped, as a slicing machine can contaminate a loaf with mold spores, and wrappings encourage condensation and thereby moisture and mold. Double baking retards mold growth by removing extra moisture. When stowing the bread, separate the loaves so air can circulate around them, which is easiest to accomplish by standing them on end in a carton. Eventually the bread will start to grow "whiskers" of mold. This is not the end of its useful life—trim off the mold and continue eating it. Toast now becomes more desirable. On the next sunny day slice all the remaining loaves, lay the slices on the cabintop to dry, turn them, and stow them in tins or heavy sealed plastic bags. If they are dry enough, they will keep for weeks more. In the U.S., where bread is expensive and preservatives prevent molding, we stock up for a passage at a day-old bakery goods store. Most of it will be far older when we eat it.

With a boatload of hungry sailors, breakfast on *Awahnee* is a substantial meal, with either hotcakes, cooked cereal, granola, eggs, meat, French toast, or leftover fried rice commonly appearing on the table. In the Aleutian Islands we were given a start of sourdough that dated back to a sailing ship in 1910. It must have felt at home aboard *Awahnee*, for it has leavened hundreds of pounds of hotcakes and English muffins. And when Nancy makes sourdough waffles with her cast-iron waffle iron (which goes on our Primus with an asbestos pad between the burner and the iron), it takes most of the morning to cook enough to satisfy everyone.

Sourdough is not difficult to keep or use. Every two or three days when a lens of clear liquid appears in the jar, it should be "fed" equal parts of flour and water, enough to double its volume. Stir well. To make any dough—hotcake, bread, or waffle—pour out most of the sourdough culture in a large bowl and add flour, water, and a bit of sugar to make a thick liquid; let it stand overnight on the gimballed stove or another safe place. In the morning it will be all bubbly and many times its original bulk. Stir in oil, eggs, and canned milk (sour is fine) if desired. Mix together and stir in a little flour, salt, and one-eighth teaspoon baking soda per cup of flour. Add more flour or liquid until volume and consistency are as desired, and there is your dough. Soda helps the batter to rise and partially neutralizes the distinctive but sometimes too-strong sourdough flavor. In my opinion, sourdoughs are the best hotcakes, bar none. At sea when the bread is gone we often make a surplus of hotcakes at breakfast so we can eat sandwiches made of "coldcakes" for lunch.

Bread is the food most missed at sea. Cooking very dense food like bread loaves is beyond the normal capabilities of folding ovens. But beautiful English muffins can be made without an oven. I will give Nancy's recipe here because fresh bread is so delicious at sea and this can be made aboard any boat. Prepare a bread dough (we use dried yeast or sourdough) and divide it into lemon-sized pieces. Flatten each piece to a thick pancake size in a pan of loose corn meal so the corn meal sticks to the surface, top and bottom. Allow the pieces to rise. When about doubled in size, put them in a heavy skillet which has a layer of corn meal in it. Cook over low heat, rotating the muffins gently from time to time to give them even heat and keep them from sticking; remove the burnt corn meal from the skillet and add more as necessary. Turn the muffins when they are brown on one side, seven to ten minutes; five or six minutes on the other should do. The corn meal keeps the dough from touching the skillet, so it cooks with dry heat, like real bread. You'll never be able to supply the demand.

EGGS

People disagree on how to preserve eggs, but most people don't even consider the best method of all. There is no need to go to great messy lengths smearing the shells with grease or waterglass. By far the easiest way is to immerse them in briskly boiling water in a wire basket for five seconds. The problem is that the permeable shell and membrane inside must be sealed. Cooking a thin layer of the white accomplishes this while also sterilizing the shell. Use eggs fresh from the farm that have never been refrigerated, if possible. We carry a 30-dozen case of eggs, and even after two months' time we rarely find a bad one. We don't bother to turn the eggs to keep them from drying out inside at the top, but we do sail hard enough to heel over.

MEAT

We carry corned beef as our basic meat supply on refrigeration-less *Awahnee*. "Bully beef" sautéed slowly with fresh ginger, garlic, or onions, plus a little of whatever vegetable is available, is the foundation of a fine meal. Whenever I find canned meat other than corned beef—and it is not common—I buy it. (Meat balls, hamburger patties, beef stew, chili con carne, and pork and beans can contain over 50 percent potatoes, beans, and/or cereal grains. Retail prices for such items are outrageous considering the ingredients.) We stocked up on canned lamb's tongues, sirloin steak tips in gravy, braised beef, smoked fish, kippered fish, roast beef—which is scarcely distinguishable from corned beef—and Spam. Whole canned chickens do not keep well on a long trip without refrigeration in my experience. Canned ham that does not require refrigeration is a welcome addition to the larder. However, bully beef is universally available and competitively priced, and we fearlessly use it wherever we would use fresh ground beef if it were available.

Heavily smoked meats and sausages will keep quite a long while —over a month—if they are dry enough to stay fairly hard. Salami, linguisa (Portuguese garlic sausage), and lup chong (Chinese pork-pineapple sausage) are all treats at sea. Just to be sure they won't mold, we string them in garlands from the gallows on the first sunny days of a voyage. If the sun is hot they will also drip grease, so the deck must be protected. Below, we give them dry, airy stowage by laying newspaper between layers of sausage in a loosely packed, ventilated box. If they mold, fear not—just rub it off with paper and salt, or discard the sausage casing before cooking. Moldy smoked meat can be salt rubbed or trimmed. A side of bacon or a fresh smoked ham will last up to ten days, or two weeks in colder climates.

To add variety to our repasts on the briny, we have rediscovered the old ways of preserving meat. It began in the New Hebrides Islands, where Madam Rouan, the wife of the French governor, signed aboard in order to visit her family in the Seychelles Islands, where she was born. She directed the local butcher to prepare a tub of fresh corned beef for the voyage. The meat was in fairly big pieces that made wonderful stews and pot roasts with leftovers that could actually be sliced and eaten cold. To corn beef you need a nonmetallic container with a tight lid; plastic is probably easiest to obtain, though wooden soy sauce tubs are excellent. Combine and stir in your corned beef tub eight cups water, one cup vinegar, one cup salt, three tablespoons sugar, a bay leaf, peppercorns, crushed garlic, and a couple of teaspoons of pickling spice. This recipe gives enough preserving solution to corn five or six pounds of meat, and has to be multiplied suitably to corn a greater quantity.

I suppose any kind of meat can be preserved this way, but it must be trimmed, for fat is impervious to the water solution of preservatives and will cause off-flavors. Meat should be boned and cut not more than two inches thick. It must be submerged in the corning solution or it will rot; a smooth rock or a plate weighted with a rock works well. The tub is then covered with its lid and stowed on deck or below.

I have corned beef, mutton, and whale with great success. The whale ribeye, all 35 kilos of it, was the gift of a whale factory manager in Japan where we tied up preparing for a journey to the Aleutian Islands. It was from a plankton-eating sei whale and tasted like beef, though it was tenderer.

Once in Chile after we had rounded the Horn from the Atlantic, we were unable to buy canned corned beef. There all canned corned beef is exported to generate foreign credit. Get some "cherky," everyone advised, it's fine at sea. Buy it in the south of Chile, they said, for the farther north you go, the more likely you will get burro. We bought 20 kilos of jerky and two cases of dried shrimp, which fed us handsomely all across the Pacific and up to Honolulu. There, before departing on our next passage, we purchased some of the leftover stores of a gold-plater that had just been delivered from Singapore, mostly Armour freeze-dried roast beef and roast pork au jus. It was a mouth-watering experience just to see the picture on the front of each foil packet of two servings. When rehydrated, heated, and served according to instructions, the verdict was, "Ummm, good. About the same as that great Chilean jerky."

Well, we haven't bought freeze-dried meat since. Jerky is easy to make, though it helps to have had some experience butchering if you begin with a live animal. You must dehydrate the meat quickly, without letting flies lay eggs in it. We bone it, cut it in strips not more than a half-inch thick, rub it with coarse salt, and put it in plastic buckets. After about 20 minutes we squeeze the meat strips dry and shake off the excess salt. Next I prefer to dip them in a sauce of hot pepper and spices like curry, black pepper, soy, and garlic so the flies will stay away, though this step is not absolutely necessary. Then we hang them on a fence to dry, far from habitation if possible. In two sunny days, taking it in or covering it at night, your jerky will be finished. Store it in an airtight container, and it will keep virtually forever.

Once, outfitting two boats simultaneously, we jerked a whole beef. Other meats can be dried also. Jerky turkey is a wonderful addition to the menu, and once, after eating all the fresh meat we could, we made jerky turtle at sea. Animals should be bought from a farmer or at auction; the meat will be fresher and the price on the hoof is a small fraction of that in a store. Killing and butchering can often be arranged for a few additional cents per pound, and is well worth it.

Before eating corned beef and jerky, you must "freshen" it by soaking it in water to remove excess salt. Corned beef doesn't require as much freshening as jerky. The process entails covering the meat with fresh water two or three times, soaking a minimum of 15 minutes each time. After the first soak removes exterior salt, dicing the jerky and parboiling it will speed the process.

The best thing to do with fish is to eat it fresh. The next best thing is to pressure cook it so that it may be eaten several days later. Then the fully cooked fish, kept in the sealed pressure cooker, can become a tuna salad, steamed fish with rice, or fishcakes. If we catch a fish bigger than what we can eat in a couple of days, we cut a large chunk to fit the pressure cooker, and cook it with a bay leaf or two and some peppercorns under pressure for 20 to 30 minutes to get the heat all the way through. Leaving the lid sealed and the weight in place, the cooker is set aside out of the sun and kept as cool as possible. It is not wise to hold the fish for a long time, but normally it is good for three or four days. When the lid is removed, check it for off-odors and do not eat it if you suspect spoilage.

We have dried fish at sea, but it is a messy business. Part of the difficulty is that salt spray accumulates as it hangs on the lifelines, so it stays moist while getting too salty. Our cat has enjoyed it, though, as did our pet bosun's bird. It is difficult to get the fish dry and really preserved unless you are sailing before a warm wind with conditions quite dry on deck. Ashore, fish strips can be dried in a single hot tropical day, and small whole split fish in two days. It should be rubbed with salt, sprinkled with pepper, and protected from moisture at night.

Cruising cooks have to know about nutrition in order to be sure their crewmates are well fed. Knowledge of nutrition has spread dramatically in response to the wide interest in organic, natural, and vegetarian food choices. Seacooks do well to take a leaf or two from vegetarian cookbooks, for supplying protein on a long voyage is not always easy. Textured vegetable protein (TVP) made from soy beans is now available in bulk from wholesale food distributors. It is a high-quality protein and is nutritionally almost equivalent to fresh meat. Sold as a dry granular substance, it can be rehydrated and seasoned to form something like hamburger. However, I find it easiest to use TVP in spaghetti sauce, tamale pie, or beans, where I toss it in the pot liquid along with onions, a couple of bouillon cubes, and spices. It is light and easy to store and does not spoil if kept dry, an excellent item to have aboard.

In the days of sailing ships live sheep, pigs, and goats were carried aboard to supply meat, and sometimes a cow was brought along to give milk for the captain's children. *Awahnee* has been given chickens, ducks, sheep, and a goat at various island departures. However, animals do not travel well aboard a small boat, and are best eaten quickly. One cruising boat I know of arrived in the Marquesas from the Galapagos with a goat that had become a pet, and another had a hen who thought she was entitled to roost on the bunkboard of a little girl's berth.

In any developed country good meats in variety are obtainable. On tropical islands where the stores are without refrigerated cabinets or frozen food sections, the choices are limited. Fresh meat is goat, sheep, pork, and sometimes cattle. On all tropical islands, it seems, inhabitants prefer the meat of young goats, and I heartily agree. It is far superior to the rangy old cow meat yachtsmen sometimes feel privileged to find. Aside from chickens, I think goats are the most common terrestrial meat source in tropical islands of the world. Carefully prepared and properly cooked—with a teriyaki sauce or barbecued perhaps—goat meat is delicious, and it makes a lovely roast.

SEAWATER COOKING

Using seawater in cooking will certainly conserve fresh water aboard, and it may give nutritive value—after all, seawater contains every chemical element. We use one part seawater to three parts fresh water when cooking rice, oatmeal, powdered potato, and any food of that nature. When we boil eggs or vegetables that do not absorb water, like carrots, potatoes, or squash, we use straight seawater. If you want to carry it to the extreme, seawater could be used in any recipe that calls for both water and salt. Polynesians have done this for centuries.

WATER

I have taken water aboard *Awahnee* in 45 countries of the world from municipal water systems, private springs, waterfalls at the bases of cliffs, rooftop rain catchments, water barges, village pumps, and glacier melt ponds. I have bought bottled water, melted bits of iceberg collected in the dinghy at sea, siphoned water from a ship, collected rainwater off the sails and deck, and distilled seawater in the galley. Only once did the water in our main water tank become unpalatable and unpotable. That was after departure from Honolulu, when water had been taken aboard following a very heavy four-day rainstorm that had probably washed organic material into the city reservoirs. Six days out we were pumping a black flocculent precipitate into our cups along with water so foul-smelling we stopped drinking it even in tea or coffee. We were left with 60 gallons of good water in plastic jerrycans, eight people aboard, over 3000 miles to go to Japan, and no wind. After 18 days of calms and zephyrs we got all the rain we wanted at the tail end of a typhoon. The entire passage, 4300 miles from Honolulu to Kobe, Japan, took 35 days.

In small villages and on low islands in particular, look first before filling your tanks. Many times I have declined to do so, after learning a lesson at Takaroa in the Tuamotus. After taking on some water, I wanted to see what level remained in the reservoir because the village needed rain—and I noticed bones and hermitcrab shells scattered over the bottom. As soon as I returned on board, I chlorinated the tank with two teaspoons of chlorine laundry bleach (universally available) to 100 gallons of water, to achieve a level of approximately one part per million. It did not foul. In isolated areas we use stream water, but we taste and smell it carefully. If there is any doubt because of cloudiness or nearby habitation, we chlorinate it slightly. If we are short and can find only brackish water, we reserve it for cooking and drink the remaining good water.

I have found it best to carry three 50-foot lengths of small (three-eighths-inch diameter) garden hose in order to get water aboard conveniently for filling my tanks and, where it is abundant, for washing down, showering, and laundry. Sometimes, especially at big-ship berths, it is impossible to find a valve with hose thread. You might have to carry water or have the harborboard turn on a main that could be four inches in diameter—they sell water to ships by the ton. (One short ton is 250 gallons U.S. measure.) Remember that you can always reduce pressure and control volume by letting it flow into a bucket and siphoning out of the bucket with your hose. In fact, I often take on water this way even when there is a tap with hose thread in order to guard against excessive pressure on a tank when it comes full. Tanks should have large breathers, in my estimation at least half the diameter of the filling hose. They can double as an overflow pipe, but should not lead too high above the top of the tank to avoid sudden damaging pressure if the tank is overfilled. One of my galvanized tanks swelled enough in this manner to pull away from the baffle plates, breaking all the rivets that were holding them. The breather led about four feet higher than the top of the tank.

A long drop in a siphon hose, more than 30 feet, for example, can also build up damaging pressure. To reduce this I sometimes deliberately make a loose connection between the inboard end of the filling hose and the tank filling intake. On my boat this is clear plastic hose so I can see the water running, located above the galley sink where spilled water goes harmlessly down the drain.

CHAPTER 12

Lines and knots

All lines aboard *Awahnee* are of synthetic fiber, except one line of one-inch-diameter fine manila hemp given us by the bosun of a departing British ship. Since synthetic lines are very strong and do not rot they are far superior to vegetable-fiber line for boat use. They must, however, be guarded against chafe. Personally, I have seen few of them break that were not already weakened from wear or tied so that they cut themselves.

I prefer Dacron for sheets and halyard tails because it stretches least. Standard three-strand laid rope is ordinarily used, but various types of braided and woven line that are practically kink-proof are especially good for use as sheets. They seldom foul blocks, they coil easily, and they rarely tangle. Since these lays of line cannot easily be married with wire, they are not popularly used for halyard tails but may be used full length. Careful selection of the block and its leads is necessary because a foul lead or a poorly designed block with wearing edges can destroy a synthetic halyard in a single storm.

Nylon is favored by many sailors for anchor rodes and mooring lines because it can stretch up to 40 percent of its length, thereby passing sudden tensions less abruptly to the cleats. On *Awahnee* I use polypropylene for mooring lines and anchor rodes. Although it is not quite as strong or stretchy as nylon, it floats. It almost never fouls on the propellor or rudder, or on coral, rocks, or debris on the bottom. It should be weighted to keep it from catching other boats, however. Floating polypropylene line also makes a non-fouling tow-line, which is a good and sometimes vital thing to have. While we visited Chile in 1966, 52 men were lost when their tug, on a rescue mission, went on the rocks after her nylon tow-line sank and fouled the propellor.

When I switched to synthetic line, I found I also had to change some of the knots, bends, and splices I had used on hemp and flax lines—knots that seamen have used for hundreds of years. Synthetic line's elasticity, greater strength, and hard, slick finish, which reduces friction, combine to make standard knots, bends, and splices unreliable. Some knots will crawl and work themselves loose under varying tensions. Others tighten and cannot be untied at all. When we sailed across the Great Australian Bight in 1962, our old main had been resewn and fitted with new reef points, which were nylon instead of manila. They untied themselves repeatedly until necessity mothered the improvisation of a new reef knot in the slippery line.

In springy, slick line three-quarters-inch in diameter or larger, it is difficult to draw a knot up tight enough to set it. A properly tied knot, even if it is quite loose, is the first requirement in using large line. Seizing the knot is insurance that it will draw up and stay tied under strain. I usually keep a short length of small stuff clove-hitched around one strand of my large lines close to the working end where it is always at hand to seize a knot. Sometimes in a hurry, I open the lay of the rope and tuck the end of the line through instead of seizing the knot. This is good only as a stopgap because the distorted line will be damaged or fail under heavy strain.

BASIC KNOTS

Knowledge of knots is one of the marks of a seaman, and it is a knot properly tied that may someday save a boat or a life. A proper knot does what it is meant to, then can be readily untied. Knots will only hold 45 percent (reef knots) to 75 percent (round turn and two half hitches) of the strength of the line itself, and can destroy lines when the strain is too great.

There are hundreds of knots, but in my opinion five of them will meet all ordinary needs aboard a small boat:

• The overhand knot and its variations

• The bowline and variations, including the sheet bend

• The half hitch and its variations

• The rolling hitch

• The masthead knot.

Practice the knots you think you will need and teach your crew and family. Many people are eager to learn but don't have the chance to. Make a game of it. It's worth the time spent.

The overhand knot. The single overhand knot, the simplest of all knots, is the basis of many others, including the reef knot and the bowline. A reef or square knot is a double overhand knot, but because a reef knot can tighten so much that it cannot be undone, or, in other situations, work itself loose, I do not use it. The surgeon's knot is better. It is the same as a reef knot except that the first overhand turn passes around a second time to prevent slipping. In my opinion, it is better to avoid this type of knot altogether for lashing down gear on deck. Instead, make one end of the line fast, take tight turns around the gear, and finish off with a round turn and two half hitches on the cleat or deck fixture.

The figure eight is a variation of the overhand knot. It is used as a stopper knot to keep the end of a sheet or halyard from passing through a block or fair lead, or to keep the bucket lanyard from slipping through your hand. It can always be untied, even after jamming.

The bowline. The bowline is the first knot we teach a lubberly crew member. When he can flip a bowline in a piece of line with his eyes closed or behind his back, we know he's getting salty. The bowline is a jamming knot which gets tighter under strain, and it is as sure as any knot when set firmly. It requires a slack line for tying and untying, but will hold whether or not there is tension on the line. It is difficult to set or firm down a bowline in large-diameter line. I remember my embarrassment before the gathered village of Uturoa on Raiatea when my one-inch synthetic anchor rode tied to the bower anchor separated from the three-quarter-inch nylon extension. This was in the days before I had a diesel engine, and the old gasoline mill wasn't working. We had sailed in the pass through the coral reef, dropping our offshore anchor, and fallen off to come smartly alongside, our big French flag flying festively. It was market day, with the whole countryside in attendance on the town wharf. Everything was all set: a man ready to snub the anchor rode, the halyards manned for dousing the sails at the last minute, the mooring lines led through the chocks ready to be tossed ashore. Then it all went wrong. As we set the anchor, one of the bowlines joining the anchor rode and the extending line slipped and untied, causing 25 tons of *Awahnee* to scrape against the pier, which was so high our stanchions took all the force. A horrible schmozzle ensued. By the time things settled down, it was raining and overcast, so dark that diving for the anchor was out of the question. We had to drag the grapnel all afternoon in the deep Uturoa harbor before recovering my prized Northill anchor. The cause of it all was my failure to set properly or to seize the bowline in the heavy synthetic line.

A bowline on a bight will provide an attaching point anywhere along a long line. A double bowline is used where chafe is unavoidable. Both of these bowlines make a good chair lift, one leg through each loop, with a safety line added around the person's chest.

The sheet bend, a knot which is used to join lines together, is nothing more than a bowline tied with two lines. On lines of different diameters or on slippery lines, double or triple sheet bends give extra safety and can be untied more easily. On large line the end of the line should be seized. A sheet bend is often used through the eye of a mooring line or an existing bowline to extend the length of the line. This is faster and surer and uses less line than two bowlines. Sheet bends, like bowlines, require slack for untying.

The half hitch. The basis for many knots, the half hitch must be used carefully, as it can pull into a knot so tight that it has to be cut away. A clove hitch is good in a line under steady tension but unreliable in slippery line that is alternately slack and tight. A bowline would be better. I use a clove hitch to fasten a topping lift some distance from the end of my spinnaker pole, but I rotate the knot to the bottom of the pole and make a bowline with the end of the line and the standing part of the topping lift. A clove hitch will not slip along the tapered pole, and it provides a good bearing surface for the occasional heavy load on a topping lift. This is also a good rig for a boat boom.

Half hitches jam when the standing part of the line stretches under strain, becoming smaller in diameter. This causes the half hitches to tighten. When tension is released, the line returns to full size and jams on the hitches so they cannot be untied either with the line relaxed or returned to its previous tension. A round turn and two half hitches (in the form of a clove hitch) punishes a line less than any other knot because it distributes the strain over a large length of the line before the sharp turns of the knot receive tension. Two or three round turns relieve tension at the knot even more. What I have found best is to take one round turn around a mooring bollard or ring, continue as if to make a second round turn but instead pass the end of the line around the standing part and back around the bollard in the reverse direction. I then put the hitches on the standing part of the line. This is effective when working with lines under great tension, such as tow-lines. The greater the strain, the more reversing turns are laid on. The multiple turns and reversed direction reduce the tension on the end of the line and lessen the danger of the half hitches jamming. This hitch can be slacked off while under tension, but you must stand well clear.

The fishermen's bend is an excellent knot where friction and wear are great, as in making line fast to a shot of anchor chain. It doubles the turns of line and is closely akin to a round turn and two half hitches, except that the first hitch passes through the round turn. The dead end should be seized. The fisherman's bend can take very great strain without pulling up hard. The Brussels or buntline bend is neater and lighter than a bowline for attaching a sheet to the clew of a sail. It is a jamming knot that can usually be untied when the line is slack by tumbling the first turn, but not if pulled too tight.

The rolling hitch. Another type of jamming knot, the rolling hitch is one of the few knots you can tie in a line under tension, but it is not reliable when put in a slack line. With slippery line I throw extra turns on, laying each one firm and tight. By using a rolling hitch you can re-reeve an improperly led sheet without disturbing sail trim, clap a handy billy on a halyard that needs sweating up, or take tension on a wire shroud that has broken.

The masthead knot. Though seldom used, the masthead knot can answer a pressing need if you have to rig a spar that has no metal attachments, such as a broken spinnaker pole or a jury-rigged mast. It provides the attachments for four guys, stays, or shrouds. (See Chapter 18, "Emergencies.")

When a line must run free, as in paying out a sheet, a tow-line, or an anchor rode, it is best if the line does not feed from a coil, as more often than not it will end up fouled. If there is time, flaking the line down will allow it to run free. Practically, though, the fastest way to assure that the line will run is to overhaul it from end to end by running hand over hand through the line to the end to make sure there are no tangles. As long as the lay of the line as it falls is not disturbed, it will zing out free and clear from the top of its pile. I do this with any line that has been stored in a coil or that has been disturbed by work near it. Sometimes when working with a very long line, I overhaul it in *Awahnee*'s big deckbox and lead the working end to the foredeck ready for use. A halyard coil presents a different problem because the line leads vertically. Usually if the undisturbed coil is carefully laid on deck or cabin top, it will pay out without fouling. If the coil is obviously uneven and I am in a hurry to douse the sail, I throw the coil overboard under the lifeline and let it stream in the water to straighten itself out. When lowering the large sails, I usually allow the halyard to pass inside my arm as I work the sail. Then, if it does foul, I can trap the line before the tangle goes up the mast.

You need to use caution when working with ropes under tension. Any rope—synthetic, fiber, or wire—is dangerous as it comes under strain or pays out. The extreme strength, slipperiness, and elasticity of synthetics can lead to severe accidents among inexperienced people. A half-inch anchor rode can carry you down with an anchor. A one-eighth-inch nylon fishing line can cut your hand or take off a finger if a big *aku* takes the lure at the wrong time. A tow-line or a surging mooring line can break a leg or worse. Stand clear of blocks and fittings under strain. Rig your lines with fair leads. Be wary of high tension on small cleats since the fitting itself can fail or be pulled out—a common failing with fiberglass boats. I was nearby the day a man was killed on the stern of his own boat when a bow cleat on the boat he was taking under tow pulled out of the deck and drove into his chest.

CHAPTER 13

Sailhandling

Sails move a boat. Trimming them for maximum performance is the most vital ongoing task in handling a sailing vessel.
Sails not only propel a boat, they stabilize it and confer the easy
flowing motion of a sailboat breasting the ocean swell that is so
pleasurable and so hard to describe. Understanding how sails
work and what you can do with them brings satisfaction at sea.
The various rigs we fly in different winds are presented here to
give some idea of what sails I have found useful and how I put
them to work on *Awahnee*.

CALMS

If you're becalmed, give up and take down the sails. Banging,
rubbing, and slatting around in a calm does more damage to sails
than flying them in a gale. All is not lost, however. If you can't
motor, you can do ship's work. Or while you wait for wind, you
can have a backgammon tournament, learn all the verses to the
national anthem, or lie back on deck and watch the surface sea-
life unseen in any other weather condition. There are Jesus Christ
bugs walking on the water, free-swimming crabs, Portuguese men-
of-war, purple shells that float on a raft of bubbles, and fishnet
glass balls. *Mahimahi* will gather in the shadow of your hull and
provide a target for spearsmen. You can take a swim and scrape

off barnacles that have grown on the hull during passage so that your boat can slip smoothly through the water when the merest breeze does come.

Now as never before you will appreciate lack of weight aloft, for that helps make a boat roll. In the old days square riggers were sometimes dismasted when rolling becalmed in the doldrums. I thought *Awahnee* might do the same thing as she lurched rail down to rail down in the Gulf of Panama when the period of the swell matched and reinforced the pendulum action of our keel. We were being introduced to the agony of trying to meet a deadline sailing 3,000 engineless miles from Panama to California for the start of the 1963 Transpacific Yacht Race. It remains in my memory as one of the hardest passages we ever made. We sailed against the current in light or nonexistent winds all those miles, rock-hopping inshore trying to get the advantage of a counter-current and land–sea breezes. It was a good idea in theory, but some nights we lost 15 miles in the current when it fell flat calm and we were in water too deep to anchor. It took 60 strenuous days to get to San Diego; it probably would have been as fast for us to sail to Hawaii and then back to California. But then, our choice of the coastal route had been influenced just before we cast off by an engineless schooner, square-rigged on her foremast, which we saw return to Panama tattered and with a foul bottom. She had spent 103 days at sea attempting to sail clear of the notoriously calm Gulf of Panama.

ZEPHYRS

If there's one thing that's an aggravation in sailing, it's having a wind so light you can't sail it. In many parts of the world an ocean sailor will find long periods of time and large areas in which there are only very light airs, six knots or less. You will find that the swell—and there is almost always some swell in the ocean—rolls the boat, which makes the boom swing the wind out of the main. The telltale switches back and forth with each roll. Heavy gear in the bow and stern makes her toss and pitch, killing what headway there is. The clew of the jib droops, weighted down by its hardware, and the sheet hangs limp. The jib flaps in against the shrouds and the sheet block bangs down on deck. Then the sail flaps out as the mast top oscillates, and the block snaps up with sudden tension on the sheet. Here, too, there is more wear on sailing gear than in a gale. It is a nerve-wracking business, especially when it goes on for days.

Motorsailing is the best way to make miles comfortably in light airs. By using a minimum of engine power, and therefore fuel, in combination with sails tightly sheeted, a choice of courses is available. Too much engine power completely overwhelms the force of a light wind and prevents sailing by bringing the apparent wind too far ahead. In light airs when *Awahnee*'s speed drops to two or three knots and the swell rolls the wind out of the sails, I often start the engine and operate it just above idling speed. If the wind is from ahead, this will bring my speed to about four knots using less than a half-gallon of fuel an hour. Without both sails and engine, the speed would be far less and the boat's motion uncomfortable. Balanced close on the apparent wind, a bungee cord or bicycle inner tube holding the tiller, *Awahnee* motorsails far better in light weather than when imperfectly steered by a helmsman with other things on his mind.

So if you have an engine, crank it up. Otherwise, you will embark on an exercise in ingenuity and sailing skill of the most ethereal kind. First of all, you have to discover if there really is a breeze, and this is not at all easy. On *Awahnee* the regular helmsman stays on deck and maintains a watch for wind. He watches the surface of the water for riffles. He might check the drift of cigarette smoke (this is the only time smoking is really welcome aboard my boat). A pinch of fluff from a blanket or sweater dropped from the bow or stern where the effect of rolling is minimal can detect a light zephyr. Three spinnaker-cloth telltales fly from our rigging in easy sight ten feet above deck level, from the shrouds port and starboard and from the backstay. Close attention to good telltales in light airs is as informative in my experience as an electronic wind indicator. Even in the lightest breaths of air, most sailboats align themselves stern to the wind since the bow usually has the most windage. The telltale to watch, the windward one, is on the backstay. Skill is required to interpret the irregular fluttering of a telltale in a very light stirring of wind augmented by a roll to windward.

SAILING ON THE WIND IN ZEPHYRS

You must sail the wind you have, not the wind you wish you had or the wind you think you might get. Spread the canvas best suited to what breeze there actually is. This, if I may wax philosophical, is one of the simplest and most powerful lessons a sailing man can learn, and it works in all applications to life.

The only point of sail where a boat will move in very light air is on the wind, so the course you have to sail on a zephyr may be far from the one you desire. This is because the boat's speed and the windspeed complement each other, creating an apparent wind that is stronger than the one actually blowing. It's better to move a knot or two in almost any direction than to lie rolling in the swell. When wind returns, the course can be a matter of choice. So:

1. Come on the wind.

2. Take most, not all, the weight of the boom on the topping lift and vang it. A preventer may be necessary as well to quiet the boom.

3. Trim the main to be slightly eased from close-hauled.

4. Put the best helmsman on the tiller, for a delicate touch is required—oversteering kills forward motion. Watch the bubbles in the water to detect movement. Once the boat is going, her speed will augment the wind in the sails.

5. Put up your lightest jib, whether or not it is the largest.

6. Take off clew hardware and substitute a light line for the working sheet tied directly to the clew cringle. Trim the jib until it holds its shape.

7. Come up until a sail luffs, then fall off ten degrees and hold that course.

8. If after this you cannot make the boat move, consider burning your reserve fuel and then taking off the prop. Even when I expect good winds all the way, I often remove *Awahnee's* prop at the start of a long ocean passage because she responds to every puff of wind without its drag.

SAILING BEFORE THE WIND IN ZEPHYRS

Hoisting a spinnaker strikes fear in the heart of a cruising man who doesn't know how to handle one, but nothing else will fly when the wind is light and abaft the beam. Only trial will show you the lightest wind on which your spinnaker will perform, and even in a breeze the size and direction of a sea swell may roll the boat enough to collapse it. Fall off the wind and bring the spinnaker pole way aft to minimize the area of sail behind the main, or try flying it with the main down. Remove any heavy clew and tack hardware and rig a light sheet. Try anything and everything to find what works best.

We carry a 1,580-square-foot kite and, despite its size, we have set and handed it with only three persons aboard. I used to stop it up carefully before setting it, but now, as the mad yachties of New Zealand and Australia taught us, we set it flying in the lee of the mainsail. The halyard man may experience a bit of "spinnaker uplift" sometimes, but he can always grab the mast with his legs until help comes, as I have had to do.

The classic trouble with a spinnaker is taking the monster down after the wind has come up. This is where a good helmsman is invaluable, for he keeps the wind at a constant angle over the boat. The ideal technique is to release wind pressure from the spinnaker and get it not only down but below deck to eliminate the horrors that come when folds of the sail on deck catch wind or, worse, blow over the side and catch water. On *Awahnee* we do the following:

1. Slack the mainsheet and fall before the wind to blanket the spinnaker.

2. Ease the afterguy to let the pole forward.

3. Release the kite from the pole. The afterguy and the foreguy remain attached to the pole. The spinnaker hangs limp behind the main or streams loosely forward without trapping wind.

4. Slack away the halyard as the spinnaker is pulled by the clew and foot right down the forward hatch onto a bunk.

In stable light conditions it is good sport to experiment with rigging an extra sail below the main boom or below the spinnaker pole to capture unused wind-power. Before the wind, anything that is up helps drive the ship. In the old days the cook hung the tea towels on the backstays to help the day's run.

TRADE WINDS

A cruising boat should be designed to sail fast on and off the trade winds, which average 15 to 25 knots across every ocean.

Augmented trades with winds to 35 knots should not present an insurmountable obstacle to good performance. Winds are steady, surface current is with the wind, and squalls can usually be weathered all standing. These winds, although varying in strength with the season, blow nearly continuously over the tropical and subtropical latitudes of the earth, except for the belt of doldrums near the equator. Many cruising sailors stay principally in trade-wind areas to spend years enjoying their regularity and warmth—avoiding, of course, passages in hurricane and typhoon seasons.

If you have twin headstays (which I heartily recommend as the handiest, strongest, and safest rig), when you decide to change headsails you can hank a second jib on the extra headstay before lowering the one flying, and have it set within seconds. This avoids all the slopping around between jibs that has to be endured on a boat with a single headstay. The doused sail can be left hanked on, ready to fly again in a moment.

Before the trades, you might use a spinnaker and full main if the swell treats you kindly. But a hard squall or an undetected wind increase at night make twin headstays, again, an attractive alternative. With a full genoa on the leeward headstay and a Yankee hanked on the windward headstay and wung out one a pole, you have a stable rig that spreads a great deal of sail, is easily raised or doused, and gives a balanced helm to the boat. This rig is easy to put up. On *Awahnee* we follow these steps:

1. Maintain a steady course before the wind.

2. Ship the pole in its mast fitting, rig a topping lift (the staysail halyard serves well) and rig an afterguy (the jibsheet is often used). Make the clew of the jib fast to the pole.

3. Top up the pole.

4. Haul aft on the afterguy, adjusting the pole to its approximate working position, and make fast.

5. Hoist the jib.

6. Adjust the course and trim the sails.

The wung-out jib scoops wind into the leeward sail, keeping it full and drawing far before the wind. If the helmsman backwinds the wung-out jib, there is no crisis—it just flaps backward between the headstay and pole. The foot of the jib acts as a foreguy on the pole, and the topping lift supports most of its weight. The jibsheet is the afterguy.

It only takes one man on the foredeck to get the pole and wung-out sail down neatly, easily, dry and under control:

1. The helmsman backwinds the sail but keeps the main and leeward jib drawing.

2. The foredeck hand rapidly eases off the halyard and topping life together until the end of the pole is a few feet above the lifeline.

3. The helmsman pays out the afterguy.

4. When the pole is close to the headstays, the foredeck hand gently slacks the topping lift until the pole rests on deck.

The jib to be wung out should not be too large. The pole, when trimmed aft, should pull the sail flat without coming against the shrouds. The sail ought to be cut like a Yankee jib with a high clew. Poling out a genoa leaves a big bulge of sail flying ahead of the headstays, which, although it does no harm, adds neither effective area nor speed and is unstable and low, giving a bad pole angle.

With this rig in the trades, *Awahnee* has sailed consistently good passages, usually averaging about 160 miles per day and once averaging 208 miles per day on a run of over 1000 miles. In our first six years of cruising, which included several voyages across the Pacific and one and a half circumnavigations, no passage exceeded 19 days. The trip that broke the spell was from St. Helena Island to Montevideo, Uruguay, 3,000 miles in 22 days.

ON THE WIND IN HEAVY WEATHER

Most skippers understand that a boat laboring in heavy wind will do better with reduced sail, but it has been my observation that the reduction is often not made soon enough or that it is not great enough to make the boat comfortable and responsive. Then, possibly as a result of hanging on to too much sail too long, reefing down is often overdone and the boat ends up undercanvassed and unable to sail well. Conversely, in improving conditions, balanced sail area should be increased to take full advantage of the wind.

You may find that it is desirable to tuck a reef in the main to reduce helm when sailing on the wind in augmented trades blowing above 25 knots. When a boat consistently buries her rail, she is laboring. With the full working jib and a single reef in the main, and occasionally the staysail, *Awahnee* sails on course in a seaway, moving easier but driving as fast as under full main. If further reduction is necessary, I can change the headsails in several different combinations before putting a second reef in the main.

To reef the main:

1. Set the boom in the gallows (lash it in place if necessary) and take the main down, gasketing it loosely.

2. Work the sail to bring the proper row of reefing grommets in line on top of the boom. Make the reefing tack fast.

3. Haul aft on the reefing clew—a tight foot is essential to the set of the sail. I pass a three-quarter-inch synthetic line made fast to the end of the boom through the clew cringle, which gives a two-to-one advantage, then take a series of turns around the boom to hold the clew down and make fast.

4. Pass the lacing line through the reefing grommets and around the boltrope on the foot of the sail. Often two men do this, starting in the middle and working both ways. Make fast one end of the lacing line.

5. Starting at the fixed end, one man sets equal tension at each grommet throughout the length of the lacing and makes it fast.

6. Top up the boom and hoist the sail.

7. With a heavy boom, use the topping lift to protect the reefed sail from the full weight of the boom. Also, cushion the sheet when jibing or tacking. The boom can develop enough force to damage the sail or other gear.

My favorite rig to weather in strong winds of about 35 knots is a #3 jib, the full staysail, and the double-reefed main. If the wind picks up more, *Awahnee* sails like a Star boat with the jib down under double-reefed main and staysail. The sail area is balanced and close to the center of lateral resistance, where it drives the boat forward. *Awahnee*'s bow, unburdened by bowsprit, sail pressure, or excess weight, rises in the swell, keeping the deck free of heavy spray. She is easy and comfortable below as she carries on to windward, capturing only a fraction of the available force of the wind. Once the sails are reefed and trimmed to harmonize the boat with the forces of wind and sea, the helm is light and responsive. This is the secret of making good to weather, long or short distances.

BEFORE THE WIND IN HEAVY WEATHER

In a smart breeze when it becomes prudent to reduce sail, twin headstays provide the opportunity to put just the right amount of wind-power to work. In strong wind, we change the leeward sail from the genoa to our second full-size Yankee jib. In still stronger wind, we put a #2 or #3 Yankee to windward and successively smaller jibs to leeward with one, two, or three reefs in the main. The wung-out jib rig can provide maximum speed in conditions under which a spinnaker could not be handled, and it will work safely and easily, hour after hour and day after day. The wung-out jib offsets so well the force of the main, which makes the boat head up, that we can steer with fingertip pressure on *Awahnee*'s tiller while making seven, eight, or nine knots.

Awahnee's best run was made before strong monsoon winds in the Indian Ocean with a wung-out jib, a #2 genoa, and a single-reefed main. She made good 359 miles in 36 hours, an average of ten knots. Over two moonless nights and the intervening day, the bow wave roared out ten yards wide on both sides, and a brilliant phosphorescent wake spun out astern for what looked like miles. I will never forget going forward at night to check the gear and finding myself looking down some 20 feet to the black water as *Awahnee* creamed along in the cresting swell. In the contemporary term, she was "surfing," but somehow I find it hard to apply that term to a 25-ton, moderately heavy displacement boat.

Before the wind, especially with a jib wung out to windward, signs that a boat is becoming overpressed are subtle. The speed is exhilarating, and she seems to be going faster and better. In increasing wind, the helm gets heavy and the course becomes erratic, and in still higher wind too much sail pressure aft of the mast creates the danger of broaching. It is time to reduce the area of the mainsail in order to lessen the tendency of the boat to round up. Reefing the main will allow you to keep control of the boat. With a jib poled out and another to leeward, it is hard work merely to come on the wind to prepare for handing the main. I use a technique for taking the main down before the wind that saves terrific wear on the rigging and sails, keeps the whole deck virtually dry, and makes miles while we reef:

1. Keep a good helmsman steering the boat on a steady course. When the main is no longer full of wind, a lot less rudder pressure will be required. Guard against jibing.

2. Slack the main halyard six to eight feet to soften the sail and take some of the draft out of it.

3. The helmsman, or, if there is another hand available, the sheet man, takes in the mainsheet to bring the boom nearly amidships.

4. Ease the topping lift and lower the boom into the gallows. Usually it must be guided down. In heavy weather I find it best to have a line fast to the weather side of the gallows. I then throw the end around the boom, recover it, and draw the boom into position over the gallows. I do this while standing to windward braced on the gallows with both hands free to work. The boom is kept under control by the line until it is dropped in the gallows, where I lash it in place. The sheet is taken up firmly and made fast. No one goes up on the cabin top to furl the main until the boom is safely under control and can't sweep across the boat. In light weather firming up the mainsheet is enough to let us guide the boom into the gallows by hand.

5. Slack away the main halyard from the windward side of the boom. Haul the sail down and make it up.

Similarly, it is practical to put up a reefed sail before the wind by reversing this process:

1. Raise the sail partially so wind pressure will steady the boom.

2. Top up the boom and ease it out under control of the recovery line and mainsheet.

3. Hoist the sail to full height. Sometimes, depending on your point of sail, you must pull aft on the leech in order to clear the headboard or battens from under either the leeward lower shroud or the spreader. In this case, keep the boom inboard until the sail is clear.

STORM WINDS

The wind is whistling, the sea is smoking, the sky is dark and overbearing. But sailing in storm winds of 50 to 60 knots is possible and sometimes vital. It is the time to consider whether your preferred destination should be changed to another more agreeable to the wind, the sea, and the ship. Safety of the ship and crew is the prime consideration, and to care for the ship is to care for the crew as well. Sail an easier course if necessary. At times you may have to sacrifice gear in the interest of safety. Once I was awakened very late as a black squall line advanced. With only three of us aboard, I elected to save a new jib and say goodbye to an old canvas main that soon departed from *Awahnee* in great snapping pieces. It's a marvel to me to this day that the new flax staysail I flew through that eight-hour squall with winds to hurricane force actually had holes blown in the middle of its panels, though not a single seam parted.

At awful times, there is no choice, and you must claw off a lee shore when embayed. Failure to do so has cost many a beautiful boat. In my mind the performance of your boat in ultimate conditions is the most important factor when considering cruising ability.

Clawing off means more than just sailing forward. The ability of a boat and crew to bring her about smartly under extreme conditions is the secret of survival. This one factor as much as any other is the reason I sail an inboard-rigged cutter. The centered effort of the stormsails and the clean ends of the hull together with the raised forward end of the keel make tacking possible in extreme winds.

One December *Awahnee* was the only yacht moving in the Mediterranean. And for good reason: it was the dead of winter and blew a gale every afternoon and night with light winds and even calms in between. This weather was new to me. The usual pattern that December was for the wind to increase to about 35 knots by afternoon with much heavier, hard-hitting squalls beginning late in the day. Sometimes the wind simply kept getting stronger and stronger, but usually we were becalmed or in light variables between dawn and late morning, when it would start all over again.

Having been delayed in Egypt, we were very late in the season to be heading through the Med and across the Atlantic to the West Indies. It was the end of November when we anchored in mid-afternoon to poor holding ground in Khanian Bay on the north shore of Crete. We decided to wait until the next morning to visit the walled city of Khania. But the onshore wind steadily increased, and by a couple of hours after dark it was howling. A heavy chop built up in the bay and began to crest over. Then I saw that my anchor bearings had changed—we were dragging. Seven-year-old Reid, Nancy, and I were the only crew, the engine was long dead, and there was no longer any shelter in the bay. We sailed the anchor out under double-reefed main and staysail. The steep chop, on the verge of breaking into waves, staggered *Awahnee* but did not prevent her from carrying through the eye of the wind on the first close tack. Only after a dozen more tacks did we clear the snarling foul ground at the bay's entrance.

Awahnee's performance that night in 1962 fixed my opinion that the cutter is the best cruising rig. Before leaving Crete, I mounted a separate storm main track on the mast and bent on the trysail, rolling it up and tying it over to the ratlines when not in use. The rest of the 1,200 miles we had to make good to the Strait of Gibraltar was one westerly gale after another. With this rig I was able to drop the double-reefed main, immediately hoist the trysail, and keep going. (Towards the end of January while we were alongside at Gibraltar, the RAF clocked a "levanter," an easterly blow, at 137 knots. The harbormaster heard 17 SOS's in the Strait, a tanker went aground at Tangier, and four or five small boats went missing with all hands.)

In the clipper ship days it was said that any fool can put sails up but it takes a seaman to know when to take them down. Essentially this is when the boat cannot be controlled well by the rudder or when she is laboring: shipping solid water aboard and sailing with her rail, stanchions, and deck gear under. On the other hand, I do not advocate taking all sail down. I am convinced that a sailboat is safer and more comfortable under control and underway in very severe conditions. A boat moving through the water rides cresting and breaking seas better than one dead in the water. To do this, I have used stormsails in various combinations:

- The *trysail* (or *storm main*), about 120 square feet, is heavily roped on all sides with a wire-reinforced luff. I set it on a pendant so the tack clears the furled working main. It is rigged with three-quarter-inch double sheets, and instead of going through tackle, they lead to the spinnaker winch on the afterdeck.

- The *triple-reefed main,* about 250 square feet, I fly when there is no time to rig the trysail on its track. I do not like to fly the main triple-reefed because this exposes it to heavy wear. The storm main gives equivalent performance in all situations except when the most critical need is to drive to windward as soon as possible.

- The *handkerchief staysail* is less than 60 square feet. This little sail is the last one to come down because of too much wind. I have sailed in weather where we made over six knots on a satisfactory course under the handkerchief alone—pulling a drogue!

- The *jib topsail*, a narrow sail set 12 feet off the deck, gives surprising additional drive (approximately two knots) when the blow is making or easing but too strong for a change from the handkerchief staysail and trysail. It is easy to douse for a quick reduction to the minimum sails.

It is my opinion, arrived at through observation and trial, that the best control and performance of my boat is achieved when the center of effort of the sails is balanced close to the center of lateral resistance. Then she responds easily to the helm, giving us the chance to maneuver and even pick up a man overboard. I repeat this because it is the crux of sailing ability in extreme conditions.

STORM SEAS

Waves in the ocean rarely curl and break over a long distance like a shorebreak, but at times this will occur in any ocean. Around the Horn, these waves are known as the "graybeards of the Southern Ocean." Breaking seas are usually relatively local; the swell builds up too steeply in one area to support its shape and crests over at the peak. This seems to happen three or four times in succession on a particular swell before the water is dispersed enough to stop breaking. The size and force of breaking waves is augmented if a cross-sea works through the dominant swells at an angle. And when the waves of the two systems both peak at their meeting, you get a giant breaking wave, but still a local, individual phenomenon. It is rare in the vastness of the ocean for a small boat to be unfortunate enough to be under one of these, but it does happen.

In these seas I instruct the helmsman to study the cresting and breaking waves carefully. In all likelihood the boat is taking them and the wind on her stern quarter, so he faces more astern than forward. After a while he becomes fairly accurate in predicting where they are going to break. First, one might break some distance astern. If it makes up again and breaks about halfway nearer the boat, the next break may be right where we are. I tell the helmsman to steer for the back of the third break in a series; by the time the boat gets there, the wave's energy is spent and the sea is only frothy and roiling. If he sees a break forming dead to weather, he is to steer us out of its way. This, of course, cannot work at night and doesn't always work during the day. On the voyage around Antarctica *Awahnee* once took a breaking sea in the cockpit that knocked the standing helmsman down and ripped the binnacle off the floor, shearing four quarter-inch bolts. But it helps, I am convinced, to try to steer in all conditions.

HEAVING-TO

I can't recall more than three times in my quarter of a million miles sailing on the ocean when it was necessary to take down all sail, give up all thought of a beneficial course, and lie to our drogues. The first was on the maiden voyage of the second *Awahnee* from New Zealand to Samoa in an augmented winter gale that resulted when two low pressure systems merged. The second was off South Africa in the blow that knocked *Awahnee* down three times and washed the cradle out from under the skiff on the cabin top. Two days later, after it had eased some, we sailed into the river port of East London, right past a meteorological station that was measuring winds up to 71 knots. The third was a five-day storm towards the end of our Antarctic circumnavigation that blew us 200 miles farther south under Australia, but nearly 800 miles eastward nearer our landfall in New Zealand.

When there is sea room, a boat should lie to a drogue and be allowed moderate forward motion. The helm should be tended so that an attempt can be made to avoid breaking seas. The ability of a boat to lie by the quarter is largely determined by the hull design, so this should be one of the major considerations in choosing a blue-water cruising boat. The boat should carry a minimal amount of sail in extreme conditions if at all possible. If the stormsail is too large or blown out, a scandalized headsail gives her a little way through the water so she can answer the rudder, and makes her stable in the seas.

Lying ahull is dangerous in extremely heavy weather, in my judgment. The seas will cause the boat to lie in the trough of the swell, where she will roll heavily as each sea passes under her, and where she is most likely to broach or be overwhelmed.

Another practice to be avoided if possible is lying to a sea anchor off the bow. A boat's greatest windage is almost always forward, and therefore she wants to blow off rather than lie head to wind. Often she pulls first to one side and then to the other, with wrenching strains and lulls in the tension of the gear. This generates punishing forces on the rudder fastenings with the helm either lashed or free, and makes it almost impossible to cook or rest below.

In monstrous seas and howling wind a boat will lie easiest by the stern quarter to one or more drogues. This allows slow forward progress with the bow streaming downwind and the vessel relatively steady, heeled to leeward. Lying dead before the wind, the boat will roll and, with less resistance to the sea, can get too much drive going straight down the face of a sea, which may result in pitchpoling. Towing warps is not effective under truly severe conditions because of their insufficient holding power.

The drogue is a great friend in troubled times. I prefer to use multiple rigs rather than one heavy drogue, which may prove absolutely unmanageable and unrecoverable. In winds of more than 80 knots and seas that were scarcely credible, *Awahnee* lay safely off Antarctica to a combination of drogues as follows:

- On the surface, a 200-foot length of one-inch line pulled a spinnaker pole fixed by a bridle and weighted with a small anchor, ten feet of light chain, and a tire.

- At mid-depth, a second line 250 feet long pulled a medium anchor and chain and two tires fixed at widely separated points by pendants.

- The deep drogue was two tires and a heavy anchor and chain at the end of 400 feet of line.

The advantage of this conglomeration is that the spar on the surface drogue disturbs the sea and dampens its impulse to break.

The deeper lines maintain a steady tension in a breaking sea that might otherwise throw unweighted surface drogues onto the afterdeck. But the principal advantage is that even though great holding power is achieved, each line can be handled separately to reduce or recover the drogues. Only twice in scores of times have the rigs fouled—once causing many hours of work and once saving a drogue that fouled after its line had parted.

The leads of drogues should be distributed to several deck fittings and can be influenced by attaching stretchy nylon lines. If a drogue is suitably arranged on a bridle, the boat can be jibed over in order to change course.

A serious deficiency of some boats that comes to light only *in extremis* is the lack of suitable places to make drogues fast. Two heavy cleats and a strong winch fore and aft are required for handling lines under heavy draft. Once on my noble 61-year-old ketch *America* I encompassed the entire cabin and cockpit coamings at deck level in order to make a drogue fast to something that wouldn't carry away.

In the ultimate storm, then, my advice is to maintain stability and control of the boat by steering the easiest course possible and towing both surface and submerged drogues for protection against breaking waves, for directional stability, and as a brake. The truism that the boat can take more than her crew is pretty accurate. Rocks sink boats much more often than the sea does. A well-designed, well-found small boat and crew can survive forces that cannot be imagined as one sits at a writing desk or in an easy chair reading. I know—I've seen it.

CHAPTER 14

Life at sea

What do you do all day at sea? You live, you breathe. You delight in the simple, powerful satisfaction that years of planning and preparation are behind you now. On a trade-wind passage with a steady warm breeze, blue sky, cumulus clouds overhead, and the horizon empty all around, you enjoy. You enjoy the exquisite sunrise. You enjoy the explosion of coffee aroma that announces breakfast while you are still in your bunk, you enjoy the realization that the sun is well up and the boat footing swiftly along. You enjoy the heat of a mid-morning watch, the cooling dash of seawater on your feet or even over your head. You take pleasure in the lift and drive of the hull beneath you and in the taut canvas above silently carrying you on your incredible way by cosmic power, accompanied by the sibilant music of the sea. You listen to it in your bunk at night, your ear only inches away from the triple encounter of wind, wave, and waterline.

You will probably learn to know your shipmates as intimately as their own families do, for at sea you review your life, talk in depth, and crystallize your thoughts. You laugh and sing and work together, just you in the world of the boat. Even when you don't feel affection, you respect your mates and tolerate their foibles, for this is a life of interdependence.

Everything you do counts: it has an immediate bearing on your personal or the general comfort, the safety and the success or failure of the passage. And there are never enough hours in the day.

You like the ten-day-old sun-dried bread with which you build fabulous sandwiches in the cockpit at noon, the hull-temperature lemonade is surprisingly refreshing, and you enjoy the tang of corned beef. You relish a heavenly freshwater shower on the after-deck in a squall. You are renewed by an afternoon nap, pleased by a good book, and comforted on night watch by the yellow glow of the cabin lamps shining in the black void before the moon rises. You are a connoisseur of sunsets, a seer of the green flash. You discern stars a scant few degrees above the horizon some nights, and if the sea is quiet you can see pathways to the brightest planets and stars reflected on it like moonglow. You witness the mystery of the universe every time you take a navigational sight.

On watch at night you hold the lives of your sleeping shipmates in the sharpness of your eye, the computer of your mind, and the palm of your hand. You participate in the mystique of the watch, the unbroken succession of helmsmen on a passage. When you balance the helm and go below into the darkened cabin to wake up your relief, you maintain the continuity that threads the events of a voyage from continent to continent. When the last watch is over and the boat lies tethered to the earth with no one manning the helm, the passage is finished, your life is changed, and triviality once again enters into your existence.

The promise and danger of the landfall thin on the horizon thrills you as the boat sails on toward the rocks, the surf, the pass, the harbor, the cold beer, the letters from home, the people, the foreign land.

You meet men whose family, culture, and entire history are totally unknown to you—and yours, as an individual, to them. You will find subtleties, values, and abilities beyond your experience in people, some of whom have hardly seen the inside of a schoolroom, and who live full and complete lives, supplied only by the goods found in a one-room store.

You will never forget the ship, how she felt at the helm or the precise location and rig of all her running gear. And for the rest of your life on the happenstance of an idle thought, a strange cloud formation, or an overheard remark, you will see her sailing in your mind's eye.

DIVIDING THE GOODIES

Food and weather are the greatest variables aboard a boat at sea. Weather is not subject to human influence, but unjust distribution of the cook du jour's fudge, pie, or cake can provoke a storm of heated feelings. We divide our goodies the way Captain Bligh did on his 3,500-mile voyage in an open whaleboat with 21 men aboard after the mutiny on the *Bounty*. Rather ceremoniously, the cook divides the prize into the necessary number of equal parts. Then another crewmember turns his back while the cook points to a portion, asking, "Who shall have this?" The other fellow names one of the crew, and this is repeated until all pieces are distributed.

We have found it best not to attempt to hold extra portions overnight, but to make the complete distribution at once. Otherwise the unallotted goodies are sometimes unaccountably half-gone by morning. An effort is also made to have fair distribution of the fruit that is not served at meals. Especially after some time at sea when the supply is waning and becoming proportionately more valued, we inventory the fruit and place a limit on how much each should eat daily. Often it works out that we have a round of oranges or mangos or apples in the mid-afternoon. This may all seem picayune, and maybe it is. But little things make a big difference, especially when you are far away from other diversion.

COOKING ABOARD

No one who has been offshore disputes that cooking is the hardest job in a small boat. To prepare every meal for days without number quickly becomes unending drudgery. The Australians and New Zealanders know this: one of the handsomest trophies for the Transtasman Race is presented to the cook on the last boat to finish.

On the theory that anyone who can boil water can learn to cook, we rotate galley duty aboard *Awahnee,* one man, one day. There is only one rule, based on nutrition and common sense: dinner must consist of meat, vegetable, and a starch. Experienced cooks take the first days and help novices at the beginning of a trip. Before the outset of a voyage we often ask someone on shore to cook a big boneless roast for us to eat the first few days. Then new cooks aren't required to deal with the stove when seasickness makes appetites unpredictable. A basic cookbook like *The Joy of Cooking* and a couple of cruising cookbooks are instruction enough in meal planning and preparation for a new cook. After he has mastered lighting the Primus stove, he is ready to concoct a gastronomic delight.

With this rotating system, no one cooks more often than every fourth or fifth day, and I never cook. Thus each person has a day or two to recover from his ordeal and another day to figure out his next salubrious menu. And salubrious they are!

The cooking day begins with the most difficult meal, dinner, and continues with breakfast the next morning and lunch, usually cold, at midday. The cook prepares the meal, washes the dishes, cleans the galley, and—after lunch so he won't contaminate food with kerosene—fills the lamps and stove. Dinner is served an hour before sundown so the galley can be cleaned during daylight. Breakfast is immediately after the dawn watch to allow the man coming off watch to eat before turning in. Similarly, lunch is at the noon change of watch. During his day in the galley, which begins and ends at 3:00 P.M., the cook stands no day watch and only one two-hour watch at night to give him plenty of time to produce his specialties. Through 219 crewmembers we've never had a bad meal at sea. But then, hunger is the best sauce.

CLEANING UP

Dishes are washed in saltwater—hot, if they are greasy—with ordinary liquid detergent. They must be dried to remove the salt, which would otherwise make an unappetizing scum on silverware. Dishtowels get damp and grimy after only a few uses, especially if the cook is gung-ho and wipes the bottoms of the pots. Dishtowels must be considered expendable, for they won't often come clean after yeoman galley service. Carry plenty of them, in dark colors.

Sponges are not a part of our galley equipment—they stay damp and get smelly and sour too easily. So do good dishcloths, although cheap, thin ones dry out even after use in saltwater. We prefer plastic scrubbers for washing dishes; they are nonabsorbent, so they don't become malodorous and unsanitary.

It isn't always easy to clean up messes on board. Paper napkins

Christopher Knight

Fiona and Teno help me gather the makings for barnacle chowder. We rowed out to pick up this bountiful float during a calm on a long passage from Hawaii to Vancouver. (Notice, in the background, the fishnet we laced from the toerail to the top lifeline with our young children in mind.)

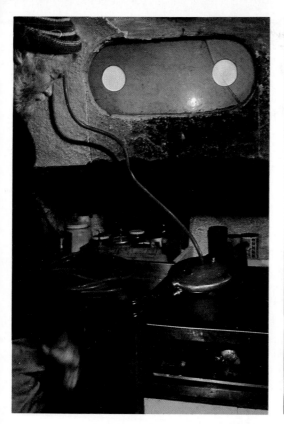
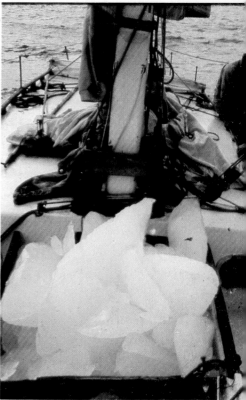

Above, left: Using a pressure cooker on *Awahnee*'s Primus stove, we distilled three quarts of water a day during the final week of the 8000-mile, 59-day last leg of our Antarctic circumnavigation. We never actually ran out of fresh water, but it was in very short supply, and I wanted to know our capacity for distilling. (Note the burnt and melted cabin insulation, testimony to a recent galley fire, and the storm shutter in place over the portlight.)

Right: A much more abundant source of water during our Antarctic voyage was the solid-state variety, collected far south of the African continent.

Facing page, top: Our vegetable bins are plastic mesh to keep produce well-ventilated. The bins slide through the rungs of the companionway ladder to stow out of the way under the cockpit. Our daughter Fiona supervises from the baby backpack.

Far left: Deception Island in the South Shetlands, an active volcano covered with glacier, has boiling hot springs at the water's edge. Here we cook dinner and heat our plum pudding Maori-style in the hot water.

Left: Turtle steak for dinner.

The cruising man's Jacuzzi.

Above: Heavy rain gave us a dinghy full of fresh water, so Reid did a laundry without having to row it ashore.

Left: Becalmed approaching Kobe, Japan, Nancy and I enjoy a hot saltwater bath in the deckbox using engine-cooling water.

Top: Open house in a Japanese fishing harbor.
Above: Three young salts greet us at Christmas Island,
rub-a-dub-dub style.

Top: Auntie Tahia welcomes me back to Tahiti in her coolest Sunday best.
Above: Passing out bananas to children on Tongareva in the Cook Islands. The diet of many atoll inhabitants consists largely of coconuts, fish, and rice. Visiting yachtsmen can bring an unaccustomed treat with a stalk of bananas or a basket of limes.

Christopher

For long passages with trade winds over the quarter, jibs flown
on twin headstays are the handiest, strongest, and safest rig.

and paper towels are bulky to stow and outrageously expensive outside the U.S. At sea fresh water is unavailable for mopping up, and even a jealously guarded cache of clean rags is gone sooner or later. We solve most clean-up problems with newspaper, which we collect before leaving on a voyage and stow under the mattresses. Not only are newspapers handy, absorbent, and disposable, they brighten our day. Many times we have all sat at a meal, bowls in hand, bent over reading the newspaper page spread out on the floor to sop up some spillage.

THE HEAD

Ah, the head. What an imposition on the already close quarters and air is this facility, necessary as it is. Independent outside ventilation unaccompanied by seawater is difficult to provide, and internal cross-ventilation imposes on the whole boat. The best tactic is to burn incense during the occupation. We favor woodsy scents like sandalwood over heavy musky ones.

I have come to think of the head as an instrument of the devil: whoever plugs it up usually can't fix it, and I get stuck with the ultimate mess. Years ago I won a notorious reputation as "Three-Squares-a-Day Griff" by trying to ration toilet paper as a measure against plugging up the pipes in the head. Now at sea we almost never use the head, and in port only when we must. The after pulpit on double-ended *Awahnee* is custom-made to function as a safe and comfortable toilet seat. Out in the air and sunlight or moonlight with *Awahnee*'s wake bubbling past beneath, using the head can be quite exhilarating. For the sake of propriety, the order to the helmsman as one goes aft is, "Keep a sharp lookout ahead."

GARBAGE AND POLLUTION

Having sailed many a voyage with sincerely concerned young people, I have had the opportunity to discuss with them the question of pollution and to act on their suggestions. Most times these have been that garbage be bagged in plastic and stowed on deck. After several warm days, during which the bags start to leak and smell, another meeting and discussion results in all cans being sunk, all glass broken and dumped, and edible garbage and paper thrown over the side. I believe that the sea can tolerate this introduction of biodegradable material from a small boat. After all, every tin can on the bottom is a home for a clutch of baby fish or an octopus.

In general, pollution of the ocean waters by floating rubbish is restricted to areas where wind and current concentrate the material. In other parts of the ocean it is possible to sail for days, weeks, or even months without sighting a single piece of plastic. Of course, in heavily travelled sea lanes the litter of hundreds of vessels and thousands of people is concentrated. An often overlooked fact is that garbage and litter dumped in ditches miles from the sea may appear at the shoreline after a major freshet or flood. This is easily seen in Hawaii at the Ala Wai Small Boat Harbor, where the Ala Wai, a small drainage canal, reaches the sea. With each big rainfall debris from the hills above is washed into the canal and ends up in the yacht basin—plastic bottles, rubber balls, glass jars, wood, paper, dead animals, and rotten fruit are common. Yachtsmen, however, often get the credit.

The people of the world who live in small villages with an agrarian economy seem unknowledgeable and unconcerned about pollution. Actually, their "pollution" is often nothing more than an agreeable contribution to the local eco-system. The household debris of coconut husks, seashells, fruit and vegetable rind, and bits of meat and fish enter the system immediately with close examination by children, dogs, chickens, and pigs. In the sea, urine and feces voided below the high water mark are biologically acceptable. The first sight of fish swimming rapidly for feces in the water may be a bit of a shock to the uninitiated Western man, but it is a fact that fish will take every bit of such debris that is not too large. Indeed, in many atoll villages, the "fare iti," or "little house," sits out on the reef over a couple of feet of water, and there you will find the greatest variety of beautiful fish, congregated for the daily offerings.

A native man is not a consumer of sophisticated goods or toxic, waste-producing materials. He lives essentially from the local land and sea and fits into the ecological system. Western man has the idea that manure of any sort causes disease and infection, but actually this is not the case. Body secretions and excretions uncontaminated by disease organisms or parasites are usually not infectious. A seldom appreciated fact is that dilution alone is an effective disinfecting process where large volumes of water and small quantities of body waste are concerned.

It is unfortunate that yachtsmen stand accused and convicted of causing pollution with their minor biodegradable wastes. Their refuse is nothing compared to the pollution of industrial wastes discharged into most developed harbors, and to the waste dumped from passenger liners, battleships, aircraft carriers, and oil tankers.

WET BUNKS AND CLOTHING

Rare is the voyage that doesn't include a wet bunk. Bedding, pillows, and mattresses wet with saltwater never really dry out until they are rinsed in fresh water, for salt crystals are hygroscopic —they absorb atmospheric moisture. This happens even after the bedding has been sun-dried, and explains the clammy feeling it acquires at night.

Prevention is the best cure, as with many matters of discomfort. On my boat we have evolved the practice of asking permission to open a hatch or port of the person who bunks beneath it. This promotes a proprietary interest on the part of the potential victim and avoids many an unpleasant surprise.

Peter Dohm, who made a long career of sailing as workaway crew, never traveled without a big sheet of plastic. Without fail, whenever he left his bunk aboard my ketch *America,* he piled his duffel in the middle of the mattress and carefully draped the plastic over it and below the level of the bedding. It was a ludicrous performance on a bright sunny afternoon, but I confess I went to bed in a damp bunk one night, and he never did.

Few sailors are so methodically pessimistic, and some get irritated when it takes the relieving watch 20 minutes to get on deck. What can you do when your bunk gets soaked? As a veteran of many a hard, wet sea voyage, I have learned it is possible to sleep dry, warm, and comfortable in a wet bunk. This magic is achieved by newspaper. When a bunk is deluged, immediately flick off or soak up standing water to lessen the damage. Newspaper is then put above and below all wet surfaces, including mattresses and pillows. If there is no dry sheet, sleep on a layer of papers atop the wet bedding. If you are out of dry pillowcases, a T-shirt does fine. After sleep, change the damp papers, and repeat until the bed is dried out. This technique worked many times over on the turbulent 59-day final leg of our Antarctic circumnavigation from the South Orkney Islands to New Zealand eastabout.

Newspaper also works in insulating you from wet clothes, keeping you warm, and absorbing some of the moisture. You can make a newspaper poncho to go over your shoulders under a wet shirt or sweater. Strips of newspaper wrapped around your feet after you have put on dry socks will protect you from wet boots, and strips around the forearms over your skivvies but under damp outerwear promote toasty warm comfort on watch.

Drying wet clothes requires ventilation; the water-saturated atmosphere of an unheated boat cabin dripping with condensation is not going to do it. This will not be a problem in a cabin heated with a stove that vents outside, of course. If you have enough spare clothes, consider putting the salty ones out in a rainsquall to rinse out and dry later. Even on cold days with weak sun, clothes free of saltwater can be dried fairly well in a protected place like inside the dinghy or in its lee. But if you are down to your last set of dry clothes without the prospect of fair weather or reaching port soon, my advice is to reserve the dry ones for below deck, and to climb back into the damp ones for standing watch.

We have found that it is hard to get warm enough to sleep comfortably when you wear damp clothes in your bunk. It is better to wear dry though scanty clothes for sleeping, even though you go to bed quite cold. However, if you lay one or two items of damp clothes beside you under the covers, in a few hours your body heat will do a surprisingly thorough job of drying them. After this, even if they are still somewhat damp, your jeans will be warm when you put them on again.

CHAPTER 15

Health

In Suva, Fiji, I met a handsome steel cruising ketch out of Montevideo with the interesting name *Estrella de José Compora*. After becoming acquainted with the three Uruguayans who sailed her, I asked the significance of this name. This is the story they told:

For several years a group of four young men worked and studied for this venture, the first world circumnavigation in a yacht by Uruguayans. In their final preparation the fear of the possibility of appendicitis became so great that they resolved as a group to have their healthy appendixes removed before sailing. Unfortunately, one of them, José Compora, died as the result of complications of the operation. And these three, resolving that José would sail with them in spirit, named their boat for him.

José's death, of course, proves nothing. But inherent fear of illness and great trusting faith in medicine are strong human traits. For a man to go to sea with a simple first-aid kit is as unrealistic as a man staying home because he could not arrange to have a physician aboard his boat.

It is my opinion that the captain should be acquainted with the personal medical situation of his shipmates and himself. I have had crewmembers aboard *Awahnee* who failed to reveal to me such serious conditions as complete night blindness, diabetes, epilepsy, gonorrhea, and gastric ulcers. This is hardly forgivable, and I now query each prospective crewmember closely.

An ocean cruising boat should have adequate supplies and information to handle accident, infection, and chance illness aboard, and her captain should have the courage to use them or authorize someone else to. In my mind, the skipper who fails to attempt medical or surgical treatment of a serious condition aboard is more derelict in his duty to his shipmates than the man who tries to treat the problem and does not effect a cure.

Medical advice from the U.S. Public Health Service is available to a boat with adequate radio gear in waters off the North American continent. The information is relayed to ships at sea by the U.S. Coast Guard, which also arranges evacuation if necessary. The Coast Guard constantly monitors 500 kHz, 2182 kHz and 156.8 MHz FM (VHF Channel 16). In the rest of the world CIRM, the Italian Radio Medical Service, provides these services free to ships of all nations as a public service. By means of a code book in different languages, the first volume in-code and the second volume de-code, information and instruction can be exchanged without using an interpreter by men who speak different languages.

CIRM watches 4265 kHz, 6420 kHz, 8685 kHz, 12748 kHz, and 17036 kHz twenty-four hours a day. If you get no answer on 2182 kHz and if direct contact cannot be made with Rome on these frequencies or relay stations in Buenos Aires and Manila, often the merchant distress frequency, 500 kHz, will provide a successful contact and relay. On more than one occasion, radio consultation has enabled untrained people to perform life-saving procedures.

At sea the means of coping with illness or accident are limited, and complete medical attention is unavailable for weeks at a time. However, don't forget that many people live long, adventurous lives without consulting a doctor except in times of serious illness. Before a voyage, someone who will sail aboard should study first aid, basic hygiene, and techniques of nursing the seriously ill or disabled. I think it is also of value to have more than a casual knowledge of tropical parasites if your cruise is to the sunny climes.

Vaccination against smallpox, tetanus, and typhoid is a must because of their prevalence in many parts of the world. In addition, vaccination against cholera, yellow fever, and other diseases should be obtained as recommended by public health authorities of the World Health Organization for the area you intend to visit. Usually this is free or at nominal cost through the port health officer at a port of entry.

Advanced First Aid Afloat by Peter F. Eastman, M.D., Cornell Maritime Press, Inc., Cambridge, Maryland, has my highest recommendation as the medical reference to have aboard a boat. It actually goes far beyond first aid with its no-nonsense directions and drawings in identifying and handling serious accident and illness, including—heaven forbid—amputation of a leg.

An even more complete though not as readable emergency medical treatise is the text used by the U.S. Merchant Marine Academy, *The Ship's Medicine Chest,* compiled by the U.S. Public Health Service and printed by the Government Printing Office, Washington, D.C. The British reference is *The Ship Captain's Medical Guide,* an official publication of Her Majesty's Stationery Office, London.

Many extensive medical kits are not really adequate for the job they may be called on to do. The one listed in *Advanced First Aid Afloat* is the most practical and complete I know of. I recommend the following additions to his kit, however, for it frightens me to think of a little yacht out of touch with the world for weeks at a time that might not have a good supply of:

1. Ophthalmic, topical, and injectable local anesthetics.

2. Sedative and pain-killing medication, including Demerol and/or morphine. (By law these must be kept in a locked cabinet.)

3. Antibiotic tablets, capsules, and injectables to help control severe infections.

4. Antihistamine medication for allergic reactions.

5. Surgical suture material, needles, and forceps.

6. A male urinary catheter.

7. Dental forceps—molar and incisor.

8. Syringes and needles for injecting drugs.

9. A Bard-Parker scalpel handle and assorted blades.

Your physician or the public health department can help you obtain these items.

It is just as vital to keep human plumbing in order as it is the ship's. Subjects that are unmentionable ashore are of genuine concern to all afloat in the same boat. Matter-of-fact discussion of normal and abnormal body functions will prevent a minor constipation from becoming an impaction of the rectum. It will remove from the cooking roster an adventurous lover who develops gonorrhea. It will stop one itchy scalp from developing into a boatload of lousy sailors. Some verbal niceties and inhibitions should be stowed ashore and reclaimed after the voyage.

SEASICKNESS

The most frequent complaint on board a small boat is seasickness. Once it strikes there is little for the victim to do but live through it. Prevention is the best cure. Take antinausea medication long before casting off for sea. In my experience, the pills should be taken at least 18 to 24 hours before sailing in order for them to be fully at work in the system when needed. Continue the medication throughout the first few days at sea according to directions, then taper off gradually. If you wait until you feel sick to take a seasickness pill, you'll probably throw up the medicine. In severe situations where pills cannot be kept in the stomach, suppositories (available by prescription) are used to administer the drug. Or a small retention enema, not more than four to six ounces of tepid water with a pill dissolved in it, will allow the medication to be absorbed. Drowsiness is often an unacknowledged but mild form of motion sickness.

Only two of the 219 crewmembers who have made ocean passages aboard *Awahnee* remained seasick for longer than two and a half days. One of them came out of it on his sixth day at sea, and the other was sick whenever we sailed heeled over.

Dry soda crackers or bread will quiet the stomach of someone feeling queasy by soaking up fluid. Fresh air helps more than anything else, and we encourage victims of *mal de mer* to stay on deck, where a little work or a short watch often helps them get over that awful feeling. Awareness that others are working the boat is more conducive to a crewmember's recovery than allowing him to succumb to total misery in a bunk down below. Throwing up is a great relief in mild cases—we encourage sufferers not to resist the urge to vomit. Once, after a new crewman barfed on my bed and pillow (while I was working on deck), I decided there was no reason for anyone to throw up below deck simply because of seasickness. No one, but no one, heaves below deck. This, the first ironclad rule on board *Awahnee,* has stood for over 15 years and I think it makes life better for everyone aboard, seasick and healthy alike.

SUNBURN

Another common problem of sailors, exposed as they often are to brilliant direct and reflected sun, is sunburn. Stinging salt spray and wind may aggravate sunburn, or can themselves burn the skin and eyes. A fresh-water wash relieves salt burns. Like *mal de mer,* sunburn can be prevented far better than treated. Sun-sensitive people and fair-skinned sailors should wear protective clothing at first, exposing their skin to the combination of sun and salt air a little longer each day. Sea and Ski is the best sunburn protection for normal skin I have used. There are several products that shield skin from all tanning rays of the sun, but some of these sting when put on sunburned or sun-sensitive skin. Many "tanning lotions" do not contain any sun screen. It is dangerous to have repeated burning, blistering, and peeling of the nose and tops of the ears. Low-grade skin cancer may result.

People who are sunburned badly enough to have blistered skin have second degree burns, and depending on how much area is blistered, they can be severely incapacitated. They need lots of fluids, rest, and warmth. Do not open the blisters unless there is some reason to. Don't put butter or other grease on a burn, use a water-miscible burn ointment or more Sea and Ski. Cold compresses on a burn will relieve pain remarkably and may very well lessen the degree of tissue destruction. Changing the watch schedule to relieve sun-sensitive crew from the midday hours until they are "sunproof" is in the best interests of all aboard.

I require everyone to have his own sunhat and suggest he bring polarizing sunglasses as well. The inexperienced and the deeply tanned sometimes try to exempt themselves, but I insist. If they don't bring their own, they will want to borrow mine. The sun blazes unexpectedly hot in the tropics when reflected from a thousand waves, and no one can work long in it without suffering eyeburn, headache, and possible sunburn.

Two other sun-related problems, heat exhaustion and heat stroke, have not occurred in our sailing. I believe this is because at sea we do not encounter extremely high temperatures and we take in sufficient salt in our food.

CONSTIPATION

The most common affliction that is potentially serious aboard a small boat is constipation. I think unaccustomed lack of bulk in the diet, relative lack of privacy at the toilet, and the sense of strangeness in a new situation all contribute. If left unattended, it can be debilitating through nausea or cramps. Raw vegetables, fresh or dried fruits, and whole-grain cereals will often work a cure in the first few days, and should be specifically included in the menu. If this is unsuccessful or if three days have passed since a bowel movement, I prefer to have the sufferer use a plain gelatin suppository or one cut from a bar of soap. This almost always works right away, though many people would rather take a laxative and wait another day. Beyond this time, the patient is in danger of becoming quite sick, and a gentle soap enema should be administered. At times, squeezing and massaging the anal region while attempting to move the bowels will break out hardened feces and success will follow. If this fails, the rectum may have to be cleared with the fingers, using a surgical glove and Vaseline lubricant. Among the crewmen aboard *Awahnee* who have been troubled with constipation, only one had further difficulty after the first bowel movement.

HELMSMAN'S REAR END

This is the term we coined for the small sea boils or pustules located in the gluteal region that so commonly afflict small-boat sailors at sea. It is best prevented and best treated by keeping dry, and to this end I advise everyone not to wear underpants. While outer pants wet with saltwater dry in the air, underwear stays damp and the skin remains soft and irritated by salt and the pressure of sitting. Helmsman's Rear End results when bacteria infect the hair follicles or pores of the skin. In warm weather, when one isn't always careful about remaining dry on watch or working on the foredeck, Helmsman's Rear End sometimes is so bad that we have a daily clinic. The pustules are opened, drained, and dotted with dilute (1 to 100) formalin, tincture of iodine or other antiseptic, which is followed by a 20-minute sun treatment of the affected area.

Saltwater boils on wrists and calves where cuffs and boots rub are a related affliction but worse because they inhibit a sailor's movements and are likely to be reopened in the course of deck work. They yield to essentially the same treatment, but may require oral antibiotics. And they must be protected from abrasion from the cuff or boot that caused them.

Sun-dried skin and ventilation with good sea air combine to eliminate problems of crotch rot and athlete's foot that may burden arriving crewmembers. No one has retained these conditions while sailing on *Awahnee* to my knowledge.

INFECTIONS

Coral cuts, insect bites, and small nicks and scratches seem more prone to infection than more serious cuts, perhaps because they don't bleed enough to wash away contaminants and possibly because they are not always adequately treated. Coral cuts head the list of troublesome common injuries. We find that aromatic spirits of ammonia immediately applied prevents infection. We keep a plastic bottle of it in the dinghy when we go diving.

We have developed a technique for dealing with infection that is much more successful than the commonly used antibiotic ointment treatment. Keeping the wound dry is the secret of success. Clean it down to the underlying healthy pink tissue by removing the scab and all pus. Use toilet paper if gauze supplies are limited. You may have to soak the scab first by putting a wet pad over it; sodium bicarbonate (baking soda) solution softens scabs better than water alone. Cover the clean wound completely with dry sulfa or antibiotic powder. Press it into the moist surface. If necessary, put on a dressing but use one that allows air circulation. Keep the wound as dry as possible. If you have no sulfa or antibiotic powder, open a capsule or crush a pill to obtain it and save the remainder for later use. Carefully wash your hands and instruments after dealing with infected wounds and dispose of waste to avoid contamination.

Staphylococcus bacteria are present on normal healthy skin, on the ground, in the air, and in salt and fresh water. When the skin is broken, staph bacteria often enter the wound, and if the body's natural defenses or the medical kit's antiseptic dressings are not successful, the wound will become infected. We all know that a bath is not a daily event for a small-boat sailor, so I recommend that everyone use an antibacterial soap like Dial, Zest, or Lifebuoy to reduce bacterial contamination on the skin. Surgical soap is too strong for regular use in bathing.

In warm, humid tropical conditions, staph bacteria thrive. Hair follicles often become sensitive and irritated. It has been my experience that applying a very small spot of tincture of iodine to an inflamed follicle will prevent it from blowing up into a pimple or serious boil. Whenever a crewman has a boil, we are all alerted to the possibility of inflamed hair follicles. This treatment is so effective that I am sure I have stopped incipient staph outbreaks aboard *Awahnee* several times. The presence of facial or body scars that indicate chronic staphyloccic infection or chronic severe pimples is enough to make me exclude a prospective crewmember.

TOOTHACHE

Toothache at sea is generally beyond one's ability to correct aboard, short of extraction. The underlying problem is of long standing and requires professional handling. Minor toothache might be controlled by brushing the teeth thoroughly, rinsing in warm saltwater, then applying oil of cloves. In desperation I once drilled one of my teeth by twirling graduated sizes of metal drills in my fingers and then Epoxied the hole. A sensitive tooth can be temporarily protected by pressing a small piece of warm paraffin or beeswax in the cavity, which will prevent heat and food contact. Though it is extremely unpleasant, severe toothache or abscess may respond to hot packs, antibiotic treatment, and time. But, if not, extraction is the only answer at sea. I once broke my own abscessed tooth off twice trying to pull it without proper instruments. Sixteen days later when we arrived at Hiva Oa in the Marquesas Islands, the doctor was away on another island. We chased him down with an all-night sail, and the next day he pulled the rest of my tooth. Never again have I sailed without dental forceps in my medical kit. If a tooth must be pulled, you must have the instrument to do it.

FISHHOOKS

Fishhook removal presents a painful problem that can be solved in more than one way. The standard method works (pushing

the hook through, cutting off the eye, and pulling the shank out),
but at the risk of leaving a wound that easily becomes infected. I
prefer to infiltrate the area for a half-inch around the imbedded
hook with local anesthetic, then gently work the hook into a position where the least tissue is caught in the barb. With a sterile
scalpel (a razor blade broken to a sharp point will do), I cut down
next to the hook and toward the barb, cutting and releasing the
tissue caught, and lift the hook out of the cut. Treatment with antiseptic or antibiotic powder and a bandage usually heals the wound.

FINGER CUTS

Longitudinally split fingers result from heavy hauling on lines,
generally halyards, when the pressure of pulling exceeds the
strength of the skin. It is painful but not serious, and heals with
antiseptic ointment and a bandage to prevent infection. Continued
work causes repeated splittings until the skin hardens and heals.
Thinning the edges next to the crack with a sharp knife or razor
blade will shorten healing time and reduce recurrence. Generally,
split fingers are the sign of a good man because you know he pulls
his weight.

Transverse splits at the joints in fingers or toes result from rope
burns, cuts, abrasions, or stretching the skin. They occur at the
soft tissue next to a callus. Healing is speeded greatly and pain
relieved by preventing movement at the edges of the crack. Wrap
and knot one or two turns of soft cotton grocer's string around the
joint right in the crack after applying antiseptic. Pain is relieved
immediately, and after four or five days healing will be nearly complete.

FISH POISONING

Fish poisoning is a complex and erratic occurrence. Experience
from one area is not necessarily useful in another. For instance, in
the Pacific *u'hu,* or parrotfish, esteemed as food, is seldom poisonous, while in the Caribbean it is commonly so. Fish that feed on
toxic growths on coral become poisonous. But you are not safe by
avoiding coral-eating fish, for the bodies of carnivorous fish often
concentrate the toxins of their prey and cause serious poisoning to
humans. Toxic coral growths are not fully understood. They are
often associated with damaged coral. If possible, consult the local
people and do as they do. In their absence, test a piece of your fish

at an anthill. Ants will either avoid poisonous fish or be killed by it in a short time. In areas where flies abound, some natives use them to test the toxicity of raw fish. Flies avoid those that are poisonous.

Fish toxins may act on the central nervous system with immediate tingling of the tongue, tingling and redness of the skin, numbness, respiratory or general paralysis, either partial or complete, temporary blindness, and, in some cases, death. Treatment is symptomatic and in my experience has been successful when antihistamines and sedatives were given over a period of two or three days.

I have never heard of a case of fish poisoning due to tuna of any type, *mahimahi* (also known as dolphin fish or dorado), or squirrelfish (*iihi* or *menpachi*). And I have never been concerned about poisoning from eating fish caught in the open ocean.

SEA-URCHIN SPINES

Some of the most common injuries encountered while sailing tropical waters are wounds from sea urchins (or *vana,* as they are called in much of the Pacific), whose sharp spines easily penetrate the skin. The purple-black variety, with thin spines up to ten inches long, are the most dangerous and diabolical. These creatures sense disturbance and point their spines toward swimmers and waders in their vicinity. The slightest contact causes severe pain, with the spines usually breaking off in the tissue. Long-embedded pieces of spine require excision, but the treatment of choice of the native peoples of the Indo-Pacific is to urinate on the injured area. Undiluted vinegar is also effective, and hot packs help relieve pain. Spines that are visible in the flesh usually disappear in three or four days, and I have never known an active infection to result.

CHAPTER 16

Vermin

Cockroaches stand very little chance of becoming, if I may borrow a term from the environmentalists, an endangered species. They are one of the oldest and most successful insects in the world. Wherever the climate is warm enough to support their habits, they are present. If you lie to a pier, they will walk up your lines. If you anchor off, the larger ones will fly aboard. Their egg capsules may crop up anywhere: in the binding of a borrowed book, in a hand of bananas, or inside the corrugations of a cardboard box. There is no avoiding them for long in the tropics.

Polynesians handle the problem by building separate eating and sleeping houses, but such an arrangement is hardly feasible on a boat. Food in regular use like butter, sugar, and jam should be kept in closed containers. Tightly cover or wrap all leftovers. Seal the holes in milk cans with little pieces of wet paper every night; it is revolting to pour a cockroach into your morning coffee along with the canned milk.

I would rather not spray insecticide in the galley where it can fall on cups and dishes, so we use two percent chlordane powder, making sure food and utensils are not contaminated. The powder can be blown with an ear syringe into cracks and crannies, behind drawers, under mattresses. It continues to act whenever a cockroach walks through it. Fumigation bombs also work well on boats.

You open all lockers and drawers, close all hatches, light the bomb, and leave for the day. If you fumigate again in two weeks to kill the newly hatched roaches, your boat should be cockroach-free until infested anew.

Cold weather is the most complete cure, although some will survive for months near the warmth of an occasionally used kerosene lamp or in the lagging of the exhaust pipe.

Sandflies—smaller than a gnat, but with a bite worthy of a man-eating tiger—are the most serious threat to comfort insects have given us. In the Marquesas Islands, where they are especially virulent, they are called "no-noes." They live in vegetation wet with fresh water, around streams, river mouths and villages, and come out only for an hour or so morning or evening, except where they are really numerous. The bites itch worse than any others I've ever had. We used to paint our bites with baking powder solution, Burroughs Solution, and any other anti-itch treatment we could think of, but still we'd wake up at night scratching ourselves raw. A camphor-based Indochinese ointment called Tiger Balm helps, but the best relief is gained from campho-phenique applied directly to the bite.

Some people, especially those who smoke, are not bitten at all, others have reactions to the bites that are delayed a day or two and, in some cases, over a week. The bites necrose in the center after a week or two, the welts go down, and a minute white scar remains. In the last century, according to an old trader, no-no bites drove one of the first missionaries in Taiohae in the Marquesas to throw himself into the sea in a hysterical frenzy.

Long sleeves and trousers help prevent bites. So does repellent. In the absence of anything else, engine oil smeared on bare skin keeps them away. No-noes do not fly far offshore. The farther west you sail in the Pacific, the less troublesome no-noes become. They don't bother people much at all in Australia.

Rats are the vermin that strike fear in my heart. If a rat comes aboard a small boat, especially a wooden one with knees, stringers, buttblocks, and frames to hide behind, he is really hard to get rid of. We've had a rat aboard *Awahnee* twice, not counting the time we came back from town one night in Auckland and saw one crawl along the bow line and jump on deck. We boarded at the stern and chased him ashore by the opposite course.

One of our rats was aboard over four months. He was a coconut island rat, small and shiny black, who stowed away at Diego Garcia in the Indian Ocean. Quick and smart, he resisted every effort we made to catch him. He used to gnaw the inside of the facing below the bunk opposite ours. I lost a lot of sleep trying to get him with a slingshot, but I never even hit him. Nancy imagined he was chewing through our anchor rode in the fo'c's'le, and he actually did ruin our storm jib making a nest. I say "he"—thank heaven no baby rats ever appeared. He disdained bacon and cheese, preferring coconut and cucumber. When we finally caught him, we were in Egypt, and had borrowed a live trap, a wire cage with a one-way door. Admiring his spirit, I decided to give him a fighting chance, and dropped him overboard at night with the shore close by, watching him swim off. He must have returned to climb up our anchor rode, for there was unmistakable evidence of a rat aboard the next few days. When cucumber lured him into the trap again, I recognized him by his notched ear. This time I finished him off properly.

Where mosquitoes are a problem, the air is so still that screens make it oppressively hot below deck and unhandy coming and going. We have never used screens on *Awahnee,* though we carried them for years. We prefer mosquito coils, which we light in the early evening when we are bothered; they last all night. They must be burned over a plate or pan to avoid the danger of a falling coal.

Flies are another matter. In the islands, flies will be about your boat all the time. Here, too, I think the discomfort and inconvenience of trying to screen them out is not worth it. Mostly, we just live with the flies, although we might spray the boat before a meal. Flies seem to take up residence rather than come and go. One of the pleasures of day sailing is getting rid of them, although when we go to sea it is sometimes two or three days before they are all gone. When there is a good breeze and we are on the wind, we organize a phalanx of towel-flapping crew to drive the flies aft through the boat, out the hatch, and up into the wind where they won't be able to fly back to the boat. This won't work unless you are sailing against a good breeze of 15 knots or so, for flies have surprising windward ability.

Centipedes aren't common pests aboard, but they can be encountered in supplies from tropical places. They are ferocious-looking: segmented with one pair of short legs at each segment, shiny black or dark brown and flattish. Large ones are about a half-inch wide and seven or eight inches long in the body. They live in dark, damp but not wet places, such as under a log or in the corner of a native-style house. Once in the Seychelles Islands, where we accepted the hospitality of showers at a beach cottage, I put on a shirt that had been hanging on the coconut thatch wall. I also put on a big centipede that crawled across my shoulders under the shirt, leaving a double trail of tiny punctures. As the shirt exploded off me, he fell to the floor without biting me. The bloody spots itched for the first day and were visible for nearly a week. When centipedes do bite, which isn't often, the result is like a wasp's sting.

Scorpions, which prefer a drier environment than centipedes, are not usually a hazard. They are soft-bodied, and sting with a poisoned barb at the end of their tail, which they hold arched over their backs. Some Asian, African, and American scorpions can give fatal stings, and children are more susceptible to them than adults. Scorpions and centipedes can come aboard a boat in a sack of kumera, a stalk of bananas, or a box of gear that has been stored in a shed for a while.

Throughout much of the world bedbugs are common. They can come aboard in a visitor's kit or in packages you might carry from one island to another, or, as happened to us, in laundry sent ashore to a washerwoman. Once established, they are very hard to get rid of. You must wash and disinfect with dilute chlordane all infested bedding, pillow tickings, mattress covers, and clothing. In addition you must scrupulously search for the creatures with a needle in every crack in the wood and paneling. Chlordane as powder or in a water solution painted in a stripe all around a bunk each day will keep them from spreading to other bunks and will kill young ones as they hatch.

Body and head lice also infest many people of the world. Lacking a specific remedy, we have successfully used DDT powder on body lice that appeared at sea, after shaving the pubic region. Head lice should be combed out of the hair, then the head shampooed and thoroughly rinsed with a dilute chlorinated hydrocarbon solution, such as chlordane, to kill the nits that remain on the hairs. A shampoo of kerosene or of an emulsion of kerosene and detergent is also effective.

CHAPTER 17

Fishing and skin diving

It is surprising how few sailors know how to troll for fish. The deep waters of all oceans are teeming with tuna, *mahimahi* (dorado), and wahoo. Closer inshore, you can catch cravalle, yellowtail, barracuda, and hake.

There is far more to trolling than tying a white rag onto a hook and trailing it at the end of a frayed line. Ocean tuna and *mahimahi* feed on flying fish, and a listless lure will not interest them at all. A good lure and speed are the secrets. When you're slicking along at seven knots with the lure skimming the surface 100 feet astern, you'll catch fish.

When I began cruising, I used rods and reels with 80-pound line, which I considered heavy sport-fishing rigs. It didn't take long to get over that idea. On my first trip south off the coast of Central America, I put out my poles, and in a few minutes it was all over. Zing, zing, zing, zing, they disappeared with four nearly simultaneous strikes. All the lines, lures, and hooks were gone. There wasn't even a back-up line to wind in.

When I arrived in French Polynesia, I bought big tuna lures and hooks on lines of 100- or 150-kilogram test monofilament. The big lure attracted big fish, and I lost a lot of gear. The largest I ever landed was a 125-pound wahoo, but we have hooked some so big we could feel their pull on the boat. Once Reid watched as the gallows, where the bitter end of the fishline is tied, bent aft several inches and then snapped upright when a big one got away. Japanese tuna boats, which we have seen in every ocean of the world, commonly catch tuna of 250 pounds and the big ones get away. Some big fish are too wary to take the lure, and I have never heard of a porpoise taking a lure. They may wonder what kind of fish *Awahnee* is as she swims along the surface without emanations of oil, gas, or motor sound.

Twice we have seen enormous fish look us over—they were interested in our hull but not in the lure we were trolling. Both times we were sailing fast in a good stiff breeze. The first was near Tonga when a billfish that must have been 20 feet long swam alongside us at the surface for perhaps 30 seconds. I never actually saw his full length because of the chop, but I will always remember that just behind his head he was nearly four feet from top to bottom. His eye was the diameter of a small grapefruit as he gazed at us about 15 feet from where I stood at the helm. The second time, we were sailing in the Wailangilala Passage in the outlying Lau Islands to Fiji when Nancy went to the stern to dip a bucket of seawater. She saw the head and bill of a marlin who had a slight overlap on us. He was nearly two feet across the back, and she could have touched him with the bucket.

My classic story of the one that got away was at Niue Island close to Tonga, where we hooked a giant on a 200-kilo monofilament nylon line and fought him for 15 minutes without a net gain of more than a yard. Then he decided to stop fooling around and parted the monofilament with one sideways lunge.

I have gradually reduced the size of my lures and increased the strength of the line until now I use a four or five-inch white feather lure with a two-ounce lead head and a hook—about one inch from point to shank—on 600-pound steel leader to a 200-kilo mono-filament nylon line. The small lure attracts fish of 20 to 50 pounds, and the big hook keeps them on the line. They are small enough to land easily with a gaff. The nylon monofilament is invisible to the fish, and it has enough spring in it to absorb the shock of the strike. It is big enough in diameter, about $\frac{3}{16}$-inch, to be pulled in without slipping out of your hands or cutting them. I keep a bit of *mahimahi* skin and a bag of white feathers in my fishing kit so I can make my own lures if I lose too many. I think it is wrong to catch more fish than we can eat, but it is amazing how fast a 35-pound *mahimahi* disappears aboard *Awahnee*—in a day and a half there is nothing left but satisfaction.

After a dark night the fish are usually hungry, and one of the duties of the dawn helmsman is to put out the lines at daybreak. With luck we will have fish for breakfast. If you hook a large fish at seven knots, you should be prepared to slow down by heading up or luffing so you won't lose him, though at that speed he may just skip along the surface unable to dive. Bring him alongside, set the gaff beneath the bulk of his body through the gillplate, and lift him aboard with both gaff and line. Once landed, a good-sized fish is hard to hold, much less control. As a result of experience I always kill it with a sharp blow or two on the head with a winch handle and get a line around his tail before releasing the gaff and hook. Fish are *never* brought into my cockpit, but are cleaned on the afterdeck, which we wet down so it can be washed easily afterwards.

If we are hungry for fish but can't sail fast enough to bring the lure to the top of the water, we sometimes fall off on a reach to go a bit faster. Or we rig a lighter lure closer astern, where the height of the gallows helps pull it at the surface. During the day we watch for birds diving and feeding, a sure indication that big fish below are feeding on smaller fry, driving them to the surface, where they become the prey of birds. If you sail through a bird flock, you'll often hook a good fish.

Mahimahi often swim in pairs. If you hook one on a single line, toss the hook out again immediately and you may well catch another. They love to lie in the shadow of flotsam, and it is they who accumulate under the hull of a becalmed or disabled boat. Lifeless lures won't make them bite, and usually they are far too big to be caught on a fly or a spoon, but you can spear them from the deck. We think they are one of the world's most delicious fish.

After you land a fish, the best way to straighten out the line is to toss it over and let the water do it. Sometimes in the process you get another strike and want to release the fish. Tuna are quite sensitive to injury, friends in the U.S. Bureau of Commercial Fisheries have told me. The best way to set one free is to release it without taking it out of the water. One man brings the fish alongside while another lies down on deck, takes hold of the fish at the gill opening, and with slack in the line takes out the hook and lets the fish go. One afternoon off the coast of Venezuela, we must have hooked a ton of 60-pound yellow-fin tuna, releasing all but the first one.

Within a day of landfall, though, we catch all the fish we can. Giving them away ashore is a greatly appreciated entrée into a village. Ocean fish aren't usually available to island people, as they often don't have the high-speed boats to catch them. In more civilized places where fish can be bought in shops, it is easy to find someone who relishes fish fresh from the briny.

We ask everyone, who sails tropical waters with us to get themselves flippers, a mask, and a snorkel so they can participate in one of the major entertainments of a yacht in beautiful warm waters, swimming on coral reefs. Many great fish stories come from the North Atlantic and the South Polar seas, but the ocean can be freely entered only in the tropics. We sometimes spend three hours a day looking, diving, collecting specimens, photographing, and spearfishing.

Yes, we see sharks. The attitude of the islanders, which we have accepted, is that sharks, too, are entitled to life. When we see a big one, eight feet or more, we leave quietly. When we are spearing fish, however, there is always the problem of what to do with the catch. Sharks are extremely sensitive to the vibrations of a fluttering injured fish and to the odor of its fluids, so do not string fish on a buoyed line or put them in a bag hung from your waist. If you cannot stow them in a dinghy anchored or tended close by, kill them. We have learned to bite them at the back of the head as islanders do: pop the head in your mouth and bite, you don't have to break the skin. It is fastest and most effective, it doesn't taste at all —just saltwater—and live fish aren't slimy.

Sharks are curious but slow to approach something big that is neither bleeding nor thrashing helplessly. When we see sharks up to our own size we continue to swim if there is no fish blood about us in the water. We watch the shark, which usually swims aimlessly some distance away. If another arrives, we agree who will watch what shark, and continue to swim as long as they don't outnumber us or approach closely. If one does, I swim to the bottom among the coral and then strongly towards it so it sees me suddenly, and I project the thought, "I'm going to stick you!" Never yet has one failed to turn away. Stay down as long as you comfortably can, and when you surface for air, be deliberate about it without splashing around. Ease back to shallower water. A shark will not usually follow. If it does, keep going until you are ashore. Shark attacks have occurred in three feet of water and less.

Our theory is that the tropical island sharks are well fed on the teeming fish of a virtually unfished reef and will not attack a large swimming creature that shows no distress. Places where they are hungry, such as the southern part of Australia and South Africa and the North Atlantic coast, are not the same at all. Follow local custom and knowledge.

Everyone who skin dives with us carries a knife in addition to his spear, but I think the spear is probably the better weapon—it could hold a shark off if you are lucky. I don't think you could kill a shark with a small "Hawaiian sling" spear, which is what we like to use for spearfishing on a reef. Killing a shark with a knife is another of those South Seas myths. Their skin is so tough it would be like trying to open up an automobile tire. Little sharks, three and a half feet on down, usually run away from a swimmer who isn't taking fish, but a four-footer gave me a scare once. He wouldn't leave me alone, and languidly but persistently tried to bite me several times. I left the water, walked the coral for a quarter-mile, and re-entered. I didn't see him again.

When you swim over the seaward edge of a reef and look down along the cliff face to hidden depths, sometimes you see bubbles rise. What's down there? If it's a big old hungry granddaddy mako shark and he sees you silhouetted against the surface, he might take you in a second. Virtually nothing can stop a 15- or 20-footer in a fast attack, even if, as some say, he has a tender nose. I hope I never find out.

Sharks may churn up the imagination, but I consider barracuda the really dangerous fish to a swimmer. The small ones in temperate waters present no serious threat, but the barracuda of the deep tropics are different. They grow to a length of five feet and more, with sharp-fanged jaws that could easily latch onto a swimmer's whole thigh. To see a silvery dozen of these fish shimmering a few yards away, each pointing directly at me as I swim past, is an unnerving experience, to say the least. It is even more so when they follow. It is true that they seldom attack, but when it happens, it is fast and furious. I believe that many so-called shark attacks are made by barracudas, one of the fastest fish in the sea.

Moray eels often lie in the coral at the bottom, protecting their territory, though at times they swim freely. It is a surprise to have one of them tear your freshly caught dinner off your spear, but don't try to spear them. They can slide along the spear and attack you. Leave them alone; they are too bony to be good eating anyhow.

There are creatures of the deep whose hostile reputation is greater than they deserve. "Man-eating clams," *tridacna* species, grow to be three feet across, but they have probably never eaten a man—they close too slowly. Besides, they live on plankton. Manta rays are also not a threat to a swimmer, though sting rays can severely wound your foot if you step on one. They fly underwater in a wave-like motion that is beautiful to watch. Big grouper fish are dangerous, but they don't usually live at levels where a skin diver swims. However, at Diego Garcia Island in the Indian Ocean, a three-and-a-half-foot red snapper with great white teeth menaced Nancy by swimming in ever diminishing circles around her. She finally speared a small fish and gave it to him as a token of her esteem before exiting. She still gets the shivers thinking of that fish.

Torch-fishing on a reef at night is an amazing experience for someone who has never seen a reef after dark. The shallow water atop the coral absolutely teems with fish, crustaceans, and mollusks of all sorts who feed on the reef. Moonless nights at low tide are best. Wear high shoes or boots for protection to the sides of your feet and ankles, for you will miss your footing many times. Walk along the reef with a pressure lamp held high, revealing a full circle of light all around you. Flashlights cast too small a beam. Shells you can simply gather: exquisite cowries, olivines, murexes, tritons, and others. Be careful of cone shells, some of which can extend a deadly poisonous barb. They may be covered with algae, which hides their identity but not their shape. Crayfish, or tropical lobsters, have no pincers and are commonly found by the light reflected from their eyes. Pick them up by the carapace, as the tails have very sharp points that can cause a bad wound. Fish on the reef are caught by stunning them with a long machete. You will probably go "torching" on the reef with an islander; don't be disappointed if all you can do is barely keep up while carrying his sack and gathering stunned fish as he joyfully gallops along the reef, striking fish as he goes.

Delicious meals are swimming around cruising people most of the time they are anchored in clean water. Small fish are eager for the hook, or can be speared. Among tropical people the world over, a five-inch to seven-inch red fish called the *menpachi,* squirrelfish, or *iihi* is prized for food. They are easily caught, and when fried crisp or baked in breadfruit leaves or fern fronds, they are sweet and delicious. A light casting rod will provide great sport trolled from a dinghy or cast from deck at anchor, but a long "Huckleberry Finn" bamboo pole will give control and action in reef pools. Artificial lures simply made in the manner of the locals will produce fish and satisfaction. With a variety of small hooks and a little sliced fish or bread, you're in business. (We also carry a throw net but it is rather tricky to use.)

Spearing is by far the most productive and interesting method for an amateur; often only two or three dives will provide a fine meal. Diving without tanks, it is best to go after small fish with a small, fast-acting spear that you can shoot more than once on a breath of air. The "Hawaiian sling" in its simplest form is a loop of surgical tubing tied to a steel spear with a barbed head. Put your thumb through the loop of tubing, stretch it out, and grab the spear. To fire it, just release your grip; the tubing will shoot the spear. Refinements are a serving on the shaft for a handhold and a triggering device that consists of an oversized hole in a block of wood to take the spear and a bent hinge for the trigger. Hawaiian slings vary from four-and-a-half or five-foot spears for close work in holes in the reef to heavy six- or seven-foot models for bigger game. There are many other kinds of spears, but none that I have seen are as fast, simple, productive and fun as a Hawaiian sling.

As a foreigner in another country, you will not find the same prejudices and aesthetic notions about food as at home, so don't let your preconceived ideas interfere with good eating. The clams, oysters, mussels, and pippies of all shores are delicious. In the Patagonian Channels and the Aleutians I was able to fill a bucket with shellfish in a few moments along the rocks after anchoring at the end of a long day's sail, even after dark. *Limu* (seaweed) is used as a seasoning in many places, and sometimes as a vegetable. Sea cucumber gonads are a delicacy in Rarotonga, and parasitic crabs that live one-to-a-sea-urchin are prized in Chile. Do as the locals do and enjoy it all.

CHAPTER 18

Emergencies

An emergency may develop on a lovely clear morning, but it seems much more likely to present itself during a hard blow at night with cold rain, poor visibility, and unseen dangers. The skipper and crew who have done their own rigging, maintenance, and installation of gear are naturally more able to devise repairs than the owner accustomed to expert and complete care of his vessel in a good boatyard. The contemporary penchant for hiring specialists for every contingency is less conducive to prompt action than the tradition of broad personal competence and "do-it-yourself" experience. And where the fully insured vessel might be left to her fate on a rocky shore, the uninsured boat is pulled to safety with sometimes only a little work, a little luck, and minimal danger.

It is essential in a developing emergency that the possible courses of action be separated into those that are feasible and those that are not. The diagnosis must come first. This is the hard part; treatment is often simple. To use time and energy bailing when the leak might be stopped is not good thinking.

FOUNDERING

When a boat is filling with water, set a bailing or pumping detail to work drying successive compartments and take the time to investigate all hull openings and areas. Often it is a hose or pipe that has failed near a hull fitting, and the treatment may be as simple as closing a hull valve or plugging a fitting. The trouble may be a stuck valve in the bilge pump itself allowing the ocean to siphon into the bilge. On more than a few boats a matchstick, toothpaste cap, or bobbypin stuck in the head valve has caused flooding.

A boat holed from striking driftwood or debris is a more serious problem. If she is in danger of sinking, bail and pump. A perfect repair can hardly be made in sinking conditions. Where the water is seen coming in, stop it with pegs, nailed battens, canvas pads, pillows, sleeping bags, or even sails held in place with struts or toms. To hell with the woodwork in a real emergency. If the leak is behind the built-in icebox, tear it out to get at the hull and stop the flow of water. Once in my experience, underwater-setting Epoxy putty that was braced quickly into position under pressure pads saved a boat after the lining was ripped out.

If the water is entering a contained space like the fo'c's'le or the head, you can build a cofferdam by boarding up the entry to a level higher than the water outside (**see drawing**). With the leak contained, you can inspect and possibly close the hole by diving over the side or rigging a collision mat. Or you may be able simply to

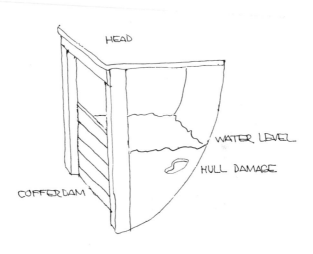

proceed to port with the damaged area flooded behind the coffer-dam. The ex-minesweeper yacht *Wild Goose,* coming to Hawaii from the South Pacific some years ago, was suddenly flooded forward when the fastenings holding a 13-inch-diameter transducer let go as the result of electrolysis, sending the transducer to Davey Jones' locker. The crew quickly shut the waterproof fo'c's'le door, and she motored the final 200 miles of her voyage with her fo'c's'le full of water.

In a more dangerous situation water pressure alone may be holding the garboard plank on. Then the only feasible action is to get the boat on the beach or the ways as soon as possible. Though careening is a shocking sight to the uninitiated, most well-designed boats will lift after being beached none the worse for the experience, and often much the better. Design factors that are dangerous include loose inside ballast, a very high center of gravity, wide open cockpits combined with broad transoms, hatches far off the center-line, and very light frames and planks. Before careening, make sure the hull is protected from lying on rocks when the tide is out, for a great deal of pressure will come on a small area.

"Fothering" a hull, a procedure named for the English lad who thought it up, is sliding a piece of heavy canvas over an underwater hole and letting the water pressure hold it against the hull. The canvas is controlled by lanyards through grommets in its corners. An awning or stormsail would do. This essentially is how I closed seven holes in the cedar planks of the first *Awahnee* after she had been aground for 13 days in the Red Sea. A heavy four-power block and tackle from her spreaders to my heaviest anchor lifted her off the coral far enough for us to dive down and nail pieces of paint-soaked canvas cut from a flax jib over the holes, the largest of which was 18 inches in diameter. Supported by pads and wood across the holes, the patches were finished with battens nailed around their perimeters. I left the last hole open until the final low tide before attempting to get her off the reef. This was to keep the water level inside the boat equal to that outside so the patches would neither burst from within nor cause her to float before we were ready.

Holes above the waterline are less critical, though they can certainly sink a boat. The way we closed the two broken portlights on the second *Awahnee* illustrates a successful method of working on material that you cannot drive nails into. We were 30 miles off the mouth of the Columbia River heading south in January 1968 from

Vancouver to San Francisco. Progress had been good on this late passage, undertaken because Coal Harbor in Vancouver had frozen over solid and it was just too cold to stay. The more favorable tack had led me incautiously close to land in the afternoon, and we were making to sea as well as we could in steadily increasing winds. The waves built up, and after midnight with the wind whistling, *Awahnee* was laboring under only the main trysail to make offshore on a course of southwest by south.

Just before dawn when the wind had moderated somewhat, *Awahnee* fell off a cresting sea, bursting two of the leeward cabin portlights and fracturing the port side of the cabin trunk. Glass and water were everywhere, and the six of us aboard were thoroughly alarmed. We pulled a sail over the oval portlight openings, which averaged 24 inches by 8 inches. Then I closed each with a piece of plywood and a gasket cut from the cabin rug. They were held in place by bolts through wooden pieces that spanned the openings on the inside. Tightening the bolts stressed the ply tightly against the outside of the cabin and sealed the gasket.

We sailed without further difficulty to San Francisco, where we learned that the Red Stack tug *Alert,* with two barges in tow, had been in the same blow. After recording 80 knots, her anemometer blew off the pilothouse, and she hove to that night for the first time in her career of towing barges to Alaska.

AGROUND

Prompt action at a grounding can prevent serious damage and get a ship afloat even on a falling tide. The shape of the keel has a great deal to do with being able to sail her off a sand or mud bank. With the bottom of the keel parallel to the waterline, she will take the ground forward and quite possibly stick there. But a boat with a descending keel often touches aft and can sail off. The jib is sheeted in hard to cause the bow to fall away from the wind, and the boat pivots on the aft end of the keel, returning to deep water.

To free a boat that is only gently aground, sometimes the keel can be swung up enough by sitting two or three or more crewmen on the outboard end of the main boom supported by the topping lift and swung out with a preventer. Ground tackle or other weight can be hung off the boom when live weight is unavailable or needed elsewhere. The ship can be lightened quickly by putting heavy gear in the dinghy or aboard another vessel.

With anchors astern, a boat can sometimes be kedged off. Weight on the foredeck will help by raising the after part of the keel. If the boat with a keel parallel to the waterline is aground at its forward end, concentrated weight on the afterdeck may do the trick.

To lessen the draft of a boat hard aground, haul her down. Any properly rigged sailboat can withstand the forces of being pulled down by the mast. Actually, before the days of drydocks and ships' ways, this was the usual method of exposing the bottom for repairs, sheathing, and painting. *Awahnee* will float in less than four feet of water hauled over, though she draws seven and a half floating upright.

To haul a boat down, reeve a line through a strong block, shackle the block to the main halyard, and haul it aloft. Make the halyard fast with a foot or two leading from the masthead sheave so the block will clear the mast and shrouds. With the dinghy, set a heavy anchor well out abeam and make the line leading through the block aloft fast to the anchor rode. Now, on deck, take a strain. Use a snatch block to take the lead to the windlass or other heavy winch, if necessary. As the mast goes over, the keel swings up— and the boat floats off sideways. Bower anchors in the right directions help greatly to bring the vessel afloat.

Similarly, if another boat is assisting, you can attach a tow-line to the mast at the spreaders when aground. A sling of soft, large-diameter rope wrapped a couple of times around the mast, padded with canvas or bedding, will avoid damaging the fittings, bruising the wood, or crushing the sailtrack. The boat will be pulled down and away from the ground and will right herself in deep water. Sometimes it is hard to convince the skipper of an assisting boat that he won't pull the rig out of your craft. On the way to drydock once, sailing just inside the windward buoys, *Awahnee* went fast aground on a rock that encroached on the channel. A passing fisherman set an anchor for us, but it dragged in the deep channel, and I couldn't get her off. Summoned by friends ashore, the Coast Guard then arrived, but the skipper declined to take a line from my mast. Though the tide was by now falling, I had to swim over to the Coast Guard boat, compose and sign a release, and swim back before he would take a draft on the line aloft. We came free gently and easily.

When rigging such a line, make the end fast to your bow so the tow can proceed with a fair lead after the line aloft has been cut

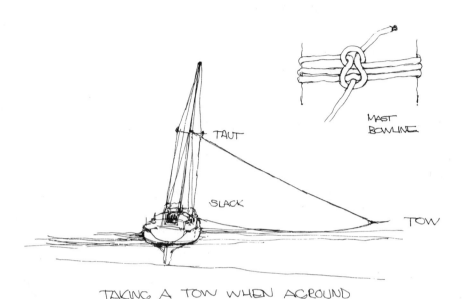

TAKING A TOW WHEN AGROUND

free. It is dangerous to try to untie it under tension. Use a short heavy line around the mast, tied in a bowline with all turns around the mast going through the knot (**see drawing**). This spreads pressure over a wider area without compressing the spar. The end of this line is then tied to a bowline in the bight of the tow-line, which will take the strain of the tow without slipping. When the boat heels from a lateral pull and swings free of the ground, a man aloft cuts the mast line. The freed vessel is out of control only for a moment as the draft on the tow-line comes properly on her bow. Before attempting the tow, make sure the lead to the bow is clear of stanchions and rails. This technique of using the mast as a lever can be applied also to raise a heeled boat off the rocks if she is not at too great an angle.

RIGGING AND SPARS

When a stay, shroud, or spreader fails, a prompt diagnosis of the situation may save the mast. You can reduce tension in the rigging and on the spars by slacking sheets, dropping sails, coming about, reefing, or rigging an auxiliary shroud or stay with a halyard. Use both ends of the halyard, not just one. Seldom at sea can permanent repairs be made to rigging, yet having short or full lengths of rigging wire, thimbles, and cable clamps aboard may allow you to restore the rigging to serviceable condition in just a few minutes.

If a shroud or stay strands or breaks aloft, reverse the wire to bring the repair to deck level. With enough length in the fully extended turnbuckle, you may only need to relay the strands, cut and serve the wire at the weak point, bend it around a thimble, fix it with cable clamps, and attach the turnbuckle directly or extended by a shackle or two. Or you can replace the end of a shroud or stay by clamping both ends of a short piece of wire cable to it by at least two cable clamps facing in opposite directions, with a thimble clamped or seized in the center of the bight of the repair wire. The cable clamps should be an eighth of an inch larger than the cable being repaired to accommodate the three wires.

Soft heavy wire, like the single strands of telephone transmission wire that are almost a quarter-inch in diameter, are strong and bend easily enough to make prompt repairs to spreaders, turnbuckles, fittings, and other hardware. Once, 600 miles south of Tasmania, a lower shroud tang broke at the mast. I made a padded wire sling over the opposite spreader, under the mainsail track, and around the mast to provide a place of reattachment for the shroud, and it held satisfactorily until we reached New Zealand. Winds exceeded 80 knots and the seas were monstrous.

The "Spanish windlass," one of the simplest ways to rig variable tension, has many applications and can even serve as a substitute turnbuckle. It is least destructive to the line if it is tight at the outset, so that few turns are needed. The Spanish windlass is the best clamp for reforming and gluing a fractured round, oval, or pear-shaped spar (**see drawing**).

If a boom breaks or a gooseneck gives way, your boat will probably sail quite well with the main loose-footed—well enough so maneuverability is not seriously impaired. Off the wind, efficiency will drop without adequate means to pole out the clew, but on a high-aspect ratio sail a spinnaker pole could be rigged to solve this problem. If the end breaks off a spar, a spinnaker pole in particular, simply tying a masthead knot and slipping it over the broken end will put the abbreviated pole back into use with attachments for the sail, topping lift, foreguy, and afterguy. (This will outlast a stainless steel strap and banding machine repair by many times.)

Dismasting is traumatic, to be sure, but its aftermath can be worse, for the spar can pound against the hull hard enough to hole it. It is necessary to get distance between the boat and the mast. Cast off all the rigging except one or two wires, bend a line on them, and pay out so the boat can lie some distance downwind of

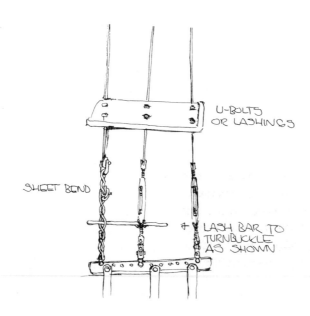

U-BOLTS OR LASHINGS

SHEET BEND

+ LASH BAR TO TURNBUCKLE AS SHOWN

SPANISH WINDLASS

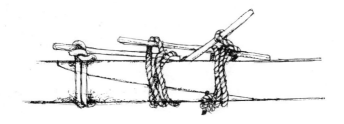

the mast. Then carefully consider your resources and possible courses of action. If you cannot lift the mast aboard or sling it alongside, you may want to tow it. Or you may buoy it with a man-overboard flag and let it lie to a sea anchor, recovering it later. In shallow water you can anchor it to the ground. If it might sink, buoy it up with flotation, and if it does sink in shallow water, buoy the spot.

You may be able to rig a spinnaker pole as a jury mast in a matter of an hour or two and be underway again. However, it takes more time to fit, glue, and screw pieces of interior woodwork carefully to construct a new mast. It takes still more time to splice wire and recut sails for a new mast, as did Miles and Beryl Smeeton and John Guzzwell aboard *Tzu Hang* off the Horn in their masterly recovery of what looked like a hopeless situation (described in the Smeetons' *Once Is Enough*). It all depends. Make sure the jury-rigged mast is well stepped on a stout temporary mast step, for it can easily bore through your cabin top or deck.

A "bully pole" is the best way to get a longish spar standing at sea. It consists of a relatively short, stout pole braced perpendicularly against the butt of the jury mast. With the mast lying on deck, masthead forward, the backstay should lead aft over the end of the vertical bully pole, which should be notched for this purpose. Equal length shrouds from the masthead are attached to the hull at the axis of rotation (an athwartships line level with the mast step) so that as the backstay, or an extension of it, is winched in, the mast remains centered. As the mast is raised, the stay's lead becomes direct, the bully pole is removed, and soon the mast is vertical.

RUDDERS

I was in the Transpacific Race once when a competitor lost his rudder close to the halfway point of the race. The skipper engaged a tug from Seattle to tow him to Honolulu. After the shock of being disabled wore off, the crew became bored slopping around in the trade winds during the several days' wait for the tug to arrive. They hoisted a steadying sail, then the main. By the time the tug got to them, they had taught themselves to steer by sail trim alone and were underway on course.

Many times it is the steering gear that fails, leaving the rudder intact but useless. Fearing this, I drilled a hole years ago in *Awah-*

nee's steel rudder to be able to attach a shackle and steering lines to it, though I have never needed to do so. I keep the hole plugged with mastic and painted over with bottom paint. On a wooden rudder such a hole should be bushed with metal.

Emergency steering without using the rudder can most easily be rigged with a steering oar—a piece of plywood or a cabinet door on the end of a spinnaker pole, perhaps. On the wind most boats can be trimmed to hold a course by sails alone, but off the wind or across it you need a steering device. A couple of shots of chain or other drag rigged well off-center astern, port and starboard, will give a degree of control, and can steer a boat quite well on even a rough passage. Aboard Ron MacAnnan's superb 83-foot classic M-boat *Pursuit,* we raced over a third of the 2,200 miles to Honolulu steering with chains assisting the emergency rudder, all the while flying the 3,600-square-foot kite and averaging over 215 miles per day. The main rudder had sheared all its drift pins in mid-Pacific. Then in the strain of steering in the Molokai Channel the rudderpost of the little auxiliary rudder folded over athwartships; we finished the race steering with a spinnaker pole as well.

ENGINES

It is surprising what a nonmechanic can do to keep an engine running. Once after a valve spring broke, I tied the valve stem up to keep it from falling into the firing chamber (sucking the valve) and continued limited operation. Parts were unavailable at Callao, Peru, the next port, unless I was willing to wait a couple of months, so I collected several valve springs from a junkyard and finally settled on one from a Mercedes diesel bus for my Yanmar engine. It worked, and I had full use of the engine all the way to Honolulu.

Another time and on another vessel I wrapped the two-and-a-half-inch shaft of a water pump with copper wire to build up a bushing so the packing could be retained. The mill ran for the couple of hundred miles to port, where repairs were properly made. And another time at an isolated island, we revitalized an engine with a rusted waterjacket by using fiberglass screen and Epoxy paste to make an internal patch.

FIRE

Fire, a real and ever-present hazard, needs immediate action. Once when called out by the yell of "Fire!" I rolled up a burning mattress with bare hands and body, carried it on deck and threw it over the side. As a former volunteer fire captain, I know that many such fires do not burn fully for the lack of oxygen available in the burning material, so it is dangerous to disturb them. Smother the fire and get it overboard before it flames up. In a galley fire where grease may be burning, water will not put it out. Use a dry chemical or CO_2 extinguisher at the base of the flames. It will work wonders. Crawl below the smoke and flames to reach the fire if necessary.

Electrical fires require double action: isolating the wires from the power source and suppressing the fire. This often requires prompt and brutal removal of lining and woodwork. Keep in mind that speed is essential and that burns and wounds heal. Do what has to be done and don't expect to do it comfortably, easily, or painlessly.

COLLECTING WATER

In a true tropical downpour, you can fill your water tanks right to the top. Seldom at sea do you have rain without wind, however, and this often makes rigging a collection awning an exercise in wet futility. Water flows off every square foot of the sails that are up; these are the source that is easiest to exploit and largest in area. Start collecting rainwater after the sails have been washed clean of salt—you can tell by tasting. On the jib I slip a split hose over the roping at the tack, which will spout a steady stream into a jerrycan. Top up the boom of the main to make the gooseneck the lowest point of the sail, and collect beneath it. I often use the dinghy, after cleaning it, upright under the mainsail gooseneck and siphon direct from it into the tanks. In addition, as I mentioned in the section on deck structures, my deck has water collection fittings, port and starboard, at the lowest point when heeled, which gives me the capacity to collect all the water that strikes above *Awahnee*'s deck.

DISTILLING WATER

Lack of fresh water is usually a situation that reaches critical proportions slowly; nonetheless, it is an emergency of the gravest kind. As long as fuel lasts, you can distill seawater on the stove to supply minimal but adequate water for a crew. On a single burner of *Awahnee*'s Primus stove we distilled three quarts of fresh water a day during the final week of the 8,000-mile, 59-day last leg of our

Antarctic circumnavigation. Though we didn't actually run out of water aboard, it was in very short supply, and I wanted to know our capacity for distilling.

We used the pressure cooker with the end of a plastic hose pushed tightly on the nipple where the weight would normally go. We filled the pot two-thirds full of seawater and put it on the gimballed stove. When it boiled, the steam ran through the hose straight up to the overhead handrail, slanting down across the galley sink and through a series of horizontal coils. By the time it arrived at the other end of the hose it had condensed into fresh water, which dripped into a plastic jerrycan. We made a little less than a quart per hour. This seemed quite slow considering the energy output of the Primus burning at full blast, but there was no leakage of steam. I concluded that we had the capacity to produce sufficient drinking water, but that it takes a great deal of energy. It would be extremely difficult to distill a significant amount of water without a proper still or a pressure cooker with its tight sealing lid fitted with a nipple.

MAN OVERBOARD

Every skipper intending to sail offshore with the lives and well-being of crewmembers in his hands should practice recovering a man overboard repeatedly until the maneuver is thoroughly understood. A beer carton makes a good dummy for it is low in the water and dark-colored. It is not difficult to recover a man if you know how, but it can be next to impossible if the first attempt is a genuine emergency. The object is to stop the boat alongside the person in the water.

The first thing to do is to get some flotation over to him—a cushion, a life ring, or anything that floats—while calling all hands on deck. *Do not change course* until you have observed the exact course that was being steered and until a flag or other highly visible object is over the side. On my boat I keep the man-overboard flags and the floating light separate and unencumbered, contrary to some opinions, because I fear their lanyards becoming entangled and preventing prompt use. Once a marker is in the water, you may change course to begin the recovery, while handling sails or starting the engine.

Post a man to watch the marker or the swimming man if he can be seen. This is a full-time job of highest priority, for low objects in the water are largely out of sight at a distance of a few yards in a seaway, and a small distant orange flag is hard to find on the featureless horizon once it has been lost from view.

Sail back to your marker or light, then steer a course opposite your original one, and you should come close to your man. Of course, you don't pick up the flotation gear and markers until the man is safely aboard, for they will continue to orient the search if you don't find him immediately. Repeated parallel passes on the original course and its opposite may be necessary.

Under sail on the wind the standard procedure is to jibe and then tack, which results in approaching the swimmer on the wind, giving maximum control and ease in stopping. Skillful handling will bring the boat to a halt, sails luffing or dropped, within an easy toss of a stout line to the man in the water. Sailing past him at a speed of a few knots may recover a strong uninjured man, but it won't suffice for anyone hurt, unconscious, or less than robust. An injured man can perhaps best be hoisted aboard in the bosun's chair or a rope sling, but again it depends largely on the weather, the crew, and the injury, if any. It may be best to bring him aboard the dinghy and then on deck. A man in the water is needed to assist in the recovery of an injured person.

Across the wind you can simply sail opposite reaches, but off the wind if the main is vanged, the spinnaker up, or the jib poled out, you have a lot of work to do just to get turned around. Throw a trail of floating objects to guide your tacks to windward to your man. In a stiff wind these will drift, so don't underestimate how far upwind you must carry on your search. Small sea anchors rigged to the life rings and other flotation gear help greatly.

Whenever anything that floats goes accidentally over the side on *Awahnee*, we have a man-overboard drill. I may be next, and I want my crew to know how to recover me. We have recovered the spinnaker pole (at night), buckets, hats, bottles of shells, a crewman who jumped over after his conch shell, another who slipped over at night while alone on watch, and my wife, who was knocked off the cabin top by the main boom in the middle of the Indian Ocean while we were sailing dead before the monsoon wind.

AVOIDING COLLISION

Through the years there has been a relentlessly widening gap between the speed, maneuverability, and size of ocean-going craft.

Large vessels commonly require a half-mile to a mile to execute a right-angle turn, and up to five miles or more to come to a stop. Large ocean-going barges are even more difficult to control and may be in a mile-long string of two or three with wire towing cables two or three inches in diameter. Given the possible dangers of encountering such hard-to-control vessels at sea, I believe it best to keep a small boat a good distance from ships whenever practicable. All vessels are required by the International Rules of the Road to keep an adequate lookout at all times when underway, as far forward and as close to the water as possible. Even so, when meeting a ship, a small-boat skipper is unwise to assume his boat is seen or to press the theoretical right of way of sail over steam.

We are admonished by the Rules of the Road to maintain course and speed, but this rule is intended for boats already near each other. Therefore I sail on a clearing course as soon as I can foresee passing close to a ship. I give the other boat a clear and uncomplicated right of way by altering course to pass astern if she is moving fast and will cross my course; if we are proceeding in nearly the same or opposite direction, I steer parallel to her course, taking care not to converge. If she is converging astern, I will diverge from her as soon as her relative course is apparent.

At night when a ship sees your lights, you at first present a problem of identification. You may be a ship with faulty lights; you may be a small craft moving at five, six, or seven knots—a fraction of the larger vessel's speed—or you may be a long-line fishing boat drifting. I sometimes, after consideration, show a ship that navigation light which gives her the right of way on her course, even though it is the incorrect light. I let her pass on her way. This I do only at a distance of miles. In any event, I would not voluntarily cross her bow or place my vessel in a position that would require her to change course.

EMERGENCY SIGNALLING

There is no practical means, save distress signals, of communicating with a ship using the gear usually aboard a yacht. I have exchanged waves with men on the deck of a bulk carrier overtaking *Awahnee* a quarter of a mile away and failed to raise an answer from her on 2181 MHz. I have never found my signal flags, with 15-inch hoists, useful even when I sailed close under a ship's stern. If you have the radio capacity and license to speak on the ship distress frequency, 500 MHz, you probably can initiate contact. Otherwise, don't count on it.

At night if I feel a ship is coming dangerously close, I shine a spotlight at her and then over my sails, repeating until I am satisfied she sees me. There are places in the world where heavy ship traffic cannot be avoided, and the ships are often so concerned with avoiding each other—easily seen on radar and in plain sight with dozens of bright lights burning—that small boats may easily go unseen. One night we were engineless and becalmed in the Strait of Gibraltar with 17 moving ships in sight. And in the Red Sea, ships used to come out of convoys through the Suez Canal in groups of 50.

South of Suez was an unhealthy place to sail because the ships jockeyed for clear going, sometimes steaming down the Gulf of Suez four and five abreast as they passed each other at anything from 18 to 30 knots. One dusk we were at the edge of the channel next to Shadwan Lighthouse, ghosting along with bare steerageway, when a ship approached heading straight for us. Outboard two more ships were passing. I couldn't tack because of the foul ground. I didn't want to jibe, for that wouldn't remove us from danger, and I wasn't moving fast enough to cross her clearly and safely. I lit my kerosene lamps and shined the 12-volt spotlight. No result. In the dusk they hardly showed. The ship was bearing down on us when I fired my Very pistol directly at her in a last desperate attempt to be seen. The ship veered off slightly, hissing past with undiminished speed. A small head wearing an officer's cap peered over the bulwark of the flying bridge high above in the gloaming, a hand waved against the sky, and then she was gone. If she had hit us, I doubt that anyone aboard would have known.

Once, arriving engineless in the Hauraki Gulf of New Zealand after Nancy had been terribly sick for 18 days, I hoisted the "W" flag at the starboard spreaders to signal that we needed medical attention. It was a ludicrous gesture. No vessel approached within miles of us as we drifted becalmed for two days and nights in the tidal streams past Great Barrier Island in and out of the Gulf. Early on the third morning we were again inside the Gulf when a fishing boat approached closer than any had before, but did not realize we were signalling. She started going off about her business. I had no flares, but fortunately there was a galvanized bucket aboard. I set an oily fire in it on deck, which brought the fisherman right over. They towed us to Auckland, a distance of some 30 miles, and Nancy was on the way to recovery in the hospital by evening.

A mirror is an excellent signalling instrument. Aground in the Red Sea, we stopped the 35,000-ton *Caltex Bahrein,* Captain Adams, with *Awahnee's* oval cabin mirror after we had signalled for four days and nights with flares, smoke, the spinnaker streaming aloft, and fires hoisted to the masthead at night, while 200 ships passed within two to five miles of us. The officer on watch said the mirror "burned onto the bridge," making an unmistakable signal. And throughout our 1975 4,000-mile voyage in company with the 74-foot ocean-going dugout canoe *Spirit of Nuku Hiva,* signal mirrors beamed the sun's rays bright and strong to draw the attention of one vessel to the other quickly.

THE DANGERS OF COMING ALONGSIDE A SHIP

If bringing a small boat alongside a ship is ever seriously considered, one must understand the dangers involved. Waves smash and wind drives against the windward side of a large vessel, while on the leeward side there is fine shelter, but the ship will be drifting surprisingly fast to leeward, and the slop may be fierce. As a result a sailboat loses her power and maneuverability, and the water holds her tight against the ship's side. If there are waves, the rigging will be rocked against the ship with the danger of smashing spreaders and mast. Also, most ships have welded brackets of various sorts that project beyond the hull high enough to clear any dock, but just in line with a lofty rig's shrouds. And if you succeed in safely pushing along the hull to the stem or stern, you find the greatest hazard of all, the high flare combined with the undercut shape of the ends of the ship. Here the only point of contact will be far aloft in your rigging. All in all, a perilous situation, and one to be steadfastly avoided.

I will never again bring a sailboat alongside a ship except in very quiet conditions or *in extremis,* where saving the lives of people aboard is the prime concern and the loss of the rigging and possibly the boat is accepted. If it is necessary to transfer people, supplies, or information, do so by small boat—either your dinghy or a lifeboat of the ship. You can communicate or make transfers without coming alongside by approaching from leeward under power, passing a line to be made fast aboard the ship, and holding a position at right angles to leeward of it some distance off. Keep your engine idling in gear while exchanges are made.

TAKING A TOW

Taking a tow is often the best way to bring a distressed boat under control. Aground, you may be pulled quickly off the bottom. Adrift, you are immediately underway. In danger, you can soon be taken clear.

Few small boats, however, carry a line long or strong enough to be used in a serious job of pulling, and many have nothing sturdy enough to make it fast to. A three-quarter-inch or one-inch diameter synthetic line or a five-inch circumference manila hawser are the minimum (including a good measure of reserve strength) for a boat about 40 feet long. Floating line seldom fouls. Multiple fastening to cleats, the anchor winch, mast, samson post, or even around the deck house or the gunwale provides a good distribution of tension and can prevent serious damage.

Preparing for a long tow in open water requires a good deal of thought and planning. It is best to rig a towing bridle with tension lines to the bow, but with the forwardmost and strongest support of the bridle aft at least half the length of the foredeck. This way the towed boat is relieved of heavy tension far forward, and her bow can lift freely in the waves. If you make a heavy towing hawser fast to any single place on a small boat, it can impart a destructive force.

It is difficult for a large vessel to go slow enough to tow even an uninjured, tight-hulled small boat without causing it discomfort or damage. Most ships require an absolute minimum of four knots for steerageway. Often they are willing to tow, but only at normal speed in order to keep to schedule. This can be anything from 18 to 30 knots, far more than the hull speed of a small boat, and will literally pull her apart. A completely disabled boat would be far better off taken aboard the ship.

Keep in mind that when accepting a tow-line, you may be agreeing to pay charges and, in many cases, salvage. By passing your line to the towing vessel, you are in a far more favorable position as far as such claims go. And don't forget that you can stop the tow at any time by merely casting off.

One afternoon in Aden during a party aboard a British naval

tug, while the bagpipes improbably skirled "Swanee River," I agreed to let the tug shoot me a line behind the naval repair ship they were going to tow up the Red Sea. It was a sobering thing the next morning as I reviewed what lay ahead. At 2:00 P.M. we had to be offshore, sailing along their expected course. They would pass us, slow down, and shoot the line. Well, we picked it up on schedule, made fast to the bridle prepared that morning, and we were away. It was a wild ride as *Awahnee* was pulled faster and faster. As the Strait of Mendel we turned into the wind and a sharp chop. We were making 10 knots against the inexorably south-going wind and current, but we were undergoing punishing discomfort to boat and crew. I signalled our trouble, but the tug had to maintain speed. We were beginning to wonder if *Awahnee*'s hull could take the punishment, when the eight-inch-circumference towing hawser parted in the middle. I waved the tug on with thanks. We were relieved to sail on, tacking into the unswerving headwind up the narrow sea.

ABANDONING SHIP

"Abandon ship!" is an order seldom heard, but it could be called at any hour as the result of cataclysmic damage. Owners and crew should think about it.

Last summer Tim Johnson, a former crewmember of mine and skipper of a boat and diving crew off the California coast, had to swim for his life along with his shipmates. They were motoring back to port one night with a full load of sea urchins when the transom of the boat apparently sheared off the hull. Tim and another man, asleep below, bundled life jackets under their arms and got on deck in time to step into the water as the boat sank beneath them. The man on watch took no flotation and was with the others only a short while before he disappeared. Tim and his mate swam for nine hours to climb ashore at one of the Channel Islands the next dawn.

The best advice is to stay with a vessel as long as she remains floating. Take to the small boat if necessary, but remain with the vessel, where you may recover food, tools, equipment, and clothing.

With planning, essentials can be removed quickly from a sinking boat. A survival kit should be stowed in an easily accessible place. It should contain water and food; an EPIRB (emergency position-indicating radio beacon), flares, matches, flashlights, and a signal mirror; clothing and life jackets; a small tarp for a boat cover; fishing gear; a tool kit; a chart and perhaps a sextant; a first-aid kit; personal valuables and papers. All these can be collected in a chest with enough flotation built into it to stay on the surface if it has to be chucked out the hatch of a sinking boat. It could be a rather permanent seat in the cabin near the companionway, held in place by wing nuts, or, as on *Awahnee,* a box under the cockpit aft of the ladder.

The flotation is, of course, your dinghy or raft. It should be unsinkable and equipped with oars, oarlocks, sail and spars, and bailers. If you rely on someone finding you in the vastness of the sea, your chances of survival are far less than if you proceed toward land or shipping lanes.

As to food and water: water is more important by far. You can easily survive for a couple of weeks without any food if you are able to conserve body heat, but three or four days in the tropic sun without water will finish off the toughest man. Evaporated canned milk is an excellent lifeboat food, for it provides liquid, protein, and carbohydrate without excess salt. Dried fruits and parched cereal grains like granola are concentrated foods that do not spoil if packed in sealed containers, even during long periods of storage.

Fishing can support life for months by providing liquid and nourishment. I know of a Tahitian man whose outboard skiff conked out on him and a companion on a trip from Mopelia to Bora Bora, about 15 miles distant, where he was to deliver a load of watermelons. Presumably they made their cargo last a long time, but it must have been no time at all compared to the 155 days of drift to Samoa. They made a fish spear of half a pair of scissors, their only tool, and a finishing batten along the gunwale. The companion survived until ten days before the skiff washed ashore.

The fishing kit should include small hooks and line and barbed spears. A folding casting rod with small lures would be good for catching the fish that gather in the shadow of the dinghy.

Tools that are indispensable are a knife (two would be better), pliers, a screwdriver, nails, screws, and perhaps a small hammer. Canvas for shelter, dinghy repair material, and caulking compound should be included in this kit, as well as light line.

Clothing should be chosen to protect against sun, wind, and cold. A wet suit may be better than actual clothes, but foul weather gear will conserve body heat well in wind and protect best from spray and rain. Sunglasses and hats are vital.

Medical supplies should include all basic materials with emphasis on prevention of sunburn, treatment of injuries, and relief of pain. Vitamin C should be included, as it is lacking in standard lifeboat kits.

All gear should be secured in or to the lifeboat. One crew I heard of prepared to abandon their trimaran, but then thought better of it and remained with the capsized vessel until they were rescued—all but one of them. The skipper's insulin was dropped overboard while loading supplies into the dinghy, and three days later he died in a diabetic coma.

Overloading the dinghy is a great danger. Some gear can be kept in the water rather than taken in the boat, such as oars, spars, and sail and watertight water and food containers that float. These items serve as a sea anchor in bad weather, but hinder progress in good weather.

Once you are alone at sea in your lifeboat with what you have managed to bring along, vital decisions must be made. Should you make for shipping lanes or land? Should you stay near the sunken vessel in case something floats up from it? I believe I would elect to stay in the area for a period of time, and then make way toward the nearest attainable land—by way of adjacent shipping lanes, if practicable.

PIRACY

Pirates exist. In Europe and the Western Hemisphere a capable yacht is a prize to men wishing to engage in smuggling. She contains valued gear unavailable by any means other than piracy to desperately poor seamen in the China Sea, the Red Sea, and the waters around Indonesia, Borneo, and the Philippines. Sometimes pirates board a yacht, toss the crew to the sharks, and take what is desired. If an inquiry eventuates, they tell a story of unfortunate collision, and there is no one to dispute it.

One blazing hot day in the desert-edged Gulf of Aden we were ghosting along with bare steerageway off the coast of Somalia. The engine hadn't worked for months. In fact it took us 12 days to sail the 280 miles in the Gulf to Aden, after a monsoon-powered Indian Ocean run of 1,040 miles from the Seychelles Islands to the entrance of the Gulf in five days flat. On this morning we had watched for hours as a large canoe slowly overtook us, the seven paddlers working steadily in the terrible heat. I was apprehensive, wondering why they worked so hard to reach us, and regretting that we were half a world from home and six months from Australia, either out of or down to the bottom of every non-necessity. Mindful of the Pilot's warning that the natives of this area are "murderous and piratical," I realized that these men had very little to lose in an attempt to improve their lot at someone else's expense. Their adobe village was barely visible on the parched shore. As they drew closer I ordered the helmsman to maintain course and steerageway. My two biggest crewmen I had remain below, to come on deck separately after the canoe was alongside so the Somalians wouldn't be sure how many of us were aboard. (We were four men, two women, and a child.)

As soon as they grasped the port toerail, big black men in ragged clothes with ceremonial scars on their faces, I gave them water. No weapons were apparent in their canoe, but an old canvas lay crumpled in its bottom. I signalled for them to remain in their boat. We found that we had no language in common. They motioned for cigarettes but we had none, only one box of tobacco and papers, which they spurned. I offered them the last of our fresh provisions, a few salt spray–blackened bananas which were rudely rejected and tossed back aboard. They rested in silence; we sailed in silence. They must have been exhausted though they didn't show it. I gave them some cans of corned beef. Soon the breeze strengthened enough for us to hoist the main. They watched this process, and as we gathered way on our offshore course they talked among themselves quietly. Then their spokesman said, "Salaam, Salaam," and they dropped off, a long paddle ahead of them.

On another occasion my friends Carl and Sumi Powell in their *Bella Kaze* were afraid to leave an emergency anchorage behind a spur of reef in the Red Sea. An Arab dhow stood off and on the only exit for two days while they rerigged a headstay after losing their bowsprit. Carl had a rifle, and while contemplating their situation, he cut two dummy rifles from spare wood, one for his wife and one for their crewman. They waited until the wind was at its most favorable slant for the day, the dhow at its farthest point, and sailed for their lives with everyone on deck, weapon in hand. The dhow came in hot pursuit. Unable to point quite as high as *Bella*

Kaze, she sheared off harmlessly to leeward. The Powells are convinced to this day that the Arabs intended to collide with *Bella Kaze,* and at the least board and strip their boat.

For this reason I do not put myself, my crew, or my boat in a disadvantageous position with any vessel I speak on the high seas. If it is a ship, I do not approach from an angle which would allow *Awahnee* to be run down; I maneuver clear and then come up on the stern quarter where I have movement and control. Nor do I sail alongside closely until after rapport is established. In preparing to sail the Red Sea I could not and did not want to carry a weapon capable of defending *Awahnee* against such hazards. So, after some thought, I took aboard a box of dynamite, caps, and underwater fuse. I reckoned that a quarter or a half stick of dynamite floated down toward a pursuing vessel would give them something to think about when it blew up, yet not cause damage. It is still the best defense I can think of for a yacht against a very unusual threat in a remote place. (And a box of dynamite might make all the difference in getting a grounded boat afloat and in deep water again, as this very box did for *Awahnee.*)

Successful response to an emergency depends on realistic appraisal of what you are able to do with what you have. It is amazing what can be accomplished by an ingenious sailor on a well-found boat. Preventive measures are best. Everyone aboard a small boat must be attentive to the equipment, its condition, use, and repair. Check to see that the through-hull valves work and the man-overboard light blinks on properly. Carry spare blocks, lumber, plywood, glue, fastenings, and underwater Epoxy. Have the oncoming watch take a minute to inspect sails, rigging, and deck stowage, and the man going below inspect the bilge and engine, if running.

And keep in mind that the emergency may not be yours. At any moment there are people adrift on the oceans of the world, people whose boats have been sunk or disabled. The watchfulness of you and your crew may prevent their emergency from becoming a complete tragedy.

CHAPTER 19

Anchoring

Every sailing man has his tales of horror, and I have mine. Enough of them relate to fouled, dragged, short-rigged, and lost anchors to demonstrate that safe anchoring is among the least understood of a seaman's skills. Whether on a weekend cruise or a voyage around the world, a casual attitude toward putting down a hook is taken at a sailor's peril. Long ago I learned that anchoring is often the best means of safeguarding not only your boat, but, in some cases, your life. Care and effort in anchoring safely are well worth the trouble, considering the alternatives.

I will never forget trying to find a safe anchorage on an unknown bottom in a rising gale and snow squalls long after dark in a particularly fearsome part of the world. We were seeking a night's shelter off the south coast of Tierra del Fuego on *Awahnee*'s passage around the Horn in 1966. We were bound from Montevideo to Honolulu, and figured a Horn passage would save time over sailing way out into the Atlantic, through the Caribbean to the Panama Canal and across the Pacfic. Besides, we had already seen the Canal years before on our first circumnavigation. And, of course, the Horn was there. . . .

It was May, the beginning of winter in the Southern Hemisphere, which is recorded as the season of mildest wind, as wind goes in that battered part of the world. Nonetheless we were prepared for ultimate conditions, and that night we got a taste. The day before, our three-man and one-woman crew had successfully passed through the Le Maire Strait between Tierra del Fuego and Staten Island, whose tidal overfalls of up to 17 feet are chillingly described in the dry language of the South America Pilot. We spent that night at anchor in Buen Suceso Bay, where Cook, Darwin, and unknown other intrepid sailing men had anchored before us. Joining their company, our spirits were high. Maybe our easy passage through the Le Maire Strait to the reassuringly named "Good Success Bay" had lulled us into thinking the worst was over; Horn Island itself lay but 87 miles west and south of us in clear water. We slept well, and in the early morning a light snow dusted us as we worked to take up the anchors. Shortly we were sailing in bright sunny weather, heeling to a strong westerly on a close reach. As the day passed, I realized we were not making good very much against the ever-increasing wind and current. Six knots through the water was yielding much less over the bottom.

This is why the Horn is so difficult to round to windward. The global force of the ceaseless westerly winds and seas in these latitudes generates a current and wave system that is one of the greatest constant forces on earth. Drake Passage, the opening between the ramparts of the Andes and their continuation in the Antarctic Peninsula to the south, is only 540 miles wide and relatively shallow. By contrast, it is 2,100 miles from Africa to Antarctica, and 1,500 miles from the Australian island of Tasmania to Antarctica. No other large land mass exists in the Southern Hemisphere to interrupt the wind and current of the Roaring Forties and below. Thus a Horn passage against the weather is one of nature's most severe tests of sailing ships. In the old days sailing men counted only their passages to windward in reckoning how many times they had been around the Horn. Ships bound from the Atlantic to the Pacific sometimes tacked for weeks against the onslaught of wind and weather before they gave up, bore away, and sailed clear around the world to reach their destination from the opposite direction. Captain Bligh on the *Bounty* did just this in 1788, having futilely attacked the elements for 30 days.

These were the conditions we now faced. The wind was making up and becoming too much for the double-reefed main and working staysail, to which we had been progressively reduced, so we put in the third reef—the first time in 95,000 miles it had been necessary to do so. At about 1630 hours in the last light of a short winter day, we made out New Island at the wide entrance of Beagle Channel, where we hoped the land would protect us from the full force of the gale.

We were wrong. Beagle Channel, at the tip of South America, is a deep, narrow cleft in the land. The last sheer mountains of the Andes drop directly down to form a channel too deep to anchor in. The cliffs on both sides acted as a wind tunnel, shunting the Pacific gale directly against us from the other end some 100 miles away. No matter how the channel turned, the wind was always full force from dead ahead. The Pilot informed us that Final Point, about six miles inside Beagle Channel, was the closest place we could expect to find a lee and bottom. The southernmost civilian habitation in the world lay 30 miles beyond Final Point.

After hours of beating through total darkness at mid-channel, we were unable to distinguish any landmarks and suspected we had made little headway. By 2200 we were cold, wet, tired, hungry, and lost. In hope of finding some place to anchor, I decided to hold the port tack toward the cliff until we found bottom on the depthmeter. We sailed closer and closer until we could see the black cliff looming overhead against the stars, and white water foaming at its base. But the depthmeter, which records to 40 fathoms, still had not registered bottom. I lost courage and came about, resigned to tack on through the night.

For the next half-hour a snow squall blotted out everything. When it cleared, we found kelp floating in the water. Usually kelp means danger, but that night it said to us, simply, "bottom"—rocky bottom, to be sure, but we were relieved nonetheless. A good-sized kelp bed will quiet breaking waves and damp a swell. When there is no other protection available, one can anchor within or behind a bed of kelp, which in the Pacific can have fronds up to 300 feet long. We sailed slowly through the bed and found bottom at eight fathoms, shelving to six. Again we passed through the kelp, tacking to windward, and detected no shoals or pinnacles to endanger anchoring. This was the best we could find, and it would have to be good enough.

Maneuvering to remain in what scant shelter there was, we prepared three anchors. It is doubtful that many sailors will end up trying to anchor at the bottom of the earth in snow squalls and gale-force winds, but the procedure we went through illustrates a successful approach to anchoring in a blow. To starboard I shackled a folding 45-pound Northill on my longest chain lead, 60 feet of $\frac{7}{16}$-inch link, and made it fast to my longest rode, 360 feet of one-inch polypropylene line. The second anchor, a 45-pound Herreshoff, was rigged to port on 30 feet of heavy chain and 300 feet of three-quarter-inch polypropylene. We set the two anchors and adjusted their rodes so that we lay to each equally, with plenty of scope. Our stern was about 500 yards from the rocks. The boat pitched in the heavy swell, and the wind showed not the slightest sign of diminishing. *Awahnee* was uneasy, and so were we.

Then we put down our insurance. I shackled the other big Northill to the main anchor chain and lowered it to the bottom, paying out a few fathoms of chain as we eased back about half a boat length on the two rodes that were already out. This chain was then seized to the stemhead fitting with several turns of light cord, and we flaked out about 25 fathoms more on deck, securing it to the windlass. This was the fail-safe: if the two anchors failed to hold, the main chain would come under tension, break the cord, and feed off the deck until it came tight as the boat dragged. The accumulation of weight and friction of all three anchors together would hold us off the rocks. And if we didn't drag, there were only a few fathoms of chain and the third anchor to pick up before recovering the other two.

Too tired to speculate on how hard the wind was blowing, the four of us went below to thaw out over *Awahnee* one-pot foul weather slumgullion: powdered potatoes with a can of corned beef and some dried onion stirred in. As we ate, the anchor chain rattled across the deck in two prolonged bursts and we knew the first two anchors were not holding. Half an hour later there was a *chunkkk* on deck and a distinct change in the pitching of the boat as we came back against the chain. Now all three anchors were working and would hold *Awahnee*—we hoped. The wind raged on undiminished, and the williwaws that accompanied the snow squalls were ferocious.

The first man on anchor watch dropped a sounding lead over at the chainplates to check for drag as the boat bucked violently in the steep swell. The rest of us tried to get warm enough to sleep. Later we awakened to hear occasional waves break, whooshing past our ears a few inches away outside the hull. The wind had shifted so that it was blowing over a fetch of some three miles from the opposite side of the channel. There was no point in considering the imponderables of the situation, so we slept fitfully on until each in turn was called for anchor watch.

In the cold light of dawn we must have been a strange sight, wind-ravaged and encrusted with rime, had there been anyone to see us. The cliffs were black even by daylight, and the waves still broke all around us in the kelp. But the leadline told us we had not dragged further. It was blowing much too hard to consider leaving a successful though fully exposed anchorage, so there was nothing to do but wait it out. We went below and had a breakfast that lasted most of the morning. By noon the wind had eased somewhat, and we decided to get underway to make another anchorage before dark, one without so close and menacing a lee shore.

The port and starboard anchors with their floating rodes came up without any great difficulty, except that dozens of long kelp streamers had wound around the rodes. As we cranked them in, one man lay on the foredeck and reached over the bow to cut the kelp away with my Italian Carabinieri sword, a prize of World War II.

The main chain was another story. Hauling with the windlass, we were unable to bring in more than half of it in an hour of tough work. The chain was fouled on the bottom. We hoisted the triple-reefed main and staysail and tried to sail it out, going strongly against it on first one tack and then the other. We gained a fathom or two, but it was putting a terrible strain on the windlass, which was lifting off the deck at its after end. To make matters worse, the pawl jumped a cog and flipped the windlass handle irretrievably overboard. Dismayed but undaunted, we used the big crescent wrench. It wasn't worth a damn. We lowered the sails and rigged a four-power handy billy from the chain to the spinnaker winch aft, bypassing the windlass altogether. The rig was about 40 feet long, so we made that much on the chain each time we winched 160 feet of line through the handy billy and two-blocked it. When we got the chain up fairly short, we hoisted the sails again and let them luff; with the shore so close, I wanted to fall off sailing as soon as the anchor broke out of the bottom.

At last it came up—in the center of a ten-foot ball of kelp which must have weighed a ton. We sailed this mass through the water while our swordsman slashed the kelp away, finally hoisting the Northill on board far out in the channel. Rid of its wrapping the anchor revealed the result of the extreme forces spent in recovering it. One fluke was torn at the welds, the stock was bent and twisted, and the half-inch stainless steel shackle was drawn out oblong.

We sailed ten miles farther into Beagle Channel to Cook's Anchorage on Picton Island, where a two-man outpost of the Chilean army, as astonished to see us as we were to find them, provided us with a weather report: "continued force eight." But it was snug there, and we rested easy.

HOW ANCHORS WORK

Through the years I have come to think of myself as an "anchor man." I *like* anchors—plenty of them, with a lot of good strong gear. The priority a racing man gives to sails I give to anchors.

I do not use heavy anchors, by customary measure. In my opinion it is wiser to have twice as many anchors aboard as are usually recommended, but they may be of medium to light weight if used with adequate chain leads. Today's small anchors are so strong that they are rarely broken or damaged, even when fouled or torn out by force. Anchors, chains, shackles, and rodes can usually take more pull than a crew can exert even with a windlass or handy billy.

All anchors, except the Japanese rock anchor, are designed so that no matter how they land on the bottom, a horizontal pull on the shank will turn them to a position for a fluke (or two flukes) to dig in the ground. For an anchor to operate properly, the pull on it must be horizontal, with no upward component. The weight and length of chain between the anchor and rode accomplishes this. When an anchored boat is blown back in a gust, pull on the rode tends to straighten and lift the chain lead. If the lead isn't long or heavy enough, it can be lifted throughout its entire length, imparting an upward pull on the anchor, which is what breaks an anchor out of the ground. The shorter the scope, the greater this likelihood. This is why the first thing to do when an anchor drags is to increase the scope.

The force that an anchor must overcome is the windage of the boat's topsides and/or the drag of its wetted surface. Windage is usually the greater force by far. Freeboard, doghouses, and flying bridges are recognized in assessing windage, but one should not overlook the accumulated cross-sectional area of stays, shrouds, running rigging, navigation lightboards, spars, lifelines, dodgers, baggywrinkles, and stowed dinghies. A clean rig is easier to hold safely at anchor in a blow and to punch to windward out of an anchorage that becomes untenable. Windward ability is safety. Many boat owners don't realize that their boats are taxed to death with windage.

Pure overwhelming weight in an anchor will not be successful in every case. Once my dinghy drifted ashore while lying to a 35-pound Danforth. Figuring its weight alone would hold the skiff, I had not bothered to set the anchor. But when the boat drifted over it, a bight of chain slipped under one fluke and jammed up short against the shank, fouling the anchor. The dinghy wound up on the rocks.

Despite attempts by various authorities, it is impossible to make specific recommendations of anchor sizes and types based on tonnage and length of a boat, since essentially it is windage and current friction that is being anchored. The clean lines and rig of a larger boat may, in fact, generate less pull on a rode than an inefficiently rigged and cluttered smaller boat.

The area of the anchor's fluke is a better indication of holding power in soft ground than weight is. In general, anchors of one-half to one pound per foot of boat length, with sufficient chain lead to prevent lifting of the anchor, will be satisfactory in moderate weather. In more severe conditions a weight of chain twice the weight of the anchor with ample scope on the rode will give a favorable angle of pull and good holding on a soft bottom. I would rather anchor to two of these sets than to one set of the much heavier gear recommended by Hiscock and others, since I can select anchors designed to hold in a given bottom, I can handle each set easily, and I can even row it out in a dinghy. To my mind this is anchoring capability.

With many anchors aboard you are in the advantageous position of being able to lose one or two complete sets and still be sufficiently equipped. One happy but miserable day in the Red Sea I sailed away from a grounding, leaving five anchors behind on the reef. *Awahnee* had been aground for 13 days; we had patched seven holes in her cedar planks and dynamited an escape channel in the reef. We set and reset six anchors that day to provide directional pull and control as we eased her back to a wide place, turned her, and—sometimes floating, sometimes dragging, sometimes moving across the wind—maneuvered her through 150 feet of jagged coral. One by one we had to cast off five anchors and rodes on the reef as we pressed to get free before the tide started to go down. Finally, after dark, we lay in the clear on our last anchor, put out as far as possible with every bit of heavy line that remained. The tide was going out by the time we had rigged the sails and taken up on the anchor. Just when the anchor broke out, she grounded again and hung on the coral. We backwinded the jib and hardened the main. *Awahnee*'s bow swung toward deep water, she heeled, and slowly, slowly, she sailed off the reef.

All night we sailed in sinking condition. Five hundred sixty times we bailed a six-gallon bucket to keep the water lower than the main cabin settees. The next morning, having achieved a desert bay, we set that last anchor as we sailed right up on the beach for careening. After repairing the patches at low tide and kedging off at the next high tide, we proceeded 140 miles to Port Tewfik, Egypt, where we replanked her starboard side and increased the anchor inventory. I know that without all those anchors aboard I would never have saved my boat.

TYPES OF ANCHORS

No one anchor is unequivocally the best in all situations. On *Awahnee,* which measures 53 feet overall and weighs 25 tons provisioned and manned for cruising, I carry ten anchors and grapnels, nine chain leads, a main chain, three rope rodes, and, in reserve, a long all-purpose line.

My opinions have changed over the years with increased experience and observation. For a long time I did not fully trust the CQR, or plow, but I have now acquired a great confidence even in small ones in difficult situations. After crossing the notoriously rough Gulf of Alaska, we once anchored in 200 feet of water to a 25-pound CQR bent to my longest chain lead with 550 feet of half-inch polypropylene line. We were waiting for a blow to ease enough for us to find the north end of the Inland Passage safely. Our anchorage was along the exposed coast under Mount Fairweather (a misnomer, needless to say) in the slight lee created by a mass of rock forced out from the cliffs by the La Perouse Glacier. We remained at that spot for 28 hours without a change in bearings.

My concern for the CQR is that it may foul on the bottom before it can dig in. The distance between the shank and the point of the fluke is much less than that of other anchors of the same weight, which may cause it to clog with weed or rubbish if it drags across the bottom. Once it has set, however, it has virtually no chance of

Awahnee's Ground Tackle Inventory

ANCHORS	WEIGHT (pounds)
CQR (plow)	25
2 welded stainless steel folding Northills	45
Herreshoff improved fisherman	40
Standard fisherman	40
Standard cast Northill	25
Collapsible grapnel	25
Stockless dinghy	10
Northill dinghy	6
Steel grapnel	6

GALVANIZED CHAIN	LENGTH (fathoms)	DIAMETER (inches)
Main anchor	60	$7/16$
Long lead	10	$7/16$
Heavy lead	5	$5/8$
2 lengths	4 each	$7/16$
4 lengths	1 to 3 each	$5/16$
Dinghy chain	$3\frac{1}{2}$	$3/16$

ROPES AND LINES	LENGTH (fathoms)	DIAMETER (inches)
Main anchor (polypropylene)	60	1
Second (polypropylene)	50	$3/4$
Third (manila)	35	1
Reserve (polypropylene)	92	$5/8$

fouling on its own rode because it turns as the direction of pull shifts. Under heavy strain a CQR will bury itself, and it may set so well that the force required to break it out will bend the shank. If I had to choose only one anchor, it would probably be the CQR.

I have great respect for Northill anchors, too. For years I have relied on them as the main anchors for *Awahnee*. The flukes have broad surfaces properly angled for penetrating in soft bottom, the wide stock drives the sharp steel points effectively into rocky ground, and once the fluke has dug in, the stock will also take hold. Northills may be the best all-purpose anchor since they are least apt to clog with debris before setting, and they will hold to a rocky bottom where a CQR is unreliable and a Danforth is downright dangerous to use. My two big stainless steel Northills are so strong and they set so deeply that tremendous effort may be required to break them out. I tend to reserve them for ultimate conditions. They are somewhat bulky to stow even when folded, but their holding power per pound is great, and they work in more varied bottom conditions than any other anchor. Their only fault, and it is a serious one, is that they can be fouled by the rode if the boat passes over them.

The Herreshoff, an improvement on the age-old fisherman anchor, bears the mark of efficient design in every curve and line, the reinforced sharpened points and lightened secondary parts. It, too, is a favorite of mine. The wide chisel-pointed flukes give good penetration and holding power. It is light and easy to stow. Unlike the CQR, however, it can be fouled by its rode.

The lightweight Danforth anchors are very popular as anchors that hold well in sand and mud bottoms when they are set properly to the full depth of their twin flukes. According to tests, they give almost as much holding power per pound as the CQR. With too short a line and no chain, however, a Danforth put over the side from a moving or drifting boat can plane on the large area of the flukes at mid-depth. Also, on coarse shingle or a rocky bottom the flukes may not dig in enough to set properly. If they are only partially engaged, leverage close to the points of the fluke can twist and bend this lightly constructed anchor. And on a very soft bottom the crown plate which supports and trips the anchor can settle into the soft mud without the flukes tilting downward enough to dig in. The anchor then lies on the bottom with its own weight centered on the crown plate, causing it to sink with the tips of the flukes above horizontal. This happened to Ted Hay, as experienced a seaman as one can find, when his ketch *Wakaya* dragged all the way across St. Mary's Bay in New Zealand, a full mile, until the flukes of his Danforth at last took the ground on the ascending lee bank.

With their long shank and stock at right angles, Danforth anchors are difficult to stow. They take up a lot of space on deck, and the stock is raised where it will foul sheets and lines unless special blocks are set at the ends. In any event, the weight of anchors on deck is anti-ballast, and on a voyage they should be stowed below. Since a Danforth might not fit in a bow anchor locker, a good place to stow one is lashed against a bulkhead with a hole drilled in the cabin sole to take the end of the stock.

The Japanese rock anchor, designed specifically for rock and coral, has been used for centuries in the Orient and is now becoming appreciated by sailors in Hawaii and on the west coast of the United States. It is a heavy medium-length iron bar bent to form a single long fluke with a double chisel-pointed small palm, and the rather long stock near the crown. When lowered to the bottom, the rock anchor touches down in a working position because of its suspension and center of gravity. The fluke is not large enough to hold on a soft bottom, but in rock this is the best anchor I have used. I credit this anchor with keeping *Awahnee* from going aground on the searing hot uninhabited coast of Somalia after we had lost a spreader and had to anchor in a 25-knot wind on a smooth rock bottom. On that occasion I had first put out a Herreshoff and then a big Northill. Both dragged, but as soon as I lowered the lighter Japanese anchor, *Awahnee* was held.

Stockless or Navy anchors are used on many large yachts and are effective principally as the restraining weight on a very heavy chain that itself does the major share of holding. Though they are heavy in proportion to their size, a long chain lead may be necessary to help the small flukes engage the ground. The principal virtue of stockless anchors is that they stow well in a hawse at the ready. The cast flukes are subject to flaws and some have broken under heavy strain. A small stockless anchor, because it has minimal bulk and no sharp points, is well suited for use as a dinghy anchor.

The collapsible four-pointed grapnel is effective in rock, heavy shingle, and coral, but in sand, mud, or clay it will resist only a slight pull. I like to use it as a lunch hook because it arms easily and positively and stows well on deck. The main reason I carry one is for dragging to recover chain and fouled anchors off the bottom.

CHAINS AND RODES

In addition to anchors, chains heavy enough and rodes long enough to transmit only a horizontal pull on the anchor are critically important to anchoring success. Besides my 60-fathom main chain, we carry nine chain leads ranging from $\frac{3}{16}$-inch to $\frac{5}{8}$-inch in diameter, and from one fathom to ten fathoms in length. Our anchor rodes and long reserve line are all polypropylene except for one manila rode, which the friendly bosun of a departing liner in an out-of-the-way port arranged to leave behind for me some years ago. Despite its propensity to absorb moisture and rot if not stowed dry, I must say that manila is a pleasure to handle.

Chain is the surest method of anchoring to a single anchor. Its holding power is much greater than an equal length of rope because, in addition to sheer strength, chain has great friction over the ground. The weight of chain suspended from the bow also quiets the boat's movement in a swell. The recommended minimum scope for chain in moderate conditions is three times the water depth; for rope it is five times. However, I much favor anchoring on a rope rode with a chain lead in all conditions but extreme foul weather. It is safer and easier to take in rope on a chain lead than a lesser length of all-chain rode. If you're losing on chain, you can't flip a turn around a bitt; you actually have to pull slack and carry it to the bitt, even from a pile of chain lying on deck. Every movement of chain is hampered by its weight.

If heavy conditions call for an all-chain rode, handling the chain over a windlass allows it to be payed out under control with a friction brake, and brought in with a pawl so that what is recovered is held. Many small boats without a windlass encumbering the foredeck have a pawl fitted to their chain chock, a serviceable arrangement when the ground tackle is light enough to lift by hand.

The bitter end of the chain should be made fast below deck near the chain locker. It should not be buried or immersed in bilge water, nor should it be permanently secured, as you may need to release it if you cannot recover your anchor. *Awahnee*'s is passed around a floor and made fast with two half hitches on itself and seized. This is only a precaution against losing the entire chain, since the weight and momentum of chain running off the bow can pull all the reserve out of the chainlocker. This may seem self-evident, but I feel it is good to mention it, as the following experience will show.

We were berthed stern-to at a long pier in Aden, south of Saudi Arabia, and enjoying the formidable hospitality of the British Navy. While there, we laid out our chain, inspected it, and marked it into five-fathom lengths. The next day the brass came aboard for an afternoon sail. Afterward, as we approached the pier, I called for the anchor to be lowered. A couple of our guests put it over and allowed the chain to run out unchecked. It clattered overboard faster and faster until the length that had been flaked on deck was gone and the rest came rocketing out of the chainlocker. I expected it to come to a jolting halt, but instead I watched in embarrassed horror as the bitter end disappeared over the side. The admiral chided Nancy, inasmuch as in the British Navy the navigator is responsible for making the chain fast in its locker. However, it was my face that was red. On a small boat the command of chain, or vice versa, at times breaks down.

Chain is usually attached to rope or cable with shackles. The threaded pin of a standard shackle is much reduced in cross-section at the threads and therefore weaker than a link of chain the same apparent diameter. Threaded stainless steel shackles are stronger than the galvanized variety but still not as strong as an equivalent chain link. The strongest shackle is the special chain shackle, which has a heavy unthreaded pin held in place by a cotter key, but this is hard to find in small sizes. A stainless or galvanized shackle that fastens with a bolt is probably as strong as chain of equal diameter, because the full diameter of the bolt bears. As a guarantee of greater strength it is a good idea to weld a large link at the end of a chain to provide room for a bigger standard shackle than would otherwise fit.

Shackles fastened to anchor chains must be seized, and this is not a job to be taken lightly. No matter how tightly a pin has been screwed in by hand, it may still come loose under strain. Unscrewed shackle pins and vanished shackles account for many anchoring emergencies. Slight irregularities frequently protrude from the threads, and these lock down on the pin when it is being screwed in. The pin will be snug until the first heavy strain comes on it and the high points become flattened. Then the pin will be slack in its threads, liable to unscrew eventually. It is therefore vital that a shackle be properly tightened and seized. Mild or stainless steel wire will work, but we often use the braided Dacron rocket cord from the line-carrying projectile guns of merchant ships. It is the best seizing cord I have found. Copper or aluminum wire should not be used on iron shackles, for the combination of metals will cause electrolysis.

In an emergency, you can put an eye at the end of a chain by tying a bowline in it and seizing the end; the same can be accomplished with two half hitches of the chain on itself with the end link bolted. Also, a heavy rope can be made fast to a chain with a double or triple sheet bend, seizing the free ends securely.

Chain can be dangerous for anchoring on a foul bottom. It hangs down heavily and can easily foul or make a full turn around some projection from the bottom. When the tide rises or the sea makes up, the snubbed chain may not have adequate scope in the deeper water. Depending on how much the tide rises, if the obstruction is not cleared there can be enough force to damage the boat or the chain itself. If this happens, the links become longer and narrower, seizing each other, which makes the chain stiff. Strain beyond this point will break the chain. Stretched chains may sometimes be repaired by driving a tapered punch into each link to release the bind, but such a chain should be used cautiously and replaced as soon as possible. Anchor chain in continual use should have worn end links cut off and should be cleaned, inspected, galvanized, and remarked into five-fathom or other lengths at least every other year.

Nylon rope, which is favored by many owners of small boats, can stretch 40 percent of its length without damage. This stretching quality encourages some people to attach a nylon rode directly to an anchor, expecting it to provide the same cushioning effect a chain lead does on the pull to the anchor. The practice is dangerous, for the pull of a taut nylon line is upward and may break out the anchor unintentionally. The great disadvantage of nylon in anchoring is that it sinks to the bottom, where it is prone to foul and chafe. Of all synthetic lines nylon is most likely to chafe on the bottom.

Through the years, I have developed ways of handling my boat that are unorthodox. Floating the end of my anchor chain lead and using floating anchor rodes are two of these. A rope rode is subject to severe chafe where it joins the chain lead, as this point continually works across the bottom while a boat is at anchor. In the South Pacific early in my cruising life a nonsynthetic rode chafed and parted on *Awahnee*. Since then, I have used a small sunken buoy at the junction of the chain lead and rode to float it off the bottom. It works beautifully. The small amount of buoyancy does not interfere appreciably with the anchor set or holding power, while chafe and fouling are virtually eliminated.

Later, when I learned of polypropylene floating line, it struck me as a splendid development. Like nylon, polypropylene doesn't absorb water or increase in weight. It stretches more than Dacron and has a great deal of yield. However, polypropylene stretches less than nylon and is about three-fourths as strong. The great value of polypropylene is that it is always clear of the bottom. It floats from the buoyed chain to the surface, or, under strain, takes a pull from the ground tackle. Besides being a superior rode, it makes a towline that won't foul rudders or propellors, a mooring line that won't sink, and a safety line that can be dragged behind for swimmers or thrown to a man overboard. If you lose a polypropylene line overboard, it won't sink. If you row an anchor out in a dinghy, a polypropylene rode will tow easily behind on the water. As with any synthetic line, it must be guarded against chafe. Perhaps the most serious objection to polypropylene anchor rode is that, floating slack on the surface, it interferes with boat traffic. This can be remedied by tying weights to the line to sink it to mid-depth. For the cruising boat lying to her own hooks in an uncrowded anchorage, polypropylene with a chain lead is unquestionably the best rode.

UNDERSTANDING ANCHORING MISHAPS

Planning, practice, and thorough understanding contribute to successful anchoring, and so does luck. The more experience and imagination you have, the more likely you are to recognize the potential for danger in an anchorage. Conditions of wind, tide, bottom, current, and traffic must be reckoned before the captain of any vessel should rest. I marvel at the owners of beautiful boats who cruise into a harbor, fix any old hook to a few fathoms of line, nonchalantly heave it over the side, and forget it. For them the lee will never change, the bottom is good holding, the scope substantial at any stage of tide. They are right sometimes, and perhaps often. But there are situations where only forethought, understanding, and work will prevent learning from painful experiences.

Even the most prudent anchoring does not assure safety. A safe quiet backwater can turn into a Chinese fire drill through a progression of events totally beyond one's control or influence. In Japan before World War II, when I was quartermaster of the 12,000-ton *President Hoover,* I witnessed a spectacle of majestic confusion. We were passing through the narrowest part of the Strait of Shimonoseki at the southwestern end of the Inland Sea. The current was running six knots or more when our bow was closely crossed by a coastal sampan some 200 feet long. Full speed astern slowed us enough to avoid collision but cost the ship her steerageway and control. The current swept her sideways out of the channel toward an anchorage of dozens of sampans and coastal freighters. Both the *Hoover*'s anchors were let go but they didn't stop her, and she dragged across the anchor chains of seven of these ships. Their chains all came taut and broke as our ship's anchors lifted them. The *Hoover* continued massively on her way until she was aground in a prohibited area with her stern against the dock of a naval arsenal. The coastal ships were carried away in the current. It happened so smoothly, so slowly, and so beyond human control that after it was all over, no one could figure out what might have been done differently.

On a smaller scale the same sort of thing can occur in any anchorage. One fall day it was blowing 40 knots in Cape Cod Bay, and small craft passing eastward through the Cape Cod Canal chose to anchor in the tiny harbor of Sandwich, the only lee for 20 miles. Gradually the basin filled. Late in the afternoon a 35-foot sloop powered in and put over an anchor. Before it took hold, the boat had turned broadside to the wind and was out of control. She drifted across the bows of two other boats, whose crews rushed on deck to look on helplessly. The sloop's anchor, snubbed short by the panicked man on the foredeck, snared both the other boats' rodes and broke out their anchors. He let out more scope, but too late—the anchors and rodes were fouled together. None of them had a spare anchor ready to put down. The sloop's auxiliary could not pull the three boats against the wind. And so the entourage drifted back with all the boats to leeward at its mercy, until the three came up against some dolphins with a sickening crunch.

When at last the rodes and anchors were untangled, the sloop powered out of the harbor and into the gale, her skipper apparently too embarrassed to try to anchor again, while a hundred sympathetic onlookers silently wished him a safe landfall.

One thing that makes working topside on *Awahnee* a pleasure is her clear deck and big deckbox, where I keep an anchor rigged whenever we are in soundings. If we find ourselves in shallow water or lost in a fog, such an anchor proves invaluable. On one occasion it saved my boat. We had to leave *Awahnee* untended in an open coastal bay. A fisherman agreed to watch her while I was away. Early one morning ten days later he called Nancy to say that *Awahnee* had come adrift and was aground at the base of a cliff in the backwash of the swell. Nancy and Reid arrived on board just 15 minutes before the peak of the tide. Within moments the ready anchor had been passed to the skiff and set in deep water. All hands and full throttle got her off just before the tide turned. Had that anchor not been ready, I am convinced they would have missed the tide, and with *Awahnee* on the rocks in the shallowing water they might never have gotten her off.

Virtually every cruising boat goes aground sooner or later, some more often than others. Their skippers may be good sailors, novices, old salts, or hotshots, but they all find it's easy to go aground. I recall a shocking time near Cross Sound, Alaska. We were bound to Juneau on our way from Japan to San Francisco, and had just weathered a bad gale in exposed water. I put in for the night in Idaho Inlet, far from aid and habitation. From the tide tables we calculated that there was another nine feet to ebb before the low. The tables also noted that the tides were subject to certain "irregularities" since the Alaskan earthquakes of 1964, but as we were anchoring in 20 feet of water at the stern, I paid no heed. We lay to a stern anchor with a bow line to a tree in the quiet fjord, went to bed, and slept peacefully for some three hours. Suddenly we were jolted awake as *Awahnee* lurched to port and came to rest with a 50° list. Thrown unceremoniously from our bunks, we struggled on deck to discover that a "tidal irregularity" had indeed left us high and dry. At low tide *Awahnee* had been precariously balanced on her keel, and one of the five of us aboard must have turned in his sleep and sent her over on her side. I was concerned about damage, so we lit up the Coleman lamp, stepped out onto the steep bank, and had a look. She was all right. There was nothing to do but wait for the tide, which couldn't have become so irregular that it wouldn't flood again. Returning to our bunks, we rigged the lee canvases to accommodate to the heel and slept through until dawn, when we were floating peacefully with the quiet Alaska-green water lapping the hull as if to say the night's event was all a dream.

Throughout the world small-boat anchorages are often in the ship harbors of ancient times, with accumulated debris of centuries on the bottom. In Saint Helena, 1,000 miles off South Africa in the South Atlantic, we anchored with the bygone spirits of Portuguese, Dutch, and English East Indiamen. The bottom was strewn with 400 years of anchors, chains, cables, and gear. The stern of a World War II wreck protruded from the roadstead. In Japan ancient fish-traps have priority over boat traffic and may occupy the middle of a channel, though they don't show up on the U.S. charts. In Alexandria, Egypt, small boats anchor near the site of the Pharos Lighthouse, one of the seven wonders of the ancient world. The skipper of a boat anchoring in these harbors must expect difficulty and fouled gear.

Nor are the bottoms of modern anchorages always less troublesome. At Kawau Island off Auckland, New Zealand, there is a bay where yachties congregate. We were warned that it was poor holding because it had a "glass bottom." I thought we were being fed some sort of Kiwi slang until *Awahnee* dragged all over the bay and we had to take refuge elsewhere. Later I learned that the glass bottom was exactly as advertised: it was 40 feet deep in beer bottles, so they reckoned.

If you cruise in tropical waters you will become well acquainted with coral reefs—beautiful, living, sometimes deadly. Coral slices the flesh of an unwary swimmer and cuts the anchor rode of an imprudent sailor. To protect my gear, I shackle a cable or chain lead around the base of a coral head and make a floating polypropylene rode fast to it. I keep several old stainless steel shrouds aboard for this purpose. If you make a three-way moor with cable and are mindful of chafe on the polypropylene, it is as close to security as you can get in coral. This is effective in rock also.

Sometimes in river mouths and rocky bays you may attempt to anchor in rocks washed clean of sand, mud, or silt. A rock anchor or Herreshoff will hold best if hooked on a big enough boulder or wide enough fissure. But on occasion these bottoms will simply reject the anchor. Once off Ua Huka in the Marquesas Islands I put over a hook in a small sheltered bay and sailed downwind in a light breeze toward the rocky beach, planning to round up sharply, when I realized that *Awahnee* wasn't slowing as I took draft on the rode. The anchor was jerking and clattering over the bottom. We put over another, which stopped the boat, and I dived to check the two of them. The bottom proved to be a bed of loose rounded rock three to six inches in diameter, incapable of providing an anchor set for holding a heavy boat. We sailed out to a coral and sand bottom which was more exposed to the wind, but it was good holding for the night. A few days later we met a chief who was painstakingly carving an engine bed for a diesel in a jaunty decked-over launch built collectively by the men of his village. A cruising boat about 35 feet long had anchored in that same bay eight months before, dragged into the breakers, holed, and sunk when the wind came up at night. Her owner and crew, considering her a total loss, departed in another yacht. But the resourceful chief and his villagers salvaged her engine and hardware to build an inter-island boat that would carry their taro and fish to market on the capital island 30 miles away.

Then there is the ultimate in inhospitable bottoms. Sailing at night was impossible when we were in the narrow and complicated Patagonian Channels of southern Chile, so we anchored each afternoon in the six weeks we were there. Once we entered a very small fjord, ghosted about a hundred yards to its head and put over a big Northill on the main chain. There was only a whisper of breeze below the high Andean cliffs. The chain hung straight down. As we made up the sails, we noticed that *Awahnee* was slowly moving backwards but we expected the chain to take up and hold us. It continued to hang straight down, so I gave it some slack. Still we glided backwards. By the time I had slacked the chain again without apparent effect, we were almost back in the main channel. We cranked up the engine and motored in again, this time tying to trees fore and aft, our lines spanning the little fjord as if it were a lock. It turned out that the bottom was smooth, glacier-polished granite, and our anchor had simply slid down and out the chute, towing *Awahnee* backwards.

HOW TO ANCHOR

Despite the complexities of ground tackle and bottoms, anchor you must. The sequence to follow is this:

1. Determine where your boat will lie.

2. Select the gear and make it ready.

3. Put down the anchor(s), set it, and pay out scope.

4. Take bearings to establish the anchored position.

5. Set an anchor watch if necessary.

Sailing Directions, tide tables, charts, word-of-mouth advice, and observation are the bases for choosing an anchorage in the first place, and a depthmeter or a leadline will inform you when you are in the preferred depth. In a tight situation when frequent soundings are required I often post a depthmeter watch. At the helm, I prefer to read the water, check the wind, sail the boat, and receive the depth report second-hand, since I find the instrument distracting. Frequently we use a leadline instead of the depthmeter. It is a simple and foolproof way to sound, and it is reassuring to hear the report, "Six fathoms, rock," "Three fathoms and a half, sand," or "Five fathoms, mud." *Awahnee*'s leadline is ten fathoms long, marked from a point eight feet above the lead, thus giving direct readings of depth below the keel. A longer leadline is hard to use when underway.

Casting the lead while under sail calls for experience—which should be acquired before the hour of need. The end of the leadline is made fast to the base of a stanchion or shroud for the obvious reason. Tapping the bottom by raising and lowering the lead several times will give some idea of its nature, and with practice one can learn to distinguish sand, mud, weed, rock, or coral. I have never been satisfied sampling the bottom with tallow or beeswax in the hollow of the lead, probably because our five-pound lead cannot hit with enough force to bring up a good sample, as the heavier ship's leads can.

To be safe in unknown water you must know the entire swinging area of your boat. Twice I have anchored and then detected submerged broken pilings within our scope. If aground or in great doubt about the safety of an area, you can sound with a lead from a dinghy before committing your vessel to unfathomed shallow water. In choosing where to lower the anchor, you must be sure there is searoom enough to get underway again if the anchor does not take the ground.

Selecting and rigging the ground tackle. As already mentioned, I always keep an anchor rigged and ready when we are in coastal waters. With this in hand, I don't always decide which particular anchor and rode combination to use until I know the depth, the swinging room, and, if possible, the type of bottom. I like to lie to two anchors off *Awahnee*'s bow, their rodes about 70 degrees apart. This has led us to the practice of making up a separate anchor set on each side of the boat. Multiple anchoring allows you to adjust the rodes to turn the boat to the best lay in the wind and waves. And it checks swinging greatly, enabling you to anchor in crowded or small areas of shelter. I often drop a third anchor astern; if the weather makes up, I can lead all three rodes to the bow and have a good set in all directions.

In crowded harbors your heaviest anchor and chain will require least scope if you choose to lie to a single anchor. A second hook placed downwind or down the tidal stream greatly reduces swinging room needed in shifting conditions. If nearby boats are lying to single anchors, however, it is better to do the same or they might swing into you.

In rigging an anchor, I lead the chain together with the first few feet of rode outboard through the chock and back aboard over the lifeline and shackle on the anchor of choice aft of the bow where there is room to lift it easily. The rode is ready to run, the junction of chain and rode is just outboard of the chock, and the chain hangs in a bight alongside (or in multiple bights outboard over the lifeline if it is long). Coiled anchor rode is so prone to fouling that we make a point of not paying out from a coil. If there isn't time to flake it down, we overhaul it into a loose pile with the lead coming off the top.

Putting the anchor down. Having found good ground and rigged the hook, it is essential that the person handling the anchor know what he is about, for he must put it over clear, get it to the bottom unfouled, pay out enough rode to minimize upward pull on the anchor when it comes under strain, and finally he must be able to recognize when it is set.

An anchor, of course, should get to the bottom as quickly as possible, since it does no good trailing in the water as you drift leeward. But there are few situations that call for throwing an anchor. One might be when you have sailed into position and your bow is blown off by a gust, in which case two men, one on the anchor and one on the chain lead, can loft a rig 20 or more feet and perhaps save making another pass. Aside from this circumstance, the first step in dropping the anchor is to slack the rode until the hook reaches the ground and then, as the boat backs or drifts down, to pay out more rode, taking only a slight strain until enough scope is out to assure a favorable angle of pull. This will prevent the chain or rode from piling on top of the anchor and fouling it. In an emergency the ready anchor can be cast over the lifelines from any point on deck to get it to the bottom as soon as possible, but the rode must be kept slack until a bight or the bitter end is properly led through the chock. Only then may strain be safely taken.

If an anchor won't set, paying out additional scope is the first action to take, but if it still will not set, it may be fouled and should be pulled, cleared, and reset. Whenever the light and weather are reasonable, I go over the side with a face mask and snorkel to check the set of my anchors. This is one of the pleasures of dropping a hook in tropical waters (but in frigid or foul harbors it is distinctly not).

I do not generally buoy anchors unless there is reason to expect them to foul on the bottom or I want to give other skippers in a crowded anchorage knowledge of my anchor placement. But if we go day sailing or on a brief jaunt down the coast, it is worthwhile to buoy a good anchor set and slip the rodes. It's a cinch to sail back, pick up the buoy, and snug down. The disadvantage of this is that a person might underestimate his requirements while away and not have sufficient reserve ground tackle on board. Ever apprehensive, I have sailed away from my main anchor chain only once, but I have often left my normal anchor sets.

When we anchor our 53-footer, the helmsman often finds it impossible to hear the man working on the foredeck. When we have crew enough, a messenger is stationed at the shrouds to transmit directions. Otherwise, a set of prearranged hand signals serves almost as well, sparing our vocal chords and preserving the dignity of silence.

Taking anchor bearings. After the anchors are holding and the boat has settled to them, you should take bearings on the shore to establish the anchored position. They need not be compass bearings, but can be near objects like a tree or a building in line with some feature of the horizon. Write them down. If an anchor watch is deemed necessary, they can be rechecked accurately.

Posting an anchor watch. Keeping an anchor watch is a vital part of good seamanship. There are times when it is necessary to anchor in less than an ideal situation—in fog, in heavy traffic, or on a lee shore with an unknown bottom—and then it is absolutely necessary to post a watch. When to do so will depend on the experience and judgment of the skipper, based on his feeling for danger. Danger isn't usually danger from the beginning; at first it's just a situation with the possibility of harm. Two lights on the horizon aren't danger. Some water in the bilge isn't danger. But with time the situation might call for action. With vigilance and recognition of jeopardy, the man on watch can save the boat and her company from distress or even shipwreck.

The primary duty of the anchor watch is just that: watching the anchoring gear. The most important task is to determine if the anchor is dragging. A well-set anchor will keep a firm, steady strain on the rode, affected only by the movement of the boat. If the bearings have changed, feel the rode by pressing on it outboard of the chock, for a dragging anchor imparts a fluctuating strain. On a rope rode this is not easily seen but can be felt as a repeated tightening and slackening of the rode; with a chain it is visible as a rather fast raising and lowering of the chain's catenary. The actual clinking sound of an anchor dragging over rocky bottom may sometimes be transmitted to a below-deck listener who places his ear to the hull beneath the waterline.

One of the simplest means of checking for drag is using a leadline, which is lowered to the bottom and made fast with enough slack in the line so it does not drag as the boat swings. If, after a while, the line leads forward when you take it up firm, the boat has dragged. Our leadline has served as an automatic anchor watch on many occasions. We put a tin can or two in a bucket on the cockpit seat and make a bight of the slack leadline fast to it. The clatter of the bucket falling to the deck when the line comes taut announces that the boat has shifted.

In more perilous conditions a proper anchor watch is set. The man on anchor watch makes his rounds at set intervals on *Awahnee.* He may spend much of his time below, but he must stay alert to any signs of a changing situation. He checks the anchor bearings and the rode, makes sure the tensions are equal on multiple rodes, and maintains chafing gear. He watches for approaching traffic and drifting objects and checks on the anchor light. (A kerosene barn lamp set in a white plastic bucket and hoisted on the staysail halyard makes a remarkably bright and wind-proof light, the answer to a sailor's prayer on a stormy night.) The man on anchor watch also keeps the halyards from slapping noisily and checks the bilge.

Not infrequently the need for a watch comes after anchoring in a hazardous location with the crew dead tired after the full duty of a difficult approach. On such occasions we set a round of half-hour watches before dividing the time remaining until morning equally among all hands. If the approach has been easy, the anchor watch is set by continuing the sea watch roster.

As she lies to an anchor, your boat will move with the rhythm of the forces acting on it. She will lift to an ocean swell or bob to a bay chop as the tidal stream flows past her hull, and she will swing port and starboard as the wind catches her bow. If suddenly she seems to be lying more quietly and with a gentler rhythm, something has changed. The boat is no longer breasting the wind and waves. She may be dragging or adrift with the anchor in deep water, or the rode may have parted. Of course, it could be only the change of tide—but nothing can be taken for granted.

ANCHORING UNDER SAIL

When we approach an anchorage under sail, we usually reduce speed by taking down the headsail, stowing it or making it up on deck in gaskets to keep the bow chocks and cleats clear. This leaves *Awahnee* moving slowly but with complete control under staysail and main. In light air with plenty of room over a good bottom, we will then drop the main just as the anchor is put over. We then fall off and run downwind under the staysail, letting the rode pay out freely. When the proper scope is nearly out, we take an increasing strain on the rode as the helmsman jibes, and *Awahnee* finishes up head to wind with the anchor holding and the staysail luffing.

In a fresh breeze there are two choices. You can drop all sails as you round up and lower the hook, keeping in mind that it takes a considerable amount of room to get underway again after everything has been dropped. Or you can round up with the sails luffing and put the anchor over, assuming the boat will back down so you can set the anchor in the right direction. Usually, however, the boat will gently forereach or drift sideways until there is scope enough to put a strain on the anchor and bring the bow to the wind. A second hook may be dropped at this time if you are across the wind far enough to give a satisfactory angle to the rodes when you fall back to the two anchors. If the anchor does not take the ground, you can trim the sheets and get underway, come about, then sail across the anchor and recover it. With a ketch and sometimes a yawl, the combination of backwinded headsail and mizzen will permit you to back down under control.

If a second anchor is to be set off the bow, sail or motor forward along the arc of the first rode. When it is perpendicular to the wind direction, put the second hook out and set it as you fall back to lie equally to the two anchors. I do not use a swivel on the rodes as I prefer to handle each separately. If they become twisted I cast one off, clear it, and make it fast again.

Once the two bow anchors are down and set, a stern anchor can be put down by easing off on the bow rodes to drift back and place the third anchor. Then the former position is taken up while paying out on the stern rode and setting its anchor. It should be given sufficient scope to allow the boat to swing somewhat on the bow anchors.

A FAIL-SAFE ANCHOR TECHNIQUE

A reserve anchor using the same principle as the leadline check for a dragging anchor greatly increases safety with little extra effort. When I feel apprehensive about an anchorage, I lower a large anchor at the bow with just enough chain to get it to the bottom. Then, so the chain will lie clear, I slack 15 or 20 feet of the rode of the working anchor and pay out chain to the reserve hook as we ease back. Now that the regular anchor won't foul the reserve one, I slack another short length of chain to the bottom, perhaps 30 feet, that will drag heavily enough on the reserve anchor to start setting it if it comes into draft. I then tie a breakaway cord to support the chain at the chock so it won't fall overboard of its own weight, flake the rest of the desired scope on deck and make it fast. If the working anchor does not hold or the boat swings widely, the reserve anchor will come under strain, the cord will break, and the chain will pay out until the boat comes up on it. This anchor is easy to pick up if it does not come into use.

If necessary, the reserve anchor can be carefully thrown ahead and to one side, clear of the working rode, or out from amidships if it has a fair lead at the bow. Or it can be put down at the end of a bowsprit and the chain dumped clear of it under the bow or at the shrouds. The important thing is to avoid fouling the anchor while giving it enough scope to take hold. If you use this technique with rope rode and a long chain lead, put all of the chain and the junction of chain and rope outside the chock. Be careful to have a fair lead from the chock through the flaked out rode to the windlass or bitt; it is easy to end up with a turn around something—the staysail stay, a stanchion, the working rode, or the pulpit.

FURTHER TECHNIQUES

Using an extra-long line. On our first voyage to Polynesia some years ago I learned the value of a very long line. One afternoon we sailed in toward the fantastic mountains and lava cores of Ua Pou to anchor under a red cliff close to a small village on the leeward side of the island. I jumped in the water just to cool off and pulled down along the chain. I was horrified to discover amidst the beautiful fish that my anchor was sitting on a smooth bare expanse of rock. The floor of the bay was like a marble slab. For 200 feet around, there was nothing for the anchor to hold to. We picked up the hook, sailed out about 500 feet and dropped the small Northill on 60 feet of chain and a long line, paying out over 500 feet of line as we sailed closer under the shelter of the cliff than before, where we rounded up and put over the big Northill on the main chain rode. This time I dived down and set it in loose coral and rock by hand. The big hook on a short scope held us close inshore, but the light anchor on the long line provided a good offing if the surf came up or the wind shifted—room enough to make sail if we were forced to leave.

Since then I have adopted the practice of dropping a light anchor on a very long line whenever entering a small or difficult anchorage, or when we must anchor just outside a surf line. My favorite for this is a 25-pound Northill on four fathoms of $\frac{7}{16}$-inch chain made fast to our longest (550 feet) polypropylene line. This gives a very low angle of pull on the anchor. Fortunately, we have never had one fail to set. We drop this anchor and allow it a good scope before giving it quite a hard strain to set it as we continue to sail closer to shore, where we drop the main anchors.

In storm conditions I frequently use a long shore line in combination with our anchors to ease their load. We pass a chain or piece of old rigging wire around a boulder, tree, or post and shackle the ends together. The line is then made fast to the shackle and protected with chafing gear if necessary. If there is nothing to make fast to, a deadman can be placed ashore to take the line. With this in mind I always carry a shovel aboard.

Anchor bridles. A bridle made fast to the anchor chain or line on a single anchor allows the boat to be turned to lie quietly in a current, cross-swell, waves, or wind, and it can be rigged off the anchor rode in use. I have a pair of stainless steel hooks that can attach a bridle to chain, and a rolling hitch works on a rope rode. The bridle is led to the stern and made fast. Anchor rode is payed out to allow the bow to swing off as desired to provide an off-center lead to make the boat more comfortable. The bridle can be adjusted at the bow or stern. Also, when a wind or current is pressing a boat to a pier, a bridle to a bower anchor can be used to hold it off, parallel to the pier.

Stern anchoring. It is often advantageous to anchor by the stern unless a boat has a big transom, since most sailboats have more windage forward than aft. The boat will lie more quietly with most of its windage to leeward, and the strain on the gear will be less. When we are lying by the stern to an anchor or drogue, I often dampen the rudder action by tying a bungee cord or bicycle inner tube to the tiller. This restricts the rudder's movement, but allows it to yield when meeting a swell.

Using a dinghy. Carrying an anchor out in a dinghy is the best means of setting a hook if you are moored, aground, or already anchored. In quiet weather and water you simply take the anchor aboard the dinghy, towing the rode behind if it is polypropylene. One method is to hook a fluke of the anchor over the dinghy's transom, or to pass the dinghy's stern line around the shank of the anchor and hold it against the stern thwart with your foot while the anchor hangs in the water. This allows the anchor to be dropped without fuss, just by lifting your foot.

It is a hard job to row upwind towing a long rode into a fresh breeze. It is easier to take all the anchoring gear aboard the dinghy, row out, put the hook over and pay out rode as you return to the boat. Be careful: the load is often large and unstable, with the anchor and chain on top, since they have to go out first. If the dinghy is big enough, another person's weight can keep it more stable while he helps get the gear out clear. If there is a forward rowing position (very advantageous), the forward man can provide the

Norwegian steam while the other can concentrate on anchoring.

Taking a chain rode upwind in a dinghy in a fresh breeze can be virtually impossible, even with a small outboard engine. Often the weight and friction of a bight of chain over the bottom are simply too great. If you must attempt it, though, take the anchor and about two-thirds of the scope into the dinghy. Hold the chain fast with your foot against the center of the after thwart and pull strongly away while chain is paid out from the boat as far as you can pull it. Continuing to bend the oars, let about 20 feet of chain out of the dinghy in a burst. This will allow further headway. When the drag almost stops the dinghy, let out another burst of chain, repeating until all chain is laid out, rowing nonstop all the while. Then drop the anchor clear of the chain. Don't underestimate the amount of chain needed for adequate scope, since the chain invariably will not be straight on the bottom.

Doing it yourself. Setting an anchor without a dinghy can be accomplished by supporting it with flotation gear and swimming it out when you are unable to put an anchor out from your boat. And a relatively heavy anchor can be walked out on the bottom, since its weight gives your feet traction submerged.

Scowing. Many times on unyielding rock or coral bottoms we scow an anchor by making chain fast to the crown of the anchor and seizing it to the other end of the shank with wire or line. This guards against being unable to break the anchor out, for a strong pull after shortening the scope will break the seizing and draw the anchor up by its crown. The total strength of the seizing should be about one-third the strength of the rode. Scowing allows full use of the anchor's strength because the seizing assures pull in the proper direction, but a boat should not be allowed to swing on a scowed anchor, as the seizing could chafe through and leave you with a reversed anchor. Scowed anchors are used only for temporary anchoring.

BREAKING OUT ANCHORS

If it has not been fouled or set too deeply, an anchor breaks out as you pull up on it. If the set is heavy and deep, it will be hard to tell when it has broken out from the bottom. Usually the first sign is the bow falling off the wind to one side or the other and the boat drifting while the rode is straight down. After an anchor is broken out, it can be brought up much more rapidly by hauling hand over hand on the rode than by working the windlass. I often drag the anchor and chain through the water in reverse when I pick up my hook under power to wash them and keep them clear of the hull while bringing them aboard.

If you can recover your anchors and get underway without using the engine, you have passed an acid test in boathandling. The first step is to single up, that is, to recover all but one anchor. Usually this can be done by slacking enough rode to pull up short on the extra anchors and heave them up. In light wind the next step is to put up working sail and tack up to the remaining anchor, taking in rode as you sail. In stronger stuff the boat will sail faster than you can haul the rode, and it is better to sail up on the anchor on main and staysail in a cutter rig, or haul up with the main luffing if you have no staysail. Usually by the second or third tack the boat will pass close over the anchor. When you get little additional slack on the rode with another tack, snub the line. If you are lucky, the anchor will break out immediately, the rode streaming slightly aft as the boat holds a steady course. Keep sailing slowly while you bring the anchor on deck, which is best done by reaching outboard of the lifelines or pulpit and lifting it aboard.

Anchors that refuse to break out of the bottom present another body of anchoring problems and solutions. Frequently they foul on the bottom or on some man-made object. A firm tension of several hundred pounds on the rode, with the boat's surging motion from waves, sailing and/or motoring, will often work a fouled anchor free. To lift fouled cable or chain so the anchor can be cleared, raise the anchor as high as possible and pass a bight of line around the fouling gear to support its weight. Then slack away on your anchor rode and work the hook free. When this is done, one end of the bight is cast off and the fouling material drops back to the bottom.

If the anchor has fouled on a very heavy object, you may not be able to lift it with your own gear. When time and conditions permit, you can dive down and pass a line around it or grapple it, take up short at low tide, and make fast. As the tide rises, the flotation of the boat will exert a lifting force of tons and you may be able to free the hook. But be alert to the possibility of damage, for the strain can tear a winch, bitt, chock, anchor roller, or rail right off the boat.

In rough rock with edges and fissures, which may be hidden by a layer of sand, the anchor can jam so tightly that it cannot be wrenched or twisted out by lifting on the end of the shank. This, of course, is the force that normally breaks an anchor out. A hook fouled like this must be drawn out, reversing the direction of pull that set it. If you buoyed the anchor with a strong enough line to the crown, you can haul it clear. Otherwise, you can try to hook it with a small grapnel and draw it out. Ultimately, you may have to dive and pry the anchor free with a wrecking bar. If it is necessary to dive for fouled gear, the boat should be put on another anchor so the diver can work with a slack rode and not be endangered when the boat surges. Most of the time skin-diving gear will suffice, but I keep a scuba tank for these situations, and I've been successful in water 70 feet deep.

Sometimes an anchor may have been set without complication, but the chain or rode may have fouled. Outcroppings of rock, coral, or wreckage can rise well above the surrounding bottom, holding a turn of the rode or catching it underneath. No matter how well your anchor was set or how much scope was used, if the rode fouls, your boat will be left surging against a short length of rode leading down sharply. When the weight and buoyancy of the boat are thrown against this short lead, it may part, or damage deck fittings (particularly an off-center anchor roller mounted on a bowsprit, a lubberly arrangement if there ever was one, good only under light strain or in carrying a ready anchor).

At the least, extreme strain with short scope may ruin either rope or chain. The first action is to slacken the rode and return to a comfortable, safe scope. If there is not enough rode remaining to do this, bend on a heavy line with a rolling hitch, seizing the knot well, and pay out. With a man on deck playing the tension on the rode, the boat can often be maneuvered carefully to unwind the fouling turn. Gentle manipulation and perseverance pay off; use a diver or a man in the dinghy with a face mask or look-box to direct the operation. If this doesn't work, you can pay scope out freely, sail or motor away from the direction of the last wrap, and fetch up on the rode quite firmly.

Sometimes, after exhausting your ingenuity and patience, there is nothing to do but surge a fouled rig repeatedly to tear it free or break it. And if that doesn't work, you must either cut free (it doesn't take long to hacksaw a link of chain underwater if you have no boltcutters) or buoy it and return to battle another time.

The captain of a boat must always be alert to the possibilities of any given situation, and must be prepared to do whatever is necessary to safeguard his boat and crew. Above all, he must be able to respond quickly should the situation worsen. The flexibility offered by the gear we keep aboard *Awahnee* lets us solve almost any anchoring problem. Naturally, a smaller boat will not carry so extensive an inventory as *Awahnee*'s. But one thing is certain: no boat can stint on ground tackle or its proper use and always reach home port safely.

CHAPTER 20

Arriving

Though flag etiquette can be a hassle, it is appreciated by many people, not the least of whom are the officials you must meet before being allowed ashore in a foreign country. Having been unable to buy, for example, an Australian flag in Noumea or a South African flag in Darwin, we collected a kit of scraps of spinnaker cloth from a sailmaker. We stitch up the national flag before arriving in the local waters of a new country. This flies at the starboard spreader with the "Q" flag beneath it as you sail into the quarantine anchorage. Properly, when under sail, your country's flag should be flown at the peak of the gaff, or where that would be if you do not have a gaff-headed main. When the sails are furled your flag of registry is hoisted on a staff at the stern. However, most yachts fly their national colors at the stern whether underway or not.

Tradition decrees that your national flag never be hoisted before the courtesy flag of the nation you are visiting, and that they be flown every day from 8:00 A.M. until sundown. What every protocol-conscious yachtsman needs is a roller-furling flag controlled by a timer-connected photoelectric cell so the colors will always be unfurled in the morning and struck at sundown whether anyone is aboard or not.

The hardest ordeal for many cruising people is the assault of bureaucrats on the peace and freedom of sailing after arrival at a far shore. The paperwork required to enter a foreign port can be formidable: crew list in quadruplicate, list of firearms and ammunition, provisions list, health inspection certificate, "de-rat" certificate, customs declaration, fresh stores list, general inventory, liquor and tobacco inventory, and declaration of intended stay and itinerary in local waters.

Whenever you go from one political entity to another, you must arrive at a port of entry where health, immigration, and customs officials are stationed. Passports, visas, and health cards are dealt with everywhere, no matter how remote.

The quarantine anchorage or wharf is marked on detailed charts of major ports, and its location described in the applicable Pilot. In small places, it is usually at the seat of government. In any event, it is improper to go ashore until the doctor has visited the boat or you have been directed to do so. This can mean a considerable wait for a sea-weary crew. It is preferable to arrive during working hours Monday through Friday. Extra-hours clearance is simply impossible in most places, and where it can be arranged it often requires a fat fee.

At anchor, a small vessel is sometimes not noticed. I recommend a large, bright "Q" flag of spinnaker cloth that will fly in the lightest breeze. (Since you and your crew are an unknown quantity on arrival, you are in quarantine until the authorities are satisfied that you carry no disease; hence the requirement that you fly the "Q" flag until cleared.)

Sometimes the skipper must go ashore to telephone the authorities. I usually do this by phoning the customs office, who round up the other officials. Often they will come alongside in a launch if you are anchored off, but sometimes they must hazard your dinghy.

The doctor may actually examine everyone aboard for signs of communicable disease, but usually the examination is just a perfunctory confirmation that everyone has a valid certificate of smallpox vaccination. He may request your de-rat certificate, a piece of paper granted ships that have been inspected for rats with none found. If you ever have the opportunity to acquire one of these, do so—it will help.

Many island groups are completely free of animal-carried diseases like rabies and psittacosis, and they have protective rules that are understandably stringent. If you take a dog or cat from a rabies-infected area (North America, Europe) to Tonga or Tahiti, you are required to see that the animal never leaves the vessel. In New Zealand yachtsmen must post a bond of several hundred dollars as a guarantee that their animal will not take shore leave, to be forfeited along with the animal's life if it does. And I hear that in Australia the officials now give a yachtsman the choice of summarily putting his pet to death or leaving the country. Parrots of all types are dealt with similarly. In fact, animals aboard a small boat are hardly worth the trouble they create with the authorities, even if you have a docile cat with saltwater running in its veins.

The immigration officer invariably wants a crew list, sometimes in triplicate or quadruplicate. I always have these prepared listing the name of the boat, our last port, our date of departure, and everyone aboard, along with their nationality, passport number, and age. Sometimes the immigration officer will take all the passports to his office until departure, but usually he will stamp them and leave them in the possession of their owners.

If anyone is to be removed from the crew list, the immigration officials must be consulted, for it is their responsibility to prevent people from remaining in their country who cannot support themselves. Some places, notably French Polynesia, may require all crew to post a bond covering the price of a plane ticket home before they are granted visas. It is far better to get visas before arriving in a country so rules like this don't come as a surprise.

Next comes the customs officer. He may merely ask you if you have anything to declare. This means, do you intend to sell or otherwise dispose of any goods you have brought into the country. However, he can require you to:

1. fill out a cargo manifest, which provides certification that you are not a commercial vessel.

2. provide a list of the make, manufacture, and ownership of all optical and electronic gear aboard, which must, of course, be aboard when the boat departs.

3. list all ship's stores, which some countries require to remain unused during your stay, as you are expected to buy locally produced food or pay duty on what you have imported and used.

4. place liquor, cigarettes, and tobacco in a locked cabinet, which he seals, as a guarantee that you will pay local prices and taxes on these goods during your stay.

5. list all firearms and ammunition aboard, which are likely to be taken ashore and kept by the police until departure.

6. let him inspect the medical kit for prohibited or excessive drugs.

In addition, he may, for no apparent reason, decide to search your boat for contraband. This, believe me, is no fun, and there is no compensation for the time and effort it takes and the disruption it causes. *Awahnee* has been searched three times: once when the authorities in Fremantle, Australia, though not disputing our story and evidence of having sailed from Tasmania westward across the Great Bight of Australia to their city on the Indian Ocean, looked for goods from Singapore aboard. Once in French Polynesia, to confirm our ammunition count. And again, years later, in New Zealand after our Antarctic voyage, when agents came aboard while I was ashore—though some of the crew were there—and took the boat apart compartment by compartment. I was severely chastised for not having several ampoules of morphine, given me by the doctor at the Russian Antarctic base, under lock and key.

Finally, a representative of the agriculture department may inspect your remaining fresh stores and confiscate those that may carry disease or insects.

After being granted *pratique* (permission to remain in harbor and visit freely ashore) the skipper ordinarily calls on the harbor authorities to find out where to anchor, how long he may stay, what the port fee is—usually nothing, or minimal—and where water and/or electricity is available. In places where there are marinas, you will surely be expected to clear the commercial harbor. Otherwise you often find yourself directed to moor among the fishing fleet. In places without facilities for small boats of relatively deep draft, you may end up in the dock reserved for small coastal steamers, ocean-going barges, or deep-sea trawlers. I like these berths, for we are surrounded by men who go to sea for their living. They understand blue-water sailors and their vessels, and we automatically participate in the easy camaraderie of all the citizens of the sea.

Official receptions are varied. In ports where once ocean-crossing small vessels were rarities and objects of admiration and curiosity, they may now be commonplace, and attitudes of the officials are often matter-of-fact. One time, after completing the immigration forms downtown, I read the sheet of paper I had been handed as I walked back to the port and was astonished to see, "Three U.S.

Americans are hereby prohibited from entering [this country]. . . ."
This actually meant, it turned out, that we were indeed free to roam
the port area but needed specific permission to travel inland. On another occasion, after crossing a different ocean, I was handed a letter
from the harbormaster which read, "Welcome, Yachtsman. You are
given 30 days free mooring in the harbor. . . ."

CHAPTER 21

The rewards of cruising

The more complicated life is, the harder it is to enjoy. The only time some people are truly happy is when they are away from things they don't understand or things they resent. Some find this feeling at the seashore, others in the mountains. I don't really think this is an escape so much as a clarification. It's when they are happy just to be alive.

It's this same yearning for simplicity, I think, that explains the deep satisfactions derived from small-boat cruising. In these times of affluence and complexity, there is hardly a level of civilized living ashore, from that of an industrial tycoon to that of a welfare recipient, where a man truly has personal control over his life. The vast majority of decisions are bound by regulations, stultifying custom, and socially instilled inhibitions. A cruising man's decisions, however, are directed by necessity and are carefully calculated to be the most agreeable compromise between the desired and the possible courses of action. The small-boat sailor can see the result of effective effort at an immediate and personal level. There is never a mystery about whether your work was all right or not. The sea soon tells you. This kind of satisfaction is limited to a boat of moderate size where hired expertise and responsibility do not replace personal control and action. You don't get it if the paid skipper takes over and you go to bed.

A sailor's world may have wide horizons, but it is finite. He knows what he can do and what is beyond his ability. When it blows up so strong the sails must be handed, he knows he is in a situation utterly beyond his control. He doesn't waste himself fruitlessly worrying about the weather, he accommodates to it by making his boat as safe and comfortable as possible, and waits until once again he can use his winches and blocks and tackle to set the sails driving his boat on course. Success is immediate and tangible: a sail that has been stitched up by hand at sea, a delicious fish dinner, a good day's run and, eventually, arrival at his destination on the other side of the ocean. Failure also is immediate and tangible: a jibsheet that chafes on the shrouds and parts in a squall, a knot that unties in use, a wet bunk under a leaking hatch, a poor day's run on a good wind because the helmsman steered all over the ocean.

When the *matangi*—the big wind—comes, you and your boat must bear the full force of nature. You must trust your boat and yourself. After experiencing a storm at sea, you are never again afraid in comparable conditions, but in your heart you always know that it could have blown harder. And it might, next time. This is not a burden that weighs on you like the tensions of a competitive job. It is just a fact.

The lesson that the sea teaches is that you must sail the wind you have, not the one you wish you had, the one you thought you would have, or the one you "ought" to have. Accept reality. Use it to your best advantage. There is nothing malicious in the sea or the boat, the wind or the rock. You may not be in command of the situation, but you can make an effective response. If you are unable to make the miles spin off the stern, make your boat sail her best in the conditions you have. If it blows too rough, make the boat comfortable and yourselves the same. It is as true today as it ever was that a good boat can take more than her crew.

Reward and a sense of proportion can be found in the daily life aboard—in the living, the breathing, the viewing. The sailing in whatever sea and wind you find out there, the training of your crew and their performance, their likes and dislikes, the landfall, good or bad, and the experiences at your destination all add spice. Relax and enjoy it. You fit.

The world is full of wonderful people, and they all contribute to the personal satisfaction realized from cruising. Virtually everyone has had dreams of visiting a far land. You will find many in your travels who have fulfilled that dream and many preparing to do so. And everywhere you will find those who would like to go but never will. Vicariously they share your adventure and the voyages of others. Often they will go far out of their way to show you their country, offer their hospitality, and help you on your way.

I have met hundreds of small-boat sailors cruising foreign shores, and there are few who have been at it for as long as ten years. Most make a trip or two and then are once again enmeshed in life ashore. On the other hand, you must search long and hard to find a cruising sailor who truly regrets casting off. I have never met one.

Satisfaction is close at hand on a boat, but you must be able to recognize it, to accept it in a simple form. As you continue to cruise, your competence and confidence will increase. You learn more about sailing every day; you will never know it all. Freedom is on every side, and along with it the need for decision, action, and results. Gradually the threshold of pleasure lowers, and you realize that you enjoy nearly everything you see. No mystery. No hidden enjoyments. The sea, the wind, the boat, the crew, you, your life.

Index

Abandoning ship, 217–219
Accommodations, 85–87
America, 29
Anchors, 227–252
   Awahnee's inventory, 230
   breaking out, 249–252
   chains and rodes, 233–236
   how they work, 227–229
   how to set, 240–249
   how to set under sail, 245–246
   reserve, 246–247
   types of, 229–233
   understanding mishaps, 236–240
Annette, 116–117
Atom, 26–27
Awahnee I:
   voyages of, 16–17, 263
   wreck of (Tuamotus), 121

Barracuda, 197
Bedbugs, 192
Bilge pumps, 75–76
Blackburn, Howard, 10
Books:
   medical, 181
   reference, 106, 108
Bow, 22
Box, masthead, 44
Bread, 132–134

Calms, 147–148
Catamarans, 19
Celestial navigation, 122–126
Centipedes, 191–192
Chafe, 54–55
Charts, 105–108
Chichester, Francis, 10
Children, 11–12
Chronometer, 125
Clew outhaul tackle, 49
Clothing, 79–81
Coaming, 30–32

Cockpit, 29–31
Cockroaches, 189–190
Collisions, avoidance of, 212–213
Coming alongside a ship, dangers of,
   215–216
Compass, 121–122
Constipation, 184
Cooking, 138, 165–166
Cook Islands, 116–117
Crew selection, 111–114
Customs, 255–256

Dampness from saltwater, 177–178
Deckboxes, 32–33
Dinghies, 81–84
Dismasting, 207–208
Dodger, 32
Dorade, 17
Drawers and bins, 88
Drogue, 161–162
Dry stores, 132

Eels, moray, 197–198
Eggs, 134
Electricity, 70–71
Electronic gear, 71–73
Engines, 67–70, 209

Fire, 209
Firearms, 76
Fish:
   for food, 137–138
   poisoning, 187–188
   and skin diving, 196–199
Fishhook removal, 186–187
Fishing, 193–199
   casting, 198–199
   spearing, 196–199
   torch-fishing, 198
   trolling, 193–196
Fittings, 39–44
   deck, 55–56

Flag etiquette, 253
Flies, 190–191
Foul weather gear, 79–80
Foundering, 200–203

Galley, 76–79
Gallows, 34–35
Garbage, 167–168
Goosenecks, 50
Grounding, 203, 238–239

Halyards, 51
Handkerchief staysail, 159
Handrails, 36
Handy billy, 76
Harbor authorities, 256–257
Hatches, 31–32
Head, 167
Heaving-to, 160–162
Heavy weather, 153–162
    before the wind in, 155–156
    heaving-to in, 160–162
    on the wind in, 153–155
    storm seas, 159–160
    storm winds, 156–159
Helmsman's Rear End, 184–185
Hull, 21–27

Immigration officials, 255
Infections, 185–187
Islander, 15

Jib, 60–62, 63–64
    topsail, 159
Keel, 24–25
Knots:
    basic, 142–146
    computing speed of boat, 126

Lamps, 88
Lice, 192
Lifelines, 35–36
Lightning, 44–45
Linen, 80–81
Lines, 53, 141–142

Mail, 108–109
Man overboard, 211–212
Mast, 38–39
Meat, 134–138

Medical kit, 181
Money:
    currency, 109–111
    earning with a yacht, 114–116
Mosquitoes, 191
Multihulls, 18–19

Navigation, celestial, 122–126
Niña, 17
Nutrition, 137

Pets, 254–255
Pidgeon, Harry, 15
Piracy, 219–221
Poles, spinnaker, 53–54
Pollution, 168
Ports, 33–34
    of entry, 254
Preventer, 48–49
Produce, fresh, 129–130
Provisioning, 127–140
    basic ingredients, 128–129
    bread, 132–134
    buying in foreign ports, 131–132
    dry stores, 132
    eggs, 134
    fish, 137–138
    meat, 134–138
    produce, fresh, 129–130
    water, 138–140
Pulpit, 35
Pursuit, 17

Rats, 190–191
Receiver, short-wave, 125
Reefing, 59–60, 153–156
Rigging:
    boom, 47
    emergency, 205–208
    strength, 56
    tuning, 45–46
Robertson, Dougal, 84
Rubrail, 29
Rudder, 25, 208–209

Sails:
    cost of, 58
    genoa and genoa staysail, 64
    ghosters, 63–64
    luff, 61

materials, 57–59
reefing, 59–60, 153–156
repair, 64–66
roller-furling, 61–62
spinnaker, 64
stormsails, 62–63, 158–159
track, 52–53
working, 58–63
Schooling at sea, 11–12
Scorpions, 192
Seasickness, 182–183
Sea urchin spines, 188
Services, international health, 180
Sextant, 122–124
Sharks, 196–197
Shrouds, 39, 44, 46
Shutters, storm, 33
Signalling, emergency, 213–215
Skin diving, 196–199
Slocum, Joshua, 10
Snorkeling, 196
Spars, emergency, 206–208
Spray, 18
Stays, 39–40
Steering, wheel, 26
Stern, 24
Stopwatch, 125
Storms (*see* Heavy weather)
Stoves, 76–78

Stowage, 89
Sunburn, 183

Tables, 88
Taffrail log, 125–126
Tahiti ketch, 18
Tiller, 25
Toerail, 28–29
Tonga, 118
Toothache, 186
Topping lift, 49–50
Tow, taking a, 216–217
Trade winds, 151–153
Trading, 116–119
Traveler, 51
Trimarans, 18–19
Trysail, 158

Vaccinations, 180–181
Ventilators, 34

Wakatoru, 19
Water:
    collection of, 210
    distillation of, 210–211
    and provisioning, 138–140
Winches, 51–53

Zephyrs, 148–151

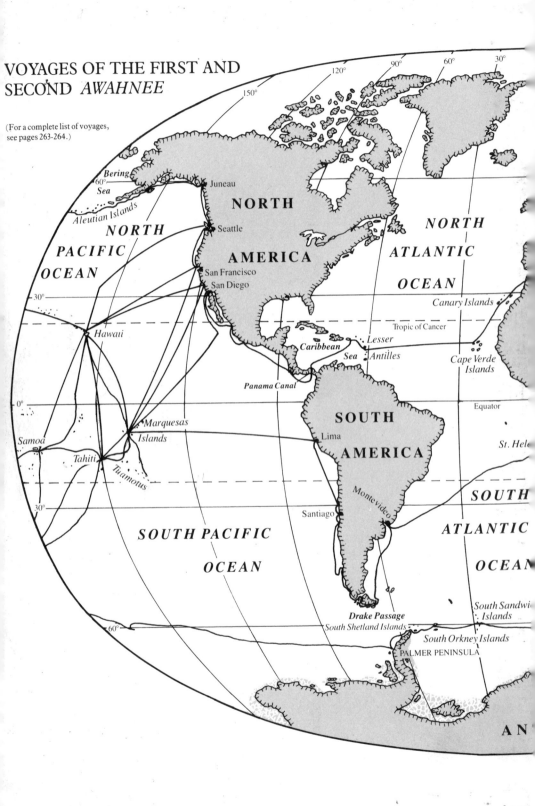

VOYAGES OF THE FIRST AND SECOND *AWAHNEE*

(For a complete list of voyages, see pages 263-264.)

NORTH PACIFIC OCEAN

Bering
Sea
Aleutian Islands
Juneau
Seattle
San Francisco
San Diego
Hawaii

NORTH AMERICA

NORTH ATLANTIC OCEAN

Canary Islands

Tropic of Cancer

Caribbean
Sea
Lesser
Antilles
Cape Verde
Islands

Panama Canal

Equator

SOUTH AMERICA

Lima

St. Hele

Samoa

Marquesas
Islands

Tahiti
Tuamotus

Montevideo

SOUTH ATLANTIC OCEAN

Santiago

SOUTH PACIFIC OCEAN

Drake Passage
South Shetland Islands

South Sandwi
Islands

South Orkney Islands

PALMER PENINSULA

AN